Reframing Cult Westerns

Reframing Cult Westerns

From The Magnificent Seven
to The Hateful Eight

Edited by
Lee Broughton

BLOOMSBURY ACADEMIC
NEW YORK • LONDON • OXFORD • NEW DELHI • SYDNEY

BLOOMSBURY ACADEMIC
Bloomsbury Publishing Inc
1385 Broadway, New York, NY 10018, USA
50 Bedford Square, London, WC1B 3DP, UK
29 Earlsfort Terrace, Dublin 2, Ireland

BLOOMSBURY, BLOOMSBURY ACADEMIC and the Diana logo are trademarks of
Bloomsbury Publishing Plc

First published in the United States of America 2020
This paperback edition published in 2021

Cover design by Eleanor Rose
Cover image: Samuel L. Jackson in a still from The Hateful Eight, 2016
(dir. Quentin Tarantino) © ArenaPAL

Library of Congress Cataloging-in-Publication Data

Names: Broughton, Lee, 1966- editor.
Title: Reframing cult Westerns: from The magnificent seven to The hateful eight /
edited by Lee Broughton.
Description: New York: Bloomsbury Academic, 2020. | Includes bibliographical references,
filmography, and index. | Summary: "This carefully curated collection focuses
on a wide range of post-classical era cult Westerns from around the world,
offering new critical insights into key films belonging to this important and
enduring film genre"– Provided by publisher.
Identifiers: LCCN 2019040275 (print) | LCCN 2019040276 (ebook) | ISBN 9781501343490
(hardback) | ISBN 9781501343513 (epub) | ISBN 9781501343506 (pdf)
Subjects: LCSH: Western films–History and criticism. | Cult films–History and criticism.
Classification: LCC PN1995.9.W4 R44 2020 (print) | LCC PN1995.9.W4 (ebook) |
DDC 791.43/6278–dc23
LC record available at https://lccn.loc.gov/2019040275
LC ebook record available at https://lccn.loc.gov/2019040276

ISBN: HB: 978-1-5013-4349-0
PB: 978-1-5013-8689-3
eBook: 978-1-5013-4351-3
ePDF: 978-1-5013-4350-6

Typeset by Deanta Global Publishing Services, Chennai, India

Contents

Acknowledgments

Thanks go to Katie Gallof, Erin Duffy, and all at Bloomsbury Academic for their help in bringing this volume to print.

Thanks also to the Archivio Fotografico della Cineteca Nazionale (Rome), Tom Betts, VG Bild-Kunst (Bonn), Ulrich Bruckner, Marco Brunello, Edward Buscombe, the Cineteca di Bologna, Christopher B. Conway, Alex Cox, Dover Publications, Glenn Erickson, Christopher Frayling, Rosaria Gioia, Mark Goodall, Emma Hamilton, Sebastian Haselbeck, Ally Lamaj, the Leverhulme Trust, the Library of Congress (Washington, D. C.), Hervé Mayer, Andrew Patrick Nelson, John Nudge, Anne-Marie Paquet-Deyris, John Power, the Reporters Associati (Rome), Viridiana Rotondi, Bill Shaffer, Laura J. Shepherd, Elisabetta Simi, Giuditta Simi, Tom Wellings, John White, Wild East Productions (New York), Jeremy Wooding, and Karen Zarker. And last, but not least, a big thank you to every one of the fine scholars who contributed a chapter to this collection.

Parts of Peter J. Hanley's chapter have previously appeared in his book *Behind-the-Scenes of Sergio Leone's "The Good, the Bad and the Ugly."* Dulmen: Il buono Publishing, 2016.

Introduction:
Cult Westerns and Cult Films

Lee Broughton

The Western Today: A Cult Genre

The Western occupies a curious space within the cinematic landscape of the twenty-first century. From the early days of cinema to the late 1950s (when Hollywood's so-called classical era came to an end), the Western was quite possibly the most popular and the most voluminous of film genres. But post-1960, the production of Hollywood Westerns began to exponentially decrease with each passing year. So much so that many observers were quick to announce the genre's death during a particularly fallow period of production at the turn of the 1980s. Those announcements regarding the genre's demise were somewhat premature, but the fact remains that relatively few Westerns are made today and those that are tend to be marginal productions. The exceptions to this rule are those mainstream-yet-still-somewhat idiosyncratic variants that are given impetus by the involvement of acutely film-literate star directors (such as the Coen Brothers and Quentin Tarantino) or "cult" character actors (such as Kurt Russell, Samuel L. Jackson, and Tommy Lee Jones). To all intents and purposes, the Western has become a cult genre in the twenty-first century.

New Westerns that receive widespread cinematic releases may be relatively few in number today, but the central tenet of the Western—the rugged hero fearlessly standing tall in the face of adversity and doing "what a man's gotta do" (be it civilizing the wilderness, protecting kith and kin, seeking revenge for those who have been wronged, rescuing a good woman, or relieving villains of their ill-gotten gains)—remains a trope that still holds the power to appeal to film fans of various stripes. Hence an ever-increasing number of postclassical-era Westerns have enjoyed an afterlife as cult Westerns via regular repertory cinema and television screenings and home video releases. Similarly academic interest in the genre has remained high. This might be because the Western's mix of instantly recognizable symbols and remarkably malleable narrative motifs ultimately enabled it to become a film form that could be readily adapted the world over. Hence, in addition to revisionist and counterculturally themed American Westerns, we also find international Westerns that foreground cultural and political symbolism that is local in nature and invariably used to allegorically discuss a variety of contemporary concerns. Westerns thus often have much of interest to tell us about their varied contexts of production.

This collection identifies key—and often previously overlooked—postclassical-era cult Westerns from around the world and reframes our understanding of them by approaching and interrogating them in new ways. The more obvious cult movie credentials of these Westerns will be briefly discussed later in this introduction, which will allow the author of each chapter to look beyond their selected Westerns' cult movie status in order to critically analyze, assess, and pass comment on previously overlooked aspects of their chosen films. While a variety of theoretical and analytical approaches will be applied to a wide range of films, the resulting chapters are grouped into three thematic sections. As well as being of academic interest in the sense that they shine a much needed light on Westerns that have attracted little in the way of detailed critical discussion previously, these thematic sections will also appeal to a broad range of general Western fans as they cover by turn classic, international, and contemporary cult Westerns.

What Is a Cult Film?

The question "What is a cult film?" has troubled film fans and academics alike for many years. Interested parties tend to know one when they see one, but because cult films can theoretically belong to any genre, be popular or art house productions, and be judged to be trash or high art and all things in between, providing a workable definition or a set of common properties is difficult. Indeed, Mark Jancovich et al. contend that "the term 'cult movies' covers a multitude of sins" while acknowledging that such films cannot be "defined according to some single, unifying feature shared by all cult movies" (2003: 1). Bruce Kawin widens the debate slightly when he notes that cult films have tended to be defined in two ways: "any picture that is seen repeatedly by a devoted audience" and any picture that is judged to be "deviant and radically different" and consequently "embraced by a deviant audience" (1991: 18). Kawin suggests that the former type—his key example is Michael Curtiz's *Casablanca* (1942)—might be dubbed "inadvertent" cult films while the latter type—his key example is Tobe Hooper's *The Texas Chainsaw Massacre 2* (1986)—might be dubbed "programmatic" cult films (1991: 19).

Casablanca is judged to be "a straightforward, conservative, unself-conscious" film that can appeal to an audience "without threatening or redefining its values in the slightest" whereas *The Texas Chainsaw Massacre 2* is judged to have set out "to be a cult film" by purposefully featuring content that sits "well outside the mainstream ideology" thus representing "a disruptive rather than a conservative force" (Kawin 1991: 19). J. P. Telotte offers a similar sense of dichotomy when he differentiates between "classical" cult films—those that possess "a broad linkage to classical cinema, in terms of both . . . narrative and . . . exhibition practices" (1991a: 39)—and the "midnight movie" variants that "challenge not only our conventional viewing practices but many norms of cinematic subject and style" (1991b: 103).[1]

Danny Peary's work provides an alternative inroad into the study and definition of cult movies by focusing on the concept of the cult film star. Electing to look at those performers "who have had [a] strong emotional impact on at least a fair-sized number of movie fans," Peary examines the careers of "character actors, pinup queens, romantic idols, porno stars, zany comics, midnight-movie favorites" and "offbeat performers who defy categorization" but have nonetheless "sparked an unusual, fiery passion in movie fans" (1991: 15). In the same year, Wade Jennings (1991) wrote an extended investigation into the cult status of a more mainstream star, Judy Garland, which sought to determine how extratextual and extra-diegetic knowledge about an actor impacts upon their fans' desire to transform them into cult icons. Further work of this nature that focuses on a variety of cult actors can be found in Kate Egan and Sarah Thomas's more recent edited collection *Cult Film Stardom: Offbeat Attractions and Processes of Cultification* (2013), which sets out to consider "how stars become cultified through a range of mediated processes and cultural sites that might differ from the traditional mode of film stardom" (Egan and Thomas 2013: 4–5).

Certainly it is possible to place some of the cult Westerns covered in this collection within the categories and approaches discussed earlier. John Sturges's *The Magnificent Seven* (1960) might easily reside at the "inadvertent" or "classical" end of the cult film spectrum while Alejandro Jodorowsky's *El Topo* (1970) might just as easily reside at the "programmatic" or "midnight movie" end of the cult film

---

[1] For more detailed reading on the latter variants, the reader is directed toward J. Hoberman and Jonathan Rosenbaum's groundbreaking book *Midnight Movies* (1991 [1983]), which offers detailed histories and critiques of a handful of the most representative examples.

spectrum. And the films under review here feature a fair number of actors who might all be described as being cult actors or cult personalities in some respect: Dean Reed, Anthony Steffen, Lee Van Cleef, John Hurt, Robert Vaughn, David Gulpilil, Tim Roth, Mads Mikkelsen, and others. Furthermore, some of the films featured here were made by cult directors—Sergio Leone, Rainer Werner Fassbinder, and Quentin Tarantino—or feature contributions from other cult personalities, such as the musicians Ennio Morricone, Leonard Cohen, and Nick Cave.

It is often necessary to probe deeper when seeking to accredit cult movie status to a film. When asking himself what makes a cult film, the cult director Joe Dante ponders a variety of possibilities: a film's sense of "unfamiliarity," its sense of obscurity, its lack of commercial success, its critical dismissal, its "extreme" content, its promotion of "terrible taste," its arty impenetrability, or its just plain terrible production values (2011: vii). Kawin suggests that "cult films offer and glory in . . . otherness—in extreme spectacles of rebellion," "wacko power," "wacko banality," "melancholy," "difference," "nostalgia for symbolism," "nostalgia for simplicity," "relentless satire," "the power of style," "unglamorized violence," "ghoul art," and "bourgeois apocalypse" (1991: 19). While Dante and Kawin provide a useful list of signifiers that could be employed in relation to some of the films under review here—for example, "arty impenetrability" might well be used to describe Alejandro Jodorowsky's *El Topo* (1970), "extreme content" rings true of Quentin Tarantino's *The Hateful Eight* (2015), "unglamorized violence" could be applied to Robert Altman's *McCabe and Mrs. Miller* (1971), "ghoul art" might work in the case of Alex Turner's *Dead Birds* (2004), "the power of style" would fit with Sergio Leone's *The Good, the Bad and the Ugly* (1966), and "melancholy" might be okay for Kristian Levring's *The Salvation* (2014)—sometimes a slightly more nuanced approach is required.

Ernest Mathijs and Xavier Mendik have provided the basis for that more nuanced approach in their edited collection *The Cult Film Reader* (2008). Mathijs and Mendik suggest that

> it is essential to carve out the elements that surround cult cinema. Typically, a cult film is defined through a variety of combinations that include four major elements:
>
> 1. *Anatomy*: the film itself—its features, content, style, format and generic modes.
> 2. *Consumption*: the ways in which it is received—the audience reactions, fan celebrations and critical reactions.

3. *Political economy*: the financial and physical conditions of presence of the film—its ownerships, intentions, promotions, channels of presentation, and the spaces and times of its exhibition.

4. *Cultural status*: the way in which a cult film fits a time or region—how it comments on its surroundings, by complying, exploiting, critiquing or offending. (2008: 1)

Mathijs and Mendik duly advise that not "all of these elements need to be fulfilled together in order to speak of a film as a cult film. But . . . each of them is of high significance in what *makes* a film cult" (2008: 1).

For Mathijs and Mendik, the anatomy of a cult film can include "innovation," "badness," "transgression," "genre," "intertextuality," "loose ends," "nostalgia," and "gore," while the consumption of cult films can involve "active celebration," "communion and community," "liveness," "commitment," "rebellion," and "alternative canonization" (2008: 2-6). Similarly, the political economy of cult films can include "production—legends and accidents," "promotion—specialist events and limited access," and "reception—tales and tails" while the cultural status of a cult film can involve "strangeness," "allegory," "cultural sensitivities" and "politics" (Mathijs and Mendik 2008: 7–10).[2] As will be seen later in this introduction when the content of the chapters that will follow are being discussed, these cues are a very useful set of tools for any interested party who wishes to test the cult movie credentials of any given film. Clearly a hard and fast "catch all" definition of what a cult film is has yet to be settled upon and may never be in light of I. Q. Hunter's warning that "cult film being a discursive category, its definition is liable anyway to change with use over time" (2016: 19). But, as Hunter notes, work does go on that seeks to make "sense of these changing definitions of cult" cinema (2016: 22). It is my hope that the contents of the volume that you are about to read will offer new and useful insights into why its eclectic range of films have—for a variety of reasons—been defined as cult Westerns.

Cult Westerns

The book opens with a part entitled "Classic Cult Westerns" and in Chapter 1 Paul Kerr focuses on one of the most popular and enduring cult Westerns,

---

[2] For more on the historical placement of cult movies, cult movie trends, and additional lines of enquiry into how they might best be defined, the reader is directed toward Ernest Mathijs and Jamie Sexton's comprehensive volume *Cult Cinema: An Introduction* (2011).

John Sturges's *The Magnificent Seven* (1960). A box office flop upon its initial release in America (though it fared better in Europe and other parts of the world), *The Magnificent Seven* is a film that—like many a cult movie—accrued its audience over time. One-off repertory cinema screenings, rereleases, and regular screenings on TV during holiday seasons kept the film visible for its growing numbers of fans. Not surprisingly, its cult movie credentials are plentiful: it is an adaptation of an existing film (Akira Kurosawa's *Seven Samurai* [*Schichinin no samurai*, 1954]) that deviates greatly from the original in terms of its location, temporal setting, mise-en-scène, and so on; its troubled and convoluted production history was played out in public via the pages of industry magazines such as *Variety*; it stars a cast of young macho male actors who would go on to become cult figures of interest themselves as their varied filmographies expanded and they became major stars; it features a raft of enigmatic characters who possess distinct personal idiosyncrasies and spout memorable and quotable dialogue; and it possesses an iconic and now instantly recognizable front title theme by Elmer Bernstein.

Here Kerr offers a welcome investigation into one of the film's cult movie aspects: its troubled production history. In the course of examining the production processes that led to the creation of *The Magnificent Seven*, Kerr references dialogue spoken by one of the film's characters when he sets himself the task of finding out why "it seemed like a good idea at the time" for Hollywood personnel to make an adaptation of *Seven Samurai* during the late 1950s. After critically discussing existing writing on the film, which has tended to suggest that *The Magnificent Seven*'s narrative is reflective of America's contemporaneous foreign policy, Kerr chooses to examine the makeup of the Mirisch Company, the independent outfit that produced the film, and the relations that the then new package-unit system of production prompted between those who came together to make *The Magnificent Seven*. Fascinatingly, in doing so he determines that the process of assembling an ensemble package of costar talent to surround its one legitimate movie star lead (Yul Brynner)—and the freelance and casualized nature of those costars' and other crew members' careers following the recent demise of the studio system—actually mirrored the film's own fictional "guns for hire" narrative.

In Chapter 2, Peter J. Hanley examines another highly popular and enduring cult Western, Sergio Leone's *The Good, the Bad and the Ugly* (*Il buono, il brutto, il cattivo*, 1966). Leone's film has some cult movie credentials in common with *The Magnificent Seven*: although it was a major box office hit upon its initial release, the film remained visible to its growing number of fans thanks to a series of one-off repertory cinema screenings, rereleases, and regular broadcasts on TV during holiday seasons; it stars a cast of macho male actors who would go on to become cult figures of interest themselves as their varied filmographies expanded and they became major stars; it features several enigmatic characters who possess distinct personal idiosyncrasies and spout memorable and quotable dialogue; and it possesses an iconic and now instantly recognizable front title theme by Ennio Morricone. But the film possesses further cult movie credentials. Its director Sergio Leone is himself a cult figure of interest, thanks partly to his personal auteurist ticks and his eminently stylish approach to filmmaking. A convoluted legal action prompted by Akira Kurosawa's objections to the unauthorized similarities that were evident between Leone's *A Fistful of Dollars* (*Per un pugno di dollari*, 1964) and his own *Yojimbo* (*Yojinbo*, 1961) led to United Artists greatly delaying the release of all three *Dollars* films in the territories where they controlled the distribution of the trilogy. Having been produced last but thematically positioned first in the *Dollars* trilogy, *The Good, the Bad and the Ugly* features enigmas and plot twists aplenty as well as a quite stunning and stylish mise-en-scène that brings the film's US Civil War setting and transgressively cynical narrative to life in a visceral and violent way.

Critics were quick to question the historical accuracy of the film's content, arguing that a lack of cultural roots, a secondhand understanding of American history, and foreign filming locations would necessarily result in a Western made by Italians being inauthentic and lacking in historical detail. Not, it would seem, in the case of a Sergio Leone film. For this chapter Hanley has carefully noted the plethora of American Civil War references that are found in *The Good, the Bad and the Ugly* and has cross-referenced them with accounts of the war found in a number of respected history books. Furthermore, Hanley has examined the aesthetics of many of the film's key props and visual flourishes and has cross-referenced them with the contents of authentic period photographs pertaining to the conflict. His findings indicate that Leone and his set designer Carlo Simi actually went to painstaking efforts in order to ensure that the film's visual representations of Civil War–related scenarios were indeed historically accurate for the most part. In addition, the film's diegetic Western locations are also found to possess historical legitimacy as they actually reference a little known episode of the war that unfolded in the West.

In Chapter 3, Cynthia J. Miller interrogates two very different Westerns that were directed by Robert Altman: *McCabe and Mrs. Miller* (1971) and *Buffalo*

Bill and the Indians, or Sitting Bull's History Lesson (1976). Beyond Altman's own status as a cult figure of interest who directed a number of idiosyncratic films, *McCabe and Mrs. Miller* might primarily owe its cult movie status to the many ways in which it transgresses the ideology and the narrative motifs of classical Hollywood Westerns: it is set in the snow country; its protagonists are an unlikeable male fool who eventually wins the audience's interest and sympathy before dying at the film's end and a drug-taking female brothel madam who fails in her efforts to make him see sense; innocent characters die unexpected and disturbing deaths; and America is shown to have been built by merciless business corporations who were prepared to commit murder in order to secure the market shares they desired. In addition, the film is distinguished by its unusual soundtrack score, which is made up of songs composed by the cult singer-songwriter Leonard Cohen. In spite of its impressive cast, years of relative obscurity awaiting rediscovery is perhaps what motivated *Buffalo Bill and the Indians, or Sitting Bull's History Lesson*'s cult film status initially. Ambitious, cynical, and satirical in equal measure, and featuring characters based on real historical figures, this Altman Western was simply too revisionist to find a mass audience in 1976 (the year in which Americans were busy celebrating the Bicentennial anniversary of the adoption of the Declaration of Independence).

Here Miller notes how the two films play to the senses in utterly dissimilar ways—*Buffalo Bill and the Indians* is a noisy shockwave of color when compared to the quiet and introspective scenes found in *McCabe and Mrs. Miller* that employ hushed grays and browns—while highlighting the equally different narrative forms and filmic styles that Altman employs in both. However, Miller argues that both films do actually speak to the tensions that are inherent in all images and portrayals of the West: their narratives strive to achieve authenticity while also seeking to reconcile their characters' lives with the landscapes they occupy—concerns that remain so central to American history and national identity. In doing so the films provide unflinching examinations of the dark side of frontier life. Altman's West is argued to be a complex landscape of the mind: not just one idea but a cluster of closely held, sometimes conflicting, values and beliefs, often perpetuated at great cost. His West draws together the imagined and the real, the familiar and the unfamiliar, hope and disillusionment. Miller concludes that Altman's Westerns cast a critical eye on the ways that history has been invented and reinvented, yet remind us that just as the mythic West is unchanging, its filmic renderings must change with time.

This part ends with Chapter 4, in which Craig Ian Mann assesses American Westerns that were released in 1980: Michael Cimino's *Heaven's Gate*, Walter Hill's *The Long Riders*, and William Wiard's *Tom Horn*. This trio of films holds much in the way of cult cache. *Heaven's Gate*'s troubled production process provoked much interest, and its subsequent failure at the box office—along with the huge financial losses incurred by United Artists—resulted in the film actually being credited with causing the death of the Western genre on film. The director of *The Long Riders*, Walter Hill, remains something of a cult figure having directed a number of films that fit readily within the cult movie idiom to varying degrees. *The Long Riders* is distinguished by its novel casting, which sees notable actor brothers playing the historical figures of the James, Younger, Miller, and Ford brothers in order to bring a striking sense of sibling similarity to the film's mise-en-scène. Many of these actors—for example, Stacy Keach, David Carradine, Dennis Quaid, and Christopher Guest—are cult thespians within their own right. *Tom Horn* is remembered as being Steve McQueen's penultimate film and one that upsets the Western genre's usual narrative patterns when his eponymous cowboy journeyman dies an unjust death at its end.

After noting that 1980 was a pivotal year for both the American Western and America itself, Mann details the profound changes that occurred politically that year. The electorate rejected Jimmy Carter's bid for a second term as president and instead turned to Ronald Reagan, a back-to-basics Republican who stood for traditional values and promised to reinvigorate an unstable economy with his pro-business policies. The year also saw *Heaven's Gate*, *The Long Riders*, and *Tom Horn* being met with varying degrees of commercial failure at the American box office. Mann explores in detail the three films' thematic preoccupations with social injustice, class warfare, and a corrupt establishment before going on to consider whether their failure at the domestic box office—and the Western's more general decline—might be attributed to the fact that the political sentiments of all three films were ideologically opposed to America's swiftly changing social, cultural, and political climate. Indeed, Mann determines that these films are "counter-Westerns" that move beyond the horrors of Vietnam and instead attack America for its increasingly materialistic and corporate society. He concludes that the films thus failed to resonate in a society where the countercultural spirit of the preceding decades was fading away in favor of a capitalist future.

Part Two entitled "Charting New Frontiers and Mapping Identity and Politics in International Cult Westerns" opens with Chapter 5 in which Matt Melia focuses on what might well be the cult Western par excellence, Alejandro Jodorowsky's

El Topo (1970). Made in Mexico and subsequently championed by none other than John Lennon, *El Topo* initially existed in English-speaking territories as a "midnight movie" during the early 1970s and the film is filled to the brim with the kind of transgressive and sometimes impenetrable content that has come to define many of the cult films that flourished on the midnight movie circuit at that time. Intertextuality (references to the work of Sergio Leone, Samuel Beckett, and others), grotesque imagery, allusions to mysticism, black humor, surreal visuals, religious symbolism, subversive sentiments, countercultural imagery, enigmatic dialogue, sex, violence, and sexualized violence all vie for attention in what is undoubtedly one of the strangest Westerns ever made. The film's distribution rights were bought by Lennon's manager, Allen Klein, who eventually withdrew *El Topo* from circulation for an extended number of years and this enforced sense of scarcity served only to add to the film's cult reputation.

In his efforts to bring new understandings of the landscape, the imagery, and the symbolism found in Jodorowsky's film, Melia traces the director's travels after the Second World War, which brought him into contact with members of the postwar liberal intellectual elite such as Andre Breton (the "Pope of Surrealism") and the mime artist Marcel Marceau and resulted in him collaborating with Fernando Arrabal in the Panic Movement (through which emerged the influence of figures such as Antonin Artaud, Jean Genet, and Samuel Beckett). Melia determines that the influence of this milieu and the zeitgeist at the time of *El Topo*'s production resulted in the concerns of two separate countercultural traditions—those of postwar Europe and the transgressive Theatres of Cruelty and the Absurd and those of the acid soaked counterculture of the late 1960s and early 1970s—being drawn together in one cinematic landscape. Melia draws comparisons between Jodorowky's own journeys of discovery and the journey undertaken by *El Topo*'s eponymous protagonist before going on to argue that the film's landscape is actually an empty interpretive space that Jodorowsky invites the viewer to fill with meaning while simultaneously presenting mythological, cosmic, and religious symbolism to assist them in their meaning-making quests.

In Chapter 6 Hamish Ford critically examines Rainer Werner Fassbinder's oft-overlooked West German Western *Whity* (1971). Perhaps more than any other Western covered in this book, *Whity*'s cult movie status might in the first instance be borne out of the fact that the film was virtually impossible to see for many years. But scarcity is not *Whity*'s only cult movie credential. Fassbinder is a cult figure in his own right, and the film itself qualifies as one of the oddest European Westerns ever produced. *Whity*'s action unfolds predominantly indoors; it features an African American character—who dies at the film's end—as its protagonist; and many of the film's characters sport obvious and ethnically coded makeup ("black face," "white face," and "brown face" variants) that function in a pointedly Brechtian way. *Whity* is also something of an exercise in genre bending since it includes elements of the family-historical melodrama, aspects of the gothic horror genre, allusions to the then-nascent Blaxploitation film cycle and art house aesthetics while also featuring a story that transgressively incorporates both queer and S&M sexualities, incestuous liaisons, and interfamily murder plots.

Whity has, perhaps unsurprisingly, continued to perplex Fassbinder fans and scholars since its temporal setting and diegetic location would appear to place it at a remove from the director's other works, which tend to critically confront the sometimes ugly truths found in West Germany's prehistory, its creation, and its economic success. However, Ford argues that *Whity* can be regarded as Fassbinder's key transitional work in which he perfects the Brecht-influenced political modernism of the films that came before while simultaneously inaugurating his famous "conversion" to melodrama's subversive potential. Ford also finds links between Fassbinder's treatment of race, sex, and class in *Whity* and a number of the director's other films. Furthermore, Ford shows that *Whity* functions as an idiosyncratic but important Western too, positing that the film is a queer genre intervention that explores many of the contradictory elements found at the Western's core and pushes them to their logical and destructive limit points.

In Chapter 7 Sonja Simonyi tackles two overlooked East German Westerns: Werner Wallroth's *Blood Brothers* (*Blutsbrüder*, 1975) and Dean Reed's *Sing, Cowboy, Sing* (1981). Again notions of scarcity and access play a part here to some extent since these films were produced within the old Soviet Bloc and were thus hard to see items for viewers based in the Western world. But the films' main point of interest—and their strongest cult film credential—is the participation of the cult musician-actor Dean Reed. An American singer-performer, Reed was a vocal supporter of leftist ideology who moved to live in East Germany in the early 1970s. He became a celebrated, state-sanctioned public personality across the whole Soviet Bloc where he was endearingly referred to as the Red Elvis. However, Reed was found dead in 1986 under mysterious circumstances that some interpreted as a suicide and others as the ultimate proof of his recent fallout with the socialist regime. *Blood Brothers* is one of a number of East German *Indianerfilms* that featured the cult actor Gojko Mitić playing heroic Native

American characters. Necessarily infused with East Germany's state-sanctioned leftist political ideology, these *Indianerfilms* have become cult favorites in the West since their revisionist narratives typically sympathize with the historical plight of Native Americans. *Sing, Cowboy, Sing* was evidently a more personal project for Reed, and it is also distinguished by the presence of another cult personality, the Czechoslovak singer-actor Václav Neckář.

Simonyi's chapter is concerned with the ways in which Reed developed an on-screen persona that referenced his real-life American cowboy identity and celebrity singing cowboy image. While Simonyi accepts that Reed's on-screen persona was made to fit with the ideological dictates of the Soviet Bloc, she suggests that a closer analysis of the two films that centrally evoked this persona in an East German context reveals a more complicated picture. In *Blood Brothers*, the celebratory foregrounding of his alluring American cowboy identity, staged through the use of classical Western tropes, ultimately serves to dilute the ideological aims of the normally wholly revisionist *Indianerfilm* cycle. By turn, in *Sing, Cowboy, Sing* Reed's image as a cowboy becomes embedded in a self-reflexively artificial frontier space and the film's distinctly mocking visual and narrative references to the *Indianerfilms* result in Reed's crude comedy actually highlighting the ways in which the Western genre was appropriated and reconfigured within the ideological context of East Germany. As such, both films illustrate the limits of Reed's American cowboy persona at the service of state socialist ideology.

The part ends with Chapter 8 in which Chelsea Wessels tackles John Hillcoat's *The Proposition* (2005), a Western whose action takes place outside of the United States. Set in Australia in the 1880s, *The Proposition* is another film that boasts impressive cult movie credentials. In the first instance, it was written by cult musician Nick Cave (who also worked on the film's soundtrack score alongside Warren Ellis); it brings a sense of "strangeness" and "displacement" to the Western since it employs much of the genre's visual iconography and many of its familiar tropes in order to tell a story that takes place within the "alien" environment of Australia's historical wild frontier; it is a particularly violent film that is set in an unforgiving landscape and the nihilistic and unflinching nature of some of its violent set-pieces imbues them with the power to cause upset and shock; its narrative features a number of unexpected plot twists and turns; and it features a number of cult actors, including John Hurt, David Gulpilil, and Ray Winstone.

Here Wessels employs a Jacques Rancière (2009) concept—"dominant fiction"—in order to examine how *The Proposition* deals with the fragmentation of Australian national identity when utilizing the Western in its attempts to address issues concerning Australia's colonial history. In *The Proposition*, the codes of the Western are employed to foreground questions of nation, space, and the myth of the past. However, Wessels argues that when these codes are used in an Australian context, the limits of the Western as a vehicle of a "dominant fiction" are exposed, and instead of creating a binding, cohesive national mythology, *The Proposition* instead articulates an understanding of the conflicting forces (essentially a triangle made up of indigenous peoples, white settlers who regard themselves as Australians and the representatives of British colonial power who wish to impose laws on them) that continue to shape Australia's national identity. Wessels determines that the Western functions differently in Australia, primarily because it has to operate in dialogue with the bushranger genre (Australia's own Western-like film form) and this dialogue exposes the limits of using the Western to establish a national mythology down under. Ultimately, Wessels argues that *The Proposition*'s employment of genre tropes actually works against the notion of a dominant fiction and in doing so the film contests any attempts to write a unified national history stemming from Australia's colonial past.

The final part of the book is entitled "Contemporary Cult Westerns and Contemporary Concerns." This part opens with Chapter 9, in which Lee Broughton examines four US Civil War–related films—Herschel Gordon Lewis's *Two Thousand Maniacs!* (1964), Sergio Garrone's *Django the Bastard* (*Django il bastardo*, 1969), George Hickenlooper's *Grey Knight* (1993), and Alex Turner's *Dead Birds* (2004)—that also incorporate supernatural elements. While it is not strictly a Western, *Two Thousand Maniacs!* is a gore-laden cult horror film directed by a cult director that satirically captures a sense of the sectional antagonisms that America was experiencing at the time of its production. The remaining three films are Westerns that possess a variety of cult film credentials. All three are exercises in genre bending as they fuse aspects of the Western with elements of the horror film. The hyper-stylish *Django the Bastard* stars a trio of cult actors in the form of Anthony Steffen, Luciano Rossi, and Rada Rassimov. *Grey Knight* is a film whose postproduction history (its producer re-edited and re-scored the film and issued a shorter version under the title *The Killing Box* [1993], which prevented the longer director's cut from being seen for several years) greatly affected its initial reception. *Dead Birds* places great emphasis on graphic and gory special effects, that are employed in both its Western and horror-themed sections, and features a plethora of unexplained enigmas.

Here Broughton draws upon the themes of three major interpretive traditions (the Reconciliation Cause, the Lost Cause and the Emancipation Cause traditions) that Gary W. Gallagher (2008) has identified as tools that Americans used—and, indeed, continue to use—in order to make sense of the US Civil War and combines their content with horror studies' take on Sigmund Freud's (2001 [1957]) work on repression, which argues that supernatural activity can represent the "return" of the repressed (the repressed usually being a painful or disturbing memory or action). By critically investigating how the Reconciliation Cause, the Lost Cause, and the Emancipation Cause traditions are employed in the films under review and considering how the films' manifestations of the supernatural might represent the "return" of the repressed, Broughton argues that the films—three American productions and one Italian production—provide wholly unorthodox representations of the US Civil War that in turn provide interesting insights into national unity, race relations, and the state of their respective nations more generally at the time of their production.

In Chapter 10 Jenny Barrett examines a trio of recent Westerns produced by non-Americans that feature the figure of the immigrant: *Jauja* (Lisandro Alonso, 2014), *The Salvation* (Kristian Levring, 2014), and *Slow West* (John Maclean, 2015). *Jauja* brings a sense of "strangeness" and "displacement" to the Western since it employs much of the genre's visual iconography and a number of its colonialist tropes in order to tell a story that takes place within the "alien" environment of Argentina's historical wild frontier. Here Danish invaders are brought into conflict with indigenous Argentineans. While it is not unusual for Westerns to feature immigrants in small or supporting character roles (usually in scenarios where they are welcomed into a community, which allows the idea that the United States is a "melting pot" of cultures to be promoted), *The Salvation* and *Slow West* are distinguished by the fact that their lead protagonists are immigrants who find America to be a violent and unwelcoming place. *The Salvation* features Danish characters and French characters (and cult figures in the form of Mads Mikkelson and Eric Cantona) while *Slow West* features Scottish, Irish, and Swedish characters.

Employing key concepts such as those of "stranger," "friend," "immigrant redeemer," "roots," and "routes," Barrett considers how the traditional promises of the America Dream hold up in this trio of films. She determines that Jon (Mads Mikkelson) in *The Salvation*, Jay (Kodi Smit-McPhee) in *Slow West* and Dinesan (Viggo Mortensen) in *Jauja* are protagonists who remain more "stranger" than "friend" because they either die or are forced to keep moving on.

For each, the route of their journey does not end with the putting down of roots. Barrett concludes that for each, their dream of settling, endorsed by faith in the American Dream, is not fulfilled. And although they are immigrant redeemers, functioning to remind other characters that there are good values to defend, none of them benefit from their act of redemption. The immigrant's settlement is violently rejected in *The Salvation*, which issues a verdict on America's rapacious exploitation of the world's resources. *Slow West* is overtly encoded as a myth whose opening words "Once upon a time" and hazy, dreamlike closure suggest that the immigrant's happy ending here is but a fairy tale. *Jauja* recasts the Western with Danish and Argentinean characters, and by inference paints the American Dream as a dream of despair for the Danish immigrant.

The part continues with Chapter 11, which sees Jack Weatherston tackling Alejandro González Iñárritu's *The Revenant* (2015). Though legitimately classed as a Western, *The Revenant* is distinguished by the fact that its narrative takes place in an earlier time frame than most genre films: its narrative unfolds in 1823 during a fur-trapping mission in the unorganized territories that would become Montana and South Dakota. Set in the snow country and featuring set-pieces that were designed to evoke a sense of immersion in the freezing landscape, the film's production was an extremely arduous affair and reports from its locations indicated that the shoot was fraught with difficulties that the cast and crew nevertheless managed to overcome. Featuring instances of extremely visceral violence, *The Revenant* gained more questionable publicity when early audiences circulated the idea that the terrifyingly authentic looking bear attack that the film's protagonist Hugh Glass (Leonardo DiCaprio) suffers also appeared to involve the bear sexually assaulting him. A noticeably good-looking film, *The Revenant*'s cult status was further secured by the knowledge that its remarkable narrative was based on a true story.

Here Weatherston critically engages with the environmental aspects of *The Revenant*'s setting and its production processes while considering the implications that they hold for the future of the Western genre on film. Weatherston notes that the film does gesture toward a notably immersive and historically accurate take on environmental authenticity but he ultimately suggests that actual interactions with the authentic in this regard tend to occur when the viewer enters into a wider, extratextual engagement with *The Revenant*. The reports of the grueling battle with nature that characterized the film's production process is one example, as is the resultant full-throated environmental advocacy that was subsequently communicated by Iñárritu and DiCaprio in a number of interviews and documentaries. By contrast, the complications of representing the primordial West on-screen are obvious: visual style and sound design have to navigate the complexities of authenticity, attempting to salvage something of the real from a mediated wilderness. Furthermore, the unreal, or hyperreal, is evident in the computer-generated animals that populate and punctuate *The Revenant*. Weatherston argues that these ghostly impressions of animals are indicative of the denuded reality of the Western ecosystem and concludes that the difficulty of making *The Revenant* in a West experiencing the wrenching dislocations of climate change points toward a precarious and contingent future for both the landscape and the Western genre itself.

The part and the book ends with Chapter 12 in which Thomas Moodie examines Quentin Tarantino's *The Hateful Eight* (2015). A cult director who possesses a self-proclaimed interest in and wide knowledge of cult movies, Tarantino loads *The Hateful Eight* with many of the properties that are associated with cult films (much as he had done with his previous Western, *Django Unchained* [2012], which Moodie also discusses here in a comparative manner). *The Hateful Eight* is intertextual in the way that it references previous cult Westerns such as Sergio Corbucci's *The Great Silence* (*Il grande silenzio*, 1968) and Joaquín Romero Marchent's *Cut-Throats Nine* (*Condenados a vivir*, 1972). Similarly, Tarantino employs music composed by Ennio Morricone, a cult composer who is best known for his working partnership with Sergio Leone. Cult films are on one level about excess and Tarantino supplies excess in a number of ways: an excessive running time; excessive dialogue, which includes the excessive use of expletives and offensive words; excessive gore and violence; and so on. The equally violent, gory, and profanity-laden *Django Unchained* had of course referenced Sergio Corbucci's original *Django* (1966) and featured a guest spot-cum-in joke involving the cult actor Franco Nero as well as featuring music by Morricone and other composers that had been lifted directly from the soundtracks of numerous Spaghetti Westerns.

Here Moodie critically analyzes *The Hateful Eight*'s cinematic and historical allusions and argues that the film operates as a broad allegory of US race relations. Indeed, he suggests that the film satirizes the societal divisions of its Reconstruction Era setting and in turn generates meanings that resonate with the contemporary moment of the film's production. Moodie argues that *The Hateful Eight*'s many references to other Western texts form part of this subversive agenda since their coexistence renders visible the political diversity inherent in their depictions and constructions of American national history on screen. After providing an overview of the ways in which the promotion of a united community has traditionally been communicated in American post–Civil War Westerns, Moodie moves on to provide a close reading of *The Hateful Eight*'s extensive dialogues on racial politics. What emerges from this analysis is the presence of a satirical strategy in which inequalities are strongly articulated only for the potential for reconciliation to be frustrated by the characters' ingrained and sustained prejudices. The resultant failure of community is ultimately presented through a violent allegory of societal collapse brought on by entrenched ideological divisions, which in the film's final moments is transcended by an ironic alliance predicated on misogyny and sadism rather than restorative communal values. The film thus subverts the unifying impulse that is common in American post–Civil War Westerns by presenting a wholly cynical vision of the United States.

This overview of Moodie's chapter is an appropriate place to note that several of this collection's chapters deal with issues of race, indigenous peoples, slavery, and colonialism. Inevitably, during the course of discussing these topics and dissecting dialogue from the films under review, problematic and, indeed, deeply offensive expressions are necessarily quoted and unavoidably reproduced. Similarly, the term "Spaghetti Western" is used in several chapters when the book's contributors are discussing Italian Westerns. Although American critics once employed the term "Spaghetti Western" in a pejorative way, it has since been used as a term of endearment by the many fans of such films, and it is employed in the same positive spirit here.

Bibliography

Dante, Joe. "Foreword." In *100 Cult Films*. By Ernest Mathijs and Xavier Mendik, vii. London: BFI, 2011.

Egan, Kate and Sarah Thomas. "Introduction: Star-making, Cult-Making and Forms of Authenticity." In *Cult Film Stardom: Offbeat Attractions and Processes of Cultification*, edited by Kate Egan and Sarah Thomas, 1–17. Basingstoke: Palgrave Macmillan, 2013.

Freud, Sigmund. *The Standard Edition of the Complete Psychological Works of Sigmund Freud Vol. XIV (1914–1916)*, edited by James Strachey. London: Vintage, 2001 [1957].

Gallagher, Gary W. *Causes Won, Lost, and Forgotten: How Hollywood and Popular Art Shape What We Know About the Civil War*. Chapel Hill: The University of North Carolina Press, 2008.

Hoberman, J. and Jonathan Rosenbaum. *Midnight Movies*. Boston: Da Capo Press, 1991 [1983].

Hunter, I. Q. *Cult Film as a Guide to Life: Fandom, Adaptation and Identity*. New York: Bloomsbury Academic, 2016.

Jancovich, Mark, et al. "Introduction." In *Defining Cult Movies: The Cultural Politics of Oppositional Taste*, edited by Mark Jancovich, Antonio Lazaro Reboll, Julian Stringer and Andy Willis, 1–13. Manchester: Manchester University Press, 2003.

Jennings, Wade. "The Star as Cult Icon: Judy Garland." In *The Cult Film Experience: Beyond All Reason*, edited by J. P. Telotte, 90–101. Austin: University of Texas Press, 1991.

Kawin, Bruce. "After Midnight." In *The Cult Film Experience: Beyond All Reason*, edited by J. P. Telotte, 18–25. Austin: University of Texas Press, 1991.

Mathijs, Ernest and Xavier Mendik. "Editorial Introduction: What Is Cult Film?" In *The Cult Film Reader*, edited by Ernest Mathijs and Xavier Mendik, 1–11. Maidenhead: Open University Press, 2008.

Mathijs, Ernest and Jamie Sexton. *Cult Cinema: An Introduction*. Oxford: Wiley-Blackwell, 2011.

Peary, Danny. *Cult Movie Stars*. London: Simon & Schuster, 1991.

Rancière, Jacques. *The Emancipated Spectator*. Translated by Gregory Elliott. London: Verso, 2009.

Telotte, J. P. "The Classical Cult Film." In *The Cult Film Experience: Beyond All Reason*, edited by J. P. Telotte, 39–41. Austin: University of Texas Press, 1991a.

Telotte, J. P. "The Midnight Movie." In *The Cult Film Experience: Beyond All Reason*, edited by J. P. Telotte, 103–5. Austin: University of Texas Press, 1991b.

Part One

Classic Cult Westerns

1

"It Seemed Like a Good Idea at the Time": Hollywood, Homology, and Hired Guns—the Making of *The Magnificent Seven*

Paul Kerr

Calvera: I don't understand why a man like you took the job in the first place. Hm? Why?

Vin: I wonder myself

Calvera: No, come on. Come on, tell me why.

Vin: It's like a fella I once knew in El Paso. One day he took off all his clothes and jumped into a mess of cactus. I asked him the same question: why?

Calvera: And?

Vin: He said it seemed like a good idea at the time.

Dialogue from The Magnificent Seven (John Sturges, 1960)

Introduction

Making any movie—let alone taking the decision to produce one in particular—is not quite the same as jumping naked into a mess of cactus but it carries its own prickly problems. This chapter will employ a critical production study of *The Magnificent Seven* (John Sturges, 1960) in order to determine why making this particular Western "seemed like a good idea at the time." I will draw in particular on the production files for the film held in the Margaret Herrick Library (MHL) in Hollywood, the collected contracts and correspondence held in the United Artists (UA) and Walter M. Mirisch Special Collections at the Wisconsin Center for Film and Theater Research (WCFTR) in Madison, the digital archive of *Variety*, interviews with surviving members of the cast and crew conducted for a Channel 4 documentary that I produced about the making of the film,

Guns for Hire: The Making of The Magnificent Seven (Channel 4, 2000), alongside autobiographies, biographies, and other accounts of the film's production.

Authors and Auteurism

Film Studies offers a literal A to Z of "theories" to "explain" the genesis of films, from Auteurism to the Zeitgeist. *Seven Samurai* (*Schichinin no samurai*, Akira Kurosawa, 1954), the film on which *The Magnificent Seven* was based, was released in the United States by Columbia in November 1956 under the title *The Magnificent Seven* (Balio 2010: 125–26). Kurosawa's "original" only began to be referred to as *Seven Samurai* in America once the remake had been announced. Appropriately enough, 1954, the year Kurosawa's classic premiered, was also the year that Francois Truffaut's celebrated article, introducing the idea of "la politique des auteurs," was first published in *Cahiers du cinema*. For the auteurist, Kurosawa is a credible "auteur" while John Sturges is not. Scan the index of virtually any academic study of American cinema and you will find a discussion of both *The Magnificent Ambersons* (Orson Welles, 1942) and *Magnificent Obsession* (Douglas Sirk, 1954) but rarely even a mention of *The Magnificent Seven*, a far more popular and arguably much more influential film. Similarly, while Preston Sturges is in the auteur canon, John Sturges is decidedly not. So perhaps, an auteurist "explanation" for the film can be dispensed with relatively swiftly. It certainly was at the time, as an early comparison of Kurosawa's "original" with Sturges's remake in *Film Quarterly* makes abundantly clear (Anderson, 1962). And no convincing case has been mounted for Sturges's status as an auteur, complete with his own signature style and thematic concerns, either in Glenn Lovell's (2008) biography of the director or in Brian Hannan's (2015) book on the film's production, though both the authors are auteurists.

Are there any other candidates for the film's authorship? The first director named in connection with the project, Yul Brynner, was its eventual star, with Martin Ritt attached as producer. It was initially announced as a Brynner project, through his company Alciona (*Variety*, 1958a) in an article which also reported that Sturges had signed a three-picture deal with the Mirisch Company. Brynner had allegedly got the idea and the directing bug from Anthony Quinn—the pair had costarred in Quinn's *The Buccaneer* (1958)—and acquired the rights from Lou Morheim, who had, in turn, secured them from the Japanese distributor. An option was agreed early in October 1957 between International Toho Company and Lou Morheim through the agency, Paul Small Artists Ltd. Inc. The agreement stipulated that "Mr Morheim's screenplay will be modern, with American names and characterizations, and set in a western (cowboy), a timberlands, oilfields, or some such backdrop" (*Variety*, 1958b).

Morheim's agent, Lilian Small, initially interested Quinn in her client's property (Morheim interview, *Guns for Hire*, 2000) and *Variety* reported that Brynner and Quinn would costar in the remake (*Variety*, 1958c). After some preproduction negotiations over the scheduling of Brynner's other on-screen commitments, the star withdrew as director to focus on playing the lead and was briefly replaced first by Anatole Litwak and then by Ritt. The latter, however, saw the project as a conventional American Western, which disappointed Morheim, so Brynner asked him how he saw it. Morheim pitched it as a Mexican Western, with Mexicans standing in for the Japanese villagers. Brynner approved this interpretation, and Alciona approached the previously blacklisted screenwriter, Walter Bernstein, who was briefed to stick closely to the original but relocate the story in Mexico, with seven gunfighters crossing the border to defend a village from bandits.

Screenwriters and even stars have also been afforded the "auteur" treatment on occasion and it is worth pausing briefly to consider their contributions to the film. Bernstein's script contains two civil war veterans, from opposing sides of the conflict, Randolph and Clayton. Quinn was originally to play the Mifune part, opposite Brynner (*Variety*, 1958c). Subsequently, Clark Gable (*Variety*, 1958d), Glenn Ford (*Variety*, 1959a), and Lloyd Nolan (*Variety*, 1959b) were all approached for this version. Even the lead role, ultimately played by Brynner himself, was initially conceived of for an older star like Gable or Spencer Tracy. Morheim and Quinn would both eventually sue Alciona and Mirisch over breach of contract (Hannan, 2015: 82). Bernstein's characters are quite different from those in the eventual film—Randolph and Clayton, Rivers (a drunk), Thayer (a bank robber), Jabe (a young sharpshooter), Bone (a quick draw gunman), and Anton (a German engineer) complete the seven. However, there are also many similarities to the finished film. The script starts with the villainous Mexicans riding into the village, though they are the local governor's men, not bandits. The seven are recruited. Bone is challenged to a duel by a rival gunman who thinks that he is faster (just like James Coburn's first scene). Rivers is only tempted to join the others because of the treasure he imagines to be behind the job (like the character of Harry Luck in the film). Jabe is initially rejected as immature, but eventually joins the others (like Chico in the film). When the seven eventually arrive in the village, they find the women are hiding in the hills (as in the eventual film). In Bernstein's script, Jabe survives, but, at the end, as he is riding off, he changes his mind and rides back to the Mexican girl. The other two survivors, Clayton and Randolph, were also the first of the seven to be introduced in this script (like Vin and Chris in the film). Bernstein's script even includes the line, "You didn't win, you lost" (Bernstein screenplay, 1959). The role of the German character, Anton Wittgenstein, in this draft, may be the one for which Horst Buchholz was originally cast—Billy Wilder, already signed by Mirisch, had cast him for his own, delayed, *One, Two, Three* (1961) and recommended him to the company. When the role was fused with Jabe to create Chico (and thus appease the Mexican censor, who was unhappy with the passivity of the Mexican villagers in Newman's draft), Buchholz seems to have been retained because he could do accents and because actors had to be signed early to avoid an impending strike by the Screen Actors Guild.

The Magnificent Seven was to have been the first film for Brynner's company, Alciona Productions (*New York Times*, 1958). When Brynner withdrew, his initial replacement was Anatole Litwak (WCFTR). The day after Alciona's announcement, it was reported that Sturges had signed a three-picture deal with the Mirisch Company (*Variety*, 1958e). Then, *Variety* reported that the Alciona film, to be produced by Paul Rudin, was about to go into production, based on Bernstein's screenplay (*Variety*, 1959c). The deal guaranteed Morheim the credit of producer or coproducer. Less than two months later (*Variety*, 1959d), the rights had been transferred to Mirisch-Alpha (Alpha was Sturges's company) with Brynner as the star and Sturges as producer-director. The Mirisch Company was then represented by Leon Kaplan of the law firm, Kaplan, Livingstone, Goodwin, and Berkowitz—the same firm also handled the affairs of John Sturges (Mirisch, 2008: 108)—and Kaplan brokered the deal between Sturges and Mirisch. With that deal, Bernstein's draft, together with the remake rights to Kurosawa's original, reverted to Mirisch while Ritt and Bernstein were summarily replaced by Sturges and Walter Newman respectively.

According to Morheim, Newman took little from Bernstein's script and went back to the original, while adapting it to a Mexican village raided by bandits but protected by "freelance cowboys" (Morheim interview, *Guns for Hire*, 2000). Walter Mirisch suggested casting James Coburn and Robert Vaughn (who had both appeared in the company's TV series, *Wichita Town* [NBC, 1959–60]). McQueen and Bronson had both been in Sturges's *Never So Few* (Sturges, 1960); Brad Dexter, Val Avery, and Bing Russell had all been in *Last Train from Gun Hill*

(Sturges, 1959). The Mexican censor, who stayed on set throughout the shoot, demanded changes to the script to ameliorate the representation of the Mexican villagers and, as Newman was unable or unwilling to travel to Mexico and/or to make such changes, another writer, William Roberts, was brought in to make the minimal necessary revisions. When the Writers Guild arbitrated on-screen credits, Newman refused to share his credit, so Roberts got a solo screenplay credit, despite having contributed least to the finished screenplay (Morheim interview, *Guns for Hire*, 2000).

Thus, *The Magnificent Seven* can claim the contributions of three writers—Bernstein, Newman, and Roberts (not to mention Kurosawa and his cowriters, Shinobu Hashimoto and Hideo Oguni), four successively attached directors (Brynner, Litvak, Ritt, and Sturges), though only one who worked throughout the production period, and five putative producers (Morheim, Ritt, Brynner's Alciona partner Paul Rudin, Sturges himself, and executive producer Walter Mirisch). But if no individual filmmaker can be cited as the only or even overriding "creator" of *The Magnificent Seven* what then can explain its production in 1960?

Capturing the Zeitgeist?

Conventional film history suggests Hollywood simply adapted a pretested plot from one national cinema market and genre to another (Martinez, 2009: 113–40). But that does not explain *why* the film *Seven Samurai* (1954) was adapted when or how it was. It could be that *The Magnificent Seven* was in some sense "authored" not by an individual filmmaker but by its relationship with the American zeitgeist—whether in terms of American imperialism abroad or American capitalism at home. This, of course, is a kind of reflection theory, but how such cinematic "reflections" of political reality are mediated, through whom and why some films allegedly reflect (or even predict) the zeitgeist in this way while others do not is rarely asked, let alone answered. Why, indeed, do particular film ideas appeal to filmmakers at particular times and then in turn appeal, if the filmmakers are lucky, to audiences? Perhaps the most influential "answer" to this question for *The Magnificent Seven* is that of Richard Slotkin (1989; 1992).

Slotkin identifies *The Magnificent Seven* as an example of what he calls "The Mexico Western," revived by *Viva Zapata* (Elia Kazan, 1952)—which had costarred Quinn—and was "developed in the largest terms by Hecht-Lancaster in their production of *Vera Cruz* (Robert Aldrich, 1954)" (Slotkin, 1989: 77). It is striking that Slotkin drops his default auteurist reflex at this point and mentions not the name of *Vera Cruz*'s director but the independent production company which produced it. But he makes nothing of this, and thus misses an opportunity to construct a more conjuncturally specific, industrially precise explanatory model. Instead he remains at the macro level. However, in the course of his plot synopsis, Slotkin makes another telling observation in passing: "Apparently the end of the wild west phase of the frontier has thrown a lot of gunfighters into unemployment" (1989: 77–78). I will return to these details in due course. It is in this context that Slotkin asserts that "the movie is a complex reflecting mechanism, not simply a device for propagating Cold War values" (1989: 76). Here Slotkin has to make a subtle maneuver, admitting that

> John Sturges' *The Magnificent Seven* was released several months before Kennedy's inauguration, and had begun production long before the 1960 presidential campaign. Obviously, we are not dealing with a case of direct influence (unless the film influenced the President). Rather, film and President share a common set of ideological premises, a common mythology and a common conception of heroic style. (1989: 76)

Slotkin proceeds to describe *The Magnificent Seven* as "officially an American remake of Akira Kurosawa's Seven Samurai—a film that itself owed a great deal to American Westerns" (1992: 474), deftly relegating Kurosawa's film to no more than a conduit for the American ideology found in earlier Hollywood films. This erasure is necessary to Slotkin's argument, which places significance on the number of members in the group. Slotkin does not want a reminder that this number derives from the Japanese original since he suggests that the protagonists are Green Berets in Western costume (Green Berets operated in teams of seven) and that the film is an allegory of American counterinsurgency (1989: 76). Slotkin also employs an auteurist approach. He never mentions that the film was produced by the Mirisch Company—it is only and always "John Sturges' *The Magnificent Seven*." And this attribution is much more than academic convention: he notes of the film's ensemble cast that "by multiplying heroes in this way, Sturges enlarges a form that had canonically focused on the single gunfighter" (Slotkin, 1989: 81). By contrast, Slotkin chooses to focus on a "single gunfighter" when he privileges Sturges and reduces a transient production team and transitional package-unit mode of production to a single filmmaker. Slotkin ignores the fact that the film had three successive screenwriters—and that the first, far from being a Cold War ideologue, was a blacklisted leftist—and implies that it was the director, rather than the production team, beginning with the multiple producers and screenwriters, who plotted the film: "In effect, Sturges has merged the conventions of the Western with the combat movie" (1989: 81). However, if such decisions are attributed not to a visionary director but to an independent production company and its freelance staff, with screenwriters, producers, and directors being hired and fired rapidly and apparently arbitrarily, quite different explanatory models might present themselves.

For Slotkin, then, *The Magnificent Seven* is "nearly an allegory of American foreign policy in Vietnam" (1989: 87). Nevertheless, he warns,

> It's vital to recall, however, that the film was made before the government decided to make Vietnam a test-case of counter-insurgency. The movie seems to anticipate both the promulgation of that policy and the crisis that tested its assumptions and called the policy into question. There is no prophetic gift involved in the process. The movie imagines its problem in these terms because it speaks out of the same ideological concerns that gave us our counter-insurgency policy: both movie and policy-makers share and exploit the same language of myth, the same images of heroism and of enemy savagery, the same narrow and essentially racist views of non-white peoples and cultures. (Slotkin, 1989: 86)

This is a serious charge to level at the three Jewish brothers who founded and ran the Mirisch Company and whose films often went out of their way to counter casual Hollywood racism. Furthermore, the one film the Mirisches produced which *did* explicitly depict insurgency, *Cast a Giant Shadow* (Melville Shavelson, 1966), did so sympathetically.

Subsequently, Slotkin amplified his argument, alleging that the film is "surprisingly prophetic" (1992: 474), that it "anticipates several aspects of the American approach to the Vietnam War" (1992: 481), and "predicts the direction in which rationalizations of American policy would move" (1992: 483). To persuade us of this, Slotkin's plot synopsis deploys anachronistic terms like "plebiscite," "Geneva settlement," "surgical strike," and "counterinsurgency" to clarify the parallels he is proposing (1989: 83–87). Here it is enough for Slotkin to suggest that "although these men are gunfighters, the form of their recruitment and association suggests that they are also commandoes, or Green Berets" (1989: 81). But if we acknowledge that they are not employees of an army but freelancers hired for a single job, the allegory—and the argument—collapses. In fact, the closest military equivalents to the seven would be mercenaries, but to acknowledge this would undermine the argument that American military ideology and foreign policy are at work in the film. Indeed, Calvera (Eli Wallach) reminds us that both his bandits and the seven "are in the same business." And it is indeed business, a job, which has brought the seven to Mexico, not a military command.

Slotkin goes on to describe the seven as a group put together "to emphasize the range and variety of skills and motives that compose such a killer elite. The common denominator is tough-mindedness and professionalism" (Slotkin, 1989: 79). As Slotkin points out, the film, and its protagonists, needs to be able to square the chivalric heroism of the classic Western with the pragmatic professionalism and mercenary materialism of their mission: "What tips Chris' balance is his discovery that the little bag of coins and the gold watch the Mexicans offer are their sole possessions. He squares his chivalric sympathies with professional hard-headedness by saying, 'I have been offered a lot for my services before, but never everything'" (1989: 79). For Slotkin, this is Green Beret professionalism and philanthropy rolled into one. But it can be understood differently. In the newly freelance employment situation following the end of vertical integration and the concomitant elimination of long-term studio staff contracts, squaring the circle between insecure employment and creative freedom was in the ideological air in Hollywood and in production companies like Mirisch. Hence, perhaps, the elision between profession and vocation.

Nevertheless, for Slotkin, *The Magnificent Seven*, despite being "drenched in ideological symbolism," is not "reducible to a determined allegory of ideology, pointing in a single direction" (1989: 88). This is an important admission, but one that seems somewhat half-hearted and a little too late. He has suggested that the film is, essentially, a premature ideological prop for counterinsurgency, ironic in that its original screenwriter was one of those attacked by the very McCarthyites who accused anti-Nazi leftists of "premature anti-fascism." While Slotkin describes this Western as articulating, indeed prematurely promoting, an aggressive American foreign policy, sociologist Will Wright (1975) sees the genre as a reflection of American domestic capitalism. While he does not discuss *The Magnificent Seven* directly, the film raises some key issues for Wright's analysis and illustrates how his model can be adapted to understand some of the ways in which films are shaped—less by a national zeitgeist and perhaps more by their production contexts.

Contexts of Production

Wright's argument is that "a clear pattern of change and development in the structure of the Western is apparent in the list of the successful films of the last forty years. This pattern of change . . . indicates that within a certain historical period only films with a specific structure were popular regardless of stars and publicity" (1975: 14). Wright goes on to divide the history of the Western into four structuring myths over four distinct periods: the classical plot (1930–55), the vengeance variation (1930–60), the transition theme (early 1950s), and the professional plot (1958–70). Wright's notion of professionalism is much the same as Slotkin's. It is the period and characteristics of the so-called professional plot which apply to *The Magnificent Seven*. For Wright, "The Professional plot extends from 1958 to 1970 and involves a group of heroes who are professionals taking jobs for money" (1975: 15) and it mirrors "the transition from a market to a managed economy" (1975: 74). Since the film was made and released in 1960 but its gestation actually began in 1958, *The Magnificent Seven* makes a fascinating test case for Wright's thesis, despite the fact that he never mentions it.

For Wright,

> All these films are about a group of heroes working for money. They are not wandering adventurers who decide to fight for a lost cause because it is right, or for the love of a girl. They are professionals, men doing a job. They are specialists who possess the unique skills used in their profession. (1975: 97)

Wright acknowledges that to relate these Western plots to their social context, he needs to demonstrate a clear correlation between the structure of the Western and the structure of contemporary American corporate institutions (1975: 130). Wright fails, however, to show how the wider American corporate culture's economic characteristics might have found their way into any particular Western. However, I argue that it is possible to identify specific transitions in the institutions, structures, and strategies of the American film industry at precisely this moment in the forms of specialization, casualization, and outsourcing to independent production companies that were being introduced. Wright's (1975) model assumes that the professional cowboy is a metaphor for the technocrat, the manager, the "technical elite" of contemporary corporate capitalism. In fact, most of the seven gunfighters are arguably more like freelance workers than managers, the equivalent of zero-hours workers rather than elite professionals, people with skills which have become anachronistic and who are suddenly all but unemployable.

Wright's structural synopsis of the professional plot breaks down into six thematic sequences: money, battle, group, independence, fight, and elite. For Wright, "the key sequence" is what he calls "independence." Like Slotkin, whose perspective also elides the industry itself, he makes nothing of this insight, thus failing to explain why the professional plot emerges in the Western—or the American economy—in 1958. However, in the specific case of the American film industry it was precisely then that post-Paramount Decree changes in Hollywood led to the creation of numerous package-unit independents, like the Mirisch Company. *The Magnificent Seven* does seem to be one of the first of the subgenre of films which could be characterized as "professional" Westerns and its genesis was, precisely, in 1958.

Following Wright, Noel Carroll (1998: 323) discusses four thematically related Mexican Westerns: *Vera Cruz*, *The Magnificent Seven*, *The Professionals* (Richard Brooks, 1966), and *The Wild Bunch* (Sam Peckinpah, 1969). According to Carroll, in each of those four films a group of American mercenaries finds itself south of the border and becomes involved in a Mexican domestic conflict. Following Slotkin, he sees the films as endorsing American counterinsurgency, though he admits that the protagonists in these films often act in support of revolutionaries and against oppression. Carroll avoids the question of origin, beyond asserting that "it is natural to suppose that they have something to do with prevailing ideological attitudes concerning international affairs" (1998: 60). Like Wright and Slotkin, Carroll equates the seven with a managerial, technocratic class when it seems more accurate to describe them as self-employed freelance laborers, albeit with specialized skills not unlike those possessed by creative workers in the film industry. *Seven Samurai* was first optioned to be remade as a Western by the screenwriter, Lou Morheim. Morheim recalled that he "envisioned a group of seven American cowboys, freelance cowboys, going down to Mexico and defending a Mexican village against bandits" (Morheim interview, *Guns for Hire*, 2000). It is suggestive that Morheim uses the anachronism "freelance" to describe the cowboys. It seems to me that an analysis that can accommodate the specifics of the industrial conjuncture in which the film was produced—the conditions of work, the mode of production, and the precise context of the film's making—might be more adequate than the promotion of either a single individual or an overarching ideology as an explanation for the 1960 production of *The Magnificent Seven*.

Studios, Production Companies, and House Styles

The idea of Hollywood "house style" and the role it played in the era of vertical integration, when the major studios had actors and production personnel on contract, has been detailed elsewhere. For instance, in an essay on the director Raoul Walsh and his 1940s films for Warner Brothers, Edward Buscombe notes that "what seems to be lacking is any conception of the relations between the economic structure of a studio, its particular organization and the kind of films it produced" (1974: 52). Buscombe suggests that "working for a studio with as distinctive a policy and style as Warners imposed a number of constraints on any director. Yet these constraints should not be thought of as merely negative in their operation. Working for the studio meant simply that the possibilities for good work lay in certain directions rather than in others" (Buscombe 1974: 60). This insight could usefully be extended to include the possibilities not only for directors but also for projects and properties themselves.

Can a comparable case be made for an independent like the Mirisch Company and its package-unit system of production—despite the fact that it neither owned nor indeed was a "studio" as such? Did the Mirisches have a business policy or strategy that can help explain why *The Magnificent Seven* was produced when and how it was? To date the best published sources on the company are a chapter in Tino Balio's (1987) excellent second volume on UA and Walter Mirisch's (2008) anecdotal autobiography. I have also published a chapter on the production of the company's classic comedy *Some Like It Hot* (Billy Wilder, 1959) (Kerr 2010) and am currently writing a book about the company (Kerr 2020). Without access to the Mirisch Company's corporate records (unavailable until the death of the last surviving brother, Walter) but aided by Walter Mirisch's own papers and those of UA, held in the Wisconsin Center for Film and Theater Research, this chapter offers an answer to Buscombe's question about "the relations between the economic structure of a company, its particular organization and the kind of films it produced," using *The Magnificent Seven* as a case study. Director Billy Wilder observed that "all the Mirisch Company asks me is the name of the picture, a vague outline of the story and who's going to be in it. The rest is up to me. You can't get any more freedom than that" (quoted in Wood 1969: 179). But far from merely freeing the filmmaker-artist from industrial chores, companies like Mirisch played a crucial role in shaping, and (despite Wilder's, or in this case Sturges's, "producer" credit) producing or co-producing, the films that carried their corporate logo. Creative freedom was not only what the Mirisches offered these producer-director "hyphenates" but also what UA offered the Mirisch Company. That this was a dependent independence, a relative autonomy, does not detract from it being more than was currently—or had perhaps even been historically—available within the vertically integrated Hollywood majors.

I want, then, to argue for the independent production company as author or, more precisely, for the conditions of production themselves to be understood as in some sense authoring *The Magnificent Seven*. That production company was the Mirisch Company (in nominal co-production with Sturges's Alpha Productions). In 1957, the three Mirisch brothers, Harold, Walter, and Marvin, had formed the Mirisch Company to produce films for UA. They had no contract writers or actors, and no studio facilities or equipment. They hired labor, facilities, and equipment by the week or month. *The Magnificent Seven* was one of their first films. The company operated as an umbrella organization providing business and legal services to newly freelance talent, primarily directors who frequently received the right of final cut. The idea was to allow filmmakers to concentrate on production while the Mirisch Company managed the logistics, arranged finance and distribution, and supervised the marketing. In return for a management fee and a share of the profits the Mirisch brothers entered into joint ventures with a variety of directors. Their assumption was that by signing up the best directors they in turn would attract the best stars.

In the 1950s Hollywood's vertically integrated studios were forced to separate production from distribution, and a wave of new independent production companies were set up to capitalize on the situation. The Mirisch Company was the epitome of this new freelance filmmaking mode which resulted in the best talent putting pictures together without studio deals. Thus, major studio-era filmmakers like Billy Wilder, William Wyler, John Ford, Robert Wise, and Anthony Mann all had deals with the Mirisch Company, which in turn was a supplier for UA. *The Apartment* (Billy Wilder, 1960) won Best Picture Oscar in 1960, and *West Side Story* (Robert Wise and Jerome Robbins, 1961) won it for them again the following year. Thus, *The Magnificent Seven* was made by an extremely ambitious company on the eve of the zenith of its industry recognition.

Janet Staiger has described how the studio system's so-called "producer mode of production" was displaced by the independents' "package mode of production" in the wake of 1948 anti-trust legislation which forced the studios to divest themselves of their theatres, while many new companies, without studios or permanent staff, emerged, renting offices and equipment and hiring freelancers. Each film was now a one-off package, made by a team assembled precisely for that production (Bordwell, Staiger and Thompson 1985: 330–35). Staiger usefully identifies seven characteristic strategies of such companies:

1. the disappearance of self-contained studios and contract staff and the development of casualization and location filming including so-called runaway production;

2. the drive to maximize attractions (multi-star packages) deploying action and spectacle;

3. the drive to minimize risk (increasing reliance on pre-sold literary, theatrical, and film properties—remakes);

4. the differentiation of films from TV—and from each other (every film a one-off);

5. the emergence of producer-director and producer/star hyphenates often on profit-sharing contracts;

6. the increasing importance at the box office of the youth demographic and of younger stars and the targeting of specific audiences; and

7. the imperative toward innovations of story (sometimes challenging censorship), stars, and director (Bordwell, Staiger, Thompson 1985: 330–35).

The Magnificent Seven deployed all seven of these characteristics. It was shot on location in Mexico (as a so-called "runaway production"), by a freelance, casualized cast, and crew, with only the director, star, and executive producer on contracts beyond that single film. It assembled an ensemble package of costar talent to surround its one legitimate movie star lead (Yul Brynner) and that assembly is mirrored in the film's own fictional narrative. Its origin in a recent art cinema and film festival hit provided it with both a narrative model and a pre-marketed storyline and functioned as something of a risk aversion strategy (characteristic of many Mirisch productions). As a one-off, the film distinguished itself from the then epidemic of multi episode TV Westerns and the deaths of so many of its leads differentiated it from the recurring and apparently "unkillable" casts of long-running Western series. And yet, ironically, it provided the launch-pad not only for three sequels but also, much later, for a TV series of its own and, eventually, a remake.

The producer-director John Sturges had a profit-sharing deal and indeed Sturges made several million dollars from the project. The ensemble package of on-screen, comparatively new, young talents assembled to complement—and contrast—the presence of the big-screen (familiar, older) star Brynner clearly functioned both to attract and to mirror the new youth-majority audience— and the casting of Steve McQueen (Vin), Robert Vaughn (Lee), James Coburn (Britt), Charles Bronson (Bernardo) and Horst Buchholz (Chico) was evidence of this. Indeed, the eventual script and cast contrasted dramatically with the older stars originally approached by Brynner and Alciona and the characters in Bernstein's original screenplay draft.

Chris's reputation with a gun attracts the six other gunmen to work with him in much the same way that the film's director attracted male action stars to the project: Walter Mirisch noted that "with Sturges we have a definite asset in attracting top male stars" (quoted in Balio 1987: 173). Similarly, Sturges admitted to modeling the role of Calvera on his old studio bosses at Columbia and MGM: "I didn't want a big tough guy because the style of that part was not that of a big tough guy. Like Cohn and Mayer, he's a conman, a negotiator . . . this hypocritical guy who sanctifies what he's doing by turning things around" (quoted in Lovell 2008: 196). This is not to recruit Sturges into the auteur pantheon through some anecdotal back door. But it is to insist that those who worked in Hollywood worked there in specific contexts and under precise contractual conditions, at particular moments and under particular pressures. Such pressures and contexts partially determined not only the ways they were employed but also the kinds of projects they were employed to work on and even the nature of their contributions to those projects.

Much is made in the film's dialogue of the fact that the seven are doing a "job as hired guns," that they "took a contract" and are to be paid "$20 for six weeks work." Vin joins up because he is broke, and the alternative, clerking in a store— "good, steady work," as one of the Mexicans informs him—is anathema. Meeting Calvera for the first time, Chris says, "Solving problems isn't in our line." Vin adds, "We deal in lead, friend." Calvera replies, "So do I, we are in the same business." And later, asked about what happens to the villagers, Calvera replies, "Can men of our profession worry about that?" The language is of business, of doing a job, of being hired professionals. As Vin explains to Chris, "You know, the first time I took a job as a hired gun, a fella told me, Vin, you can't afford to care." Or as Chris explains earlier in the film, "Men in this line of work are not all alike. Some care about nothing but money. Others, for reasons of their own, enjoy only the danger. And the competition." O'Reilly tells the children, "This is my work." And later one of the Mexican villagers says, "That is not what you were hired for." As Harry says on his first meeting with Chris, "I heard you got a contract open . . ." When Vin proposes abandoning the village, Chris is adamant. "You forget one thing. We took a contract." The Mirisch Company supported Newman's shooting script (and Roberts's minimal on-set revisions) and defended it against UA's suggested cuts when the film was in postproduction. It is particularly pertinent that the early scenes, in which the seven are "hired" and individuated, remained intact. Thus, the relative autonomy which Mirisch granted producer-directors like Sturges was mirrored by the relative autonomy the company had from UA.

The case I am arguing here is that, rather than reflecting the wider cultural zeitgeist, whether that be America's foreign policy or domestic corporate economics, *The Magnificent Seven*'s narrative embodies, in homologous structural form, its own mode of production—the package-unit mode of production deployed by independents at the end of the 1950s. I suggest that this is why the project seemed like a good idea at the time to the Mirisch Company. I use the term "homology" (I prefer it to Slotkin's term "allegory," which implies intentionality), in the sense that Raymond Williams deployed it in discussing the relationship between base and superstructure in Marxist cultural theory:

> There is the notion of "homologous structures," where there may be no direct or easily apparent similarity . . . between the superstructural process and the reality of the base, but in which there is an essential homology or correspondence of structures, which can be discovered by analysis. (1980: 33)

In Williams's sense, *The Magnificent Seven* is a (Western) homology for the replacement of the old, vertically integrated, Hollywood studios with their salaried staffs, by new package-unit independents, with a small team put together to do a particular one-off job. The cast and crew are "hired guns" in just the same way that the seven gunfighters are, paid a fee for their services for fulfilling a specific contract.

Conclusion

The Magnificent Seven was not necessarily a consciously "autobiographical" project for the filmmakers. However, such stories and such experiences relating to teams of industry professionals being brought together to work on one-off productions were, at that precise moment in Hollywood, in that specific sector of the industry, in the very air that those filmmakers breathed. But the fact that the film was made exactly in 1960—the cut-off point in Bordwell, Staiger, and Thompson's (1985) seminal account of *The Classical Hollywood Cinema*—is also suggestive. It is a pivotal film, falling between the classic Hollywood and the so-called New Hollywood and between the classical Western and the professional Western. And as such it functions too as an indicator of the way Hollywood itself was changing both as industry and as cinema.

Perhaps *The Magnificent Seven* felt like a good idea in 1958—and an exceedingly appropriate one in 1960—not because it mythologized a stage in American corporate capitalism, the development of which was far from synchronous across all of the nation's industries, and the experience of which was not necessarily particularly positive at such a transformative moment in the film industry. Nor, perhaps, because it was a story in synch with its times because of an allegedly allegorical relationship with a war not yet begun, by a president not yet elected. But, perhaps, because its story rang a bell with a community of filmmakers whose own experience of employment, whose own sense of themselves as professionals, but also, virtually overnight, as freelancers, rather than staff, was deeply destabilized. And perhaps the way that the story squared the circle between their increasingly insecure professional status and the positive spin they could put on that insecurity as creative, autonomous, vocational, elective, and even ethical—helped them to live that contradiction. That may, in part, explain why the film seems to have meant more to its makers than it did, at least on its initial release, to its American audience.

Bibliography

Note: some references to *Variety* have no page numbers, as this is how several cuttings have been preserved in the Margaret Herrick Library (MHL) production file for the film.

Anderson, Joseph L. "When the Twain Meet: Hollywood's Remake of 'The Seven Samurai'." *Film Quarterly*, Special Issue on Hollywood, 15, no. 3, Spring (1962): 55–58.

Balio, Tino. *The Foreign Film Renaissance on American Screens 1946–1973*. Madison: University of Wisconsin Press, 2010.

Balio, Tino. *United Artists: The Company That Changed the Film Industry*. Madison: University of Wisconsin Press, 1987.

Bernstein, Walter. *The Magnificent Seven* (Screenplay) in Margaret Herrick Library production file for the film, 1959 [All other quotations are from the film itself].

Bordwell, David, Janet Staiger, and Kristin Thompson. *The Classical Hollywood Cinema.* New York: Routledge & Kegan Paul, 1985.

Buscombe, Edward. "Walsh and Warner Brothers." In *Raoul Walsh*, edited by Phil Hardy, 51–61. Edinburgh Film Festival, London: British Film Institute, 1974.

Carroll, Noel. "South of the Border: The Professional Western." In *Back in the Saddle Again: New Essays on the Western*, edited by Edward Buscombe and Roberta Pearson, 46–62. London: British Film Institute, 1998.

Guns for Hire: The Making of The Magnificent Seven [Television Programme, Channel 4], Dir. Louis Heaton, UK / USA: Channel 4 Television Corporation / October Films, 2000.

Hannan, Brian. *The Making of the Magnificent Seven: Behind the Scenes of the Pivotal Western.* Jefferson: McFarland & Company, 2015.

Kerr, Paul. "'A Small, Effective Organization': The Mirisch Company, The Package Unit System and the Production of Some Like it Hot." In *Billy Wilder, Moviemaker: Critical Essays*, edited by Karen McNally, 117–31. Jefferson: McFarland & Company, 2010.

Kerr, Paul. *Hollywood's Missing Link: How the Mirisch Company Remade Hollywood.* New York: Bloomsbury, 2020.

Lovell, Glenn. *Escape Artist: The Life and Films of John Sturges.* Madison: University of Wisconsin Press, 2008.

Martinez, Dolores. *Remaking Kurosawa: Translations and Permutations in Global Cinema.* New York: Palgrave Macmillan, 2009.

Mirisch, Walter. *I Thought We Were Making Movies, Not History.* Madison: University of Wisconsin Press, 2008.

Morheim, Lou. Interview for *Guns for Hire.* Los Angeles, 2000.

New York Times, "Japanese Movie Will Be Adapted." May 13, 1958, 26.

Relyea, Robert with Craig Craig. *Not So Quiet on the Set: My Life in Movies During Hollywood's Macho Era.* Bloomington: iUniverse, 2008.

Sarris, Andrew. *The American Cinema: Directors and Directions 1929–1968.* New York: EP Dutton and Co, 1968.

Slotkin, Richard. *Gunfighter Nation: The Myth of the Frontier in Twentieth Century America.* New York: University of Oklahoma Press, 1992.

Slotkin, Richard. "Gunfighters and Green Berets: The Magnificent Seven and the Myth of Counter-Insurgency." Division II Faculty Publications. Paper 29, 1989. Available online: http://wesscholar.wesleyan.edu/div2facpubs/29 (accessed December 12, 2018).

Truffaut, Francois. "Une certaine tendance du cinema francais." *Cahiers du cinema*, 31, January (1954): 15–29.

Variety. "Brynner May Star in Jap Film Remake." March 3, (1958a): 1.

Variety. "Morheim, Story Editor Turned Prod'r Hits Best Seller Fad." September 19 (1958b): 6.

Variety. "Tony Quinn to Star in 'Magnificent Seven,'" November 6 (1958c): 1.

Variety. MHL, December 19 (1958d): (no page number).

Variety. MHL, May 21 (1958e): (no page number).

Variety. "Chatter." July 8 (1959a): 94.

Variety. "Just for Variety." July 7 (1959b): 2.

Variety. MHL, June 24 (1959c): (no page number).

Variety. "John Sturges to Rein Mirisch 7." August 19 (1959d): 2.

WCFTR, United Artists Collection, Internal United Artists memo from Robert F. Blumofe to Max E. Youngstein, "Re: Anatole Litwak," June 12, 1959. UA Addition, Box 5, Folder 4.

Williams, Raymond. "Base and Superstructure in Marxist Cultural Theory." In *Problems in Materialism and Culture*, 31–49. London: Verso, 1980.

Wood, Tom. *The Bright Side of Billy Wilder, Primarily.* New York: Doubleday, 1969.

Wright, Will. *Sixguns and Society: A Structural Study of the Western.* Berkeley: University of California Press, 1975.

2

The Historical Accuracy of Sergio Leone's *The Good, the Bad and the Ugly*

Peter J. Hanley

Introduction

The historical accuracy of Sergio Leone's *The Good, the Bad and the Ugly* (*Il buono, il brutto, il cattivo*, 1966), a Western set during the American Civil War (1861–65), has been open to scrutiny for over fifty years. In a featurette on the two-disc special edition of *The Good, the Bad and the Ugly*, film historian Richard Schickel (2004) called the historical accuracy of Leone's films into question: "All directors doing historical films make big claims about authenticity. And, and Sergio did . . . . But I also never really believe directors when they talk about authenticity of an historical kind." Similarly, film historian Patrick McGilligan (McGilligan 2002: 135) stated in a Clint Eastwood biography, "Authenticity would not be a hallmark of Leone's films. . . . The most important thing was plenty of horses and costumes and guns and blood." However, close readings of *The Good, the Bad and the Ugly*, when aligned with research into historical documentation of the American Civil War, reveal that the film is rich in historically accurate details. Furthermore, there are numerous references to Sibley's 1862 New Mexico campaign, which provides a tangible link to Civil War engagements in the West, although the plot was clearly fiction and there was no impetus to reenact specific events associated with this campaign. Instead, archive Civil War images, depicted in books or other sources, were used extensively by Sergio Leone and the film's production designer and art director Carlo Simi, as well as other colleagues, to provide historically accurate elements in scenes. Thus, the sets, props, and other visual elements are a collage of carefully researched and historically accurate elements, whereas the plot— while being set within a real historical period and real historical locations—

does not appear to be inspired by actual historical events. While acknowledging that there are examples of historical inaccuracies present too, this chapter will endeavor to reveal that, in the most part, the content of *The Good, the Bad and the Ugly* is historically accurate or inspired by historical images. Reference is made throughout to the 178 minutes long version of *The Good, the Bad and the Ugly* that was restored in 2002 (for more details regarding the various shorter versions of the film that have existed see Hanley 2016 and Broughton 2017).

Historical Setting

The vast majority of the American Civil War was fought in the East, in states such as Pennsylvania, Maryland, and Virginia (Donald 1956; Ketchum 1960; Price 1961; Macdonald 1988), whereas *The Good, the Bad and the Ugly* was, by definition of a Western, set in the West. This geographical discrepancy potentially undermined the plausibility of the plot. However, in 1862, there was a Civil War battle lasting one day on the Rio Grande (Taylor 1999), led on the Confederate side by the drunken General Sibley (Taylor 1999: 11). This battle was followed by several days of fighting in Glorieta Pass on the Santa Fe Trail (Edrington and Taylor 2000). These relatively small engagements did not escape the meticulous preproduction research undertaken by Sergio Leone and his colleagues, which included the study of archive Civil War material obtained from various sources, including the Library of Congress. For example, during the shooting of the film, *Vie Nuove* (Cinema 1966: 25) reported, together with behind-the-scenes stills taken at Elios Studios in Rome, "*Per Il buono, il brutto, il cattivo, Leone si è recato a Washington a consultare gli archivi della guerra di secession* [For *The Good, the Bad and the Ugly*, Leone went to Washington to consult the archives of the Civil War]." A brief outline of Sibley's 1862 New Mexico campaign and its many appearances in *The Good, the Bad and the Ugly* are highlighted in the next section.

Sibley's 1862 New Mexico Campaign

In 1862, Confederate Brigadier General Henry Hopkins Sibley, along with over 2,500 Texans, invaded the New Mexico Territory. Sibley is mentioned in *The Good, the Bad and the Ugly* by a hotel owner (Jesús Guzmán) as he points out the general in a column of Confederates retreating from Santa Fe. He is also mentioned by the prostitute Maria (Rada Rassimov) in Santa Ana (located southwest of Santa Fe; Hardesty 1883), while she is being brutally interrogated by Angel Eyes (Lee Van Cleef). In addition, Angel Eyes refers to Sibley in a conversation with Tuco (Eli Wallach) during the interior scene at Betterville prison camp. Sibley, a graduate of the United States Military Academy at West Point, had served at Fort Union before resigning and switching his allegiance to the Confederate States of America (Hall 2000: 21; Taylor 1999: 10). Retrospectively, the strategic aims of Sibley's ambitious campaign are not clear, although it is thought that, in addition to extending the Confederate States of America, he wanted to gain access to the raw materials and gold of the Rocky Mountains (New Mexico and Colorado) and perhaps California (Hall 2000: XI; Wooster 1996: 133; Taylor 1999: 1). The capture of California and its major ports, especially the Port of San Francisco, would have enabled the Confederacy to circumvent the Union blockade of the Confederate Atlantic and Gulf coastline (Wooster 1996: 133), which had been implemented by President Abraham Lincoln on April 19, 1861. A map depicting the Atlantic and Gulf Blocking Squadrons of the US Navy can be seen on the field desk of the artillery captain (Aldo Giuffrè) in the Battle of Langstone Bridge sequence.

Formation of Sibley's Brigade

Shortly after the outbreak of the Civil War, Sibley was promoted on May 13, 1861, to major of the 1st (United States) Dragoons, stationed in New Mexico Territory. However, on the same day he received his promotion, he resigned from the US Army with the intention to serve under the "glorious banner of the Confederate States of America" (Wooster 1996: 132). Similar to Sibley's case, Robert E. Lee was promoted to colonel on March 28, 1861, but he resigned from the US Army several weeks later, on April 20. After the onset of the Civil War, Lee was appointed to a full general in the Confederate States Army, although he declined to wear the insignia of a general. General Lee is mentioned by Tuco and Blondie (Clint Eastwood) in the scene in which they encounter Union cavalrymen. Tuco loudly calls out, "Hurrah, hurrah for the Confederacy. Hurrah, down with General Grant [General Ulysses S. Grant]. Hurrah for General." He turns to Blondie and whispers, "What's his name?" and Blondie replies, "Lee." Tuco continues in a loud voice, "Lee, Lee . . ."

After resigning, Sibley traveled along the long, arduous roads to Richmond, Virginia, the capital of the Confederacy, where, in due course, he was commissioned to the rank of brigadier general (infantry officer in command of a brigade) on July 5, 1861 (Wooster 1996: 132). Sibley, armed with firsthand knowledge of resident Federal forces, managed to win the support of Jefferson Davis, president of the Confederate States of America, for his bold plan to invade the territory of New Mexico. Full of optimism, Sibley left Richmond and arrived in San Antonio, Texas, in mid-August 1861. Initially, it proved difficult to recruit men for his brigade, and Sibley had to resort to public appeals and patriotic press (Wooster 1996: 135), but by the end of October, the recruitment and training of Sibley's brigade was essentially complete.

March from San Antonio to Fort Bliss (El Paso)

Around mid-November 1861, the Sibley brigade departed San Antonio, Texas (Thompson 2001: 9; Wooster 1996: 140). The "boys" marched from San Antonio via San Felipe Springs to Camp Hudson (also called Fort Hudson) on the Devil's River. In high definition Blu-ray frames of *The Good, the Bad and the Ugly*, Camp Hudson and Devil's River can be detected on a Texas map carried by Tuco, which he refers to while on the stagecoach with Blondie. From Camp Hudson, the Confederates headed up to Beaver Lake (Thompson 2001: 12). The Sibley brigade then marched up the Pecos River, passing Fort Lancaster along the way (Beaver Lake, Pecos River, and Fort Lancaster, as well as S. FELIPE (San Felipe Springs) and Rio Grande, can also be identified on Tuco's Texas map). The army marched to Fort Quitman in the Rio Grande Valley, and then headed to El Paso. Fort Quitman can be seen in a behind-the-scenes still showing Tuco's New Mexico map, which he consults immediately prior to being arrested by Union soldiers at the perimeter of the Langstone Bridge battlefield. Sibley's troops arrived in El Paso on December 24, 1861 (Thompson 2001: 14). After the long march along wagon ruts from San Antonio to El Paso, covering a distance of more than 500 miles, the Sibley brigade was poised to invade New Mexico (Wooster 1996: 141–47).

Invasion of New Mexico

Sibley's brigade headed north along the Rio Grande, mentioned by Tuco in the restored scene in which he consults a map, with Blondie at the reigns, after departing the mission at San Antonio. In the same scene, Tuco refers to the Sierra Magdalena (Magdalena Mountains) which lie just west of Valverde and the Rio

Grande. Along the way, Sibley's brigade passed via Mesilla, seen on a sign (Bank [of] Mesilla Est [Established] 1856) in the scene in which Blondie delivers the "wanted" Tuco to a marshal (John Bartho) and collects $2,000 reward money. Mesilla, below the thirty-fourth parallel in the New Mexico Territory, had already been declared part of the Confederate States of America in March 1861 (Taylor 1999: 5). In accord, the reward money which Blondie received in Mesilla consisted of (replica) Confederate $100 notes (Slabaugh 2001: 48).

Within several weeks of departing El Paso, Sibley encountered Colonel Edward Richard Sprigg Canby (United States) at a crossing on the Rio Grande. Canby is mentioned by a Confederate sergeant (Victor Israel) in the restored scene in which Angel Eyes visits a ruined fort. He is also mentioned by Tuco when he leads Blondie into the desert. Colonel Canby was also a graduate of West Point and his path had already crossed several times with Sibley (Taylor 1999: 13–14). They had fought together in campaigns predating the Civil War. There was even an unfounded rumor that Canby and Sibley were brothers-in-law (Edrington and Taylor 2000: 15). The garrison commanded by Canby consisted of about 3,800 men, around 1,000 of which were *Colorado Volunteers* (mentioned by the sergeant at the ruined fort; Incrocci et al. 1966). After being lured out of Fort Craig (mentioned by Angel Eyes when he questions Tuco at Betterville: "You were, ah, captured near Fort Craig"), Canby engaged Sibley on February 21, 1862, in the "Battle of Valverde," the largest Civil War battle fought in the far West (Edrington and Taylor 2000: 21). Valverde (from Spanish, meaning "green valley") is a town near the battlefield (seen on signs, Bank of Valverde and Post Office of Valverde, in the scene in which Angel Eyes walks to a stagecoach after talking to the "half soldier").

The Confederate Order of Battle included the *2nd Texas Mounted Rifles* (mentioned by the "half soldier" during his conversation with Angel Eyes; Incrocci et al. 1966), under the command of Major Charles Pyron. This regiment was also known as "Baylor's Command" in light of its previous commander, the illustrious Lieutenant Colonel John Baylor (referred to as *"Captain Baylor"* by the "half soldier"; Incrocci et al. 1966). In brief, the Battle of Valverde, involving infantry, cavalry, and artillery, was a tactical victory for the Confederates. Sibley, also known as "the Walking Whiskey Keg," was unwell and was forced to retire early from the battlefield (Taylor 1999: 74). At the end of the bloody day of February 21, Canby suffered an astoundingly high total of about 475 casualties (killed, wounded, or missing), much higher than his initial estimates, and retreated to the safety of Fort Craig. Confederate casualties amounted to about

228. However, Sibley's force had already been reduced by around 500 men before the battle at Valverde due to diseases, desertion, and transfers (Taylor 1999: 17). Arch (Archibald) Stanton, whose gravemarker holds a clue to the location of the stolen gold in *The Good, the Bad and the Ugly*, died on "3 FEBRUARY 1862" and may thus have been an early victim of Sibley's New Mexico campaign. Notably, all of the tombs in the final scene set in Sad Hill cemetery are dated 1862 or earlier. Already in February 1862, pneumonia was taking its toll on Sibley's men, who were suffering the cold winter and lacked sufficient warm clothing and blankets.

In light of their heavy losses and insufficient ammunition, the Confederates did not attempt to capture Fort Craig and its supplies. Instead, they broke camp on February 23, and headed north toward Santa Fe. Maria mentions Santa Fe when she is interrogated by Angel Eyes in Santa Ana: "He [Corporal Bill Carson] packed his things ten days ago and went away with his unit. . . . Third Cavalry, General Sibley [although the cavalry regiments were officially designated as the Fourth, Fifth, and Seventh Regiments, the men referred to them as the First, Second, and Third Regiments of the Sibley Brigade (Hall 2000: 27; Thompson 2001: 11)]. They left for *Santa Fe*." Santa Fe is also seen on a sign (Santa Fe Hotel) in the scene in which the Confederates are retreating while Tuco and three fellow bandits are encroaching Blondie's hotel room. In addition, Angel Eyes mentions Santa Fe when he questions Tuco: "Well, if you were with Sibley, that means, then, that you were, ah, coming from *Santa Fe*." On the night of February 23, the Confederates captured Socorro (name of a town in a deleted scene; Incrocci et al. 1966) with minimal resistance. Following news of the battle at Valverde, the Union sought to reinforce Fort Union with the First Regiment of Colorado Volunteers, commanded by Colonel John Slough. In the meantime, Sibley devised a plan to advance on Fort Union using three separate columns. One column would move from Santa Fe, whereas the other two columns would head northeast from Albuquerque (mentioned by one of Tuco's Mexican bandits in a restored scene), where Sibley's headquarters were located. The two columns which departed from Albuquerque passed via San Antonio. (Tuco is told by a Confederate sergeant, in a restored night time scene, that he is "*near Apache Canyon*," and that the mission at San Antonio [mentioned by the "half soldier"; Incrocci et al. 1966] is "*eighteen miles south.*") Indeed, San Antonio, New Mexico (as distinct from San Antonio, Texas) lies on the banks of the Rio Grande and is about 40 miles southwest of Apache Canyon (part of the Santa Fe Trail). Interestingly, although San Antonio, New Mexico, is not known for Franciscan missions, San Antonio, Texas, is well known for Franciscan missions that were built in the eighteenth century.

On March 26, some of the Coloradans reinforcing Fort Union continued south shortly after arriving, and they surprised one of Sibley's advancing parties in a skirmish at the mouth of Apache Canyon, which lies about fifteen miles (east of Santa Fe) along the Santa Fe Trail. Casualties were low on both sides: Three Confederates killed versus five Coloradans (Federal troops) killed, but seventy-one Confederates, and only three Coloradans, were taken prisoner (Edrington and Taylor 2000: 53). Both sides spent March 27 amassing their forces on the Santa Fe Trail: The Confederates (about 800 men) camped at Johnson's Ranch, whereas the Union troops (about 1,400 men), after exhausting supplies at Pigeon's Ranch, camped at Kozlowski's Ranch (Edrington and Taylor 2000: 63), the name assigned to the ruined fort visited by Angel Eyes (Incrocci et al. 1966). On the morning of March 28, the Union forces marched along the Santa Fe Trail and met the Confederates just west of Pigeon's Ranch at Glorieta Pass. Glorieta is mentioned in the restored scene in which a Confederate sergeant says to Angel Eyes (at the ruined fort), "If he's [Bill Carson] with the Third, they've gone to *Glorieta*." In brief, the Confederates employed superior tactics and forced a Union retreat, thereby winning the battle of Glorieta Pass, sometimes referred to as "the Gettysburg of the West" (Taylor 1999: 5). However, while the main battle raged near Pigeon's Ranch, a raiding party led by Major John M. Chivington destroyed the Confederate supply train which had been left, insufficiently guarded as in turned out, at Johnson's Ranch.

Colonel William Scurry, acting commander (because Sibley was intoxicated), decided not to chase the retreating Union force, possibly because his men were exhausted, and, also, the destruction of his supply train may have both demoralized and demotivated him. Even if Scurry had not lost his supply train at Johnson's Ranch, the Confederates would have had little chance of capturing Fort Union, a major goal of the invasion. The Confederates lacked heavy artillery, and, on the Union side, Colonel Slough had been given orders by General Canby to fall back to, and thereby reinforce, Fort Union (Edrington and Taylor 2000: 106). Canby had earlier anticipated that Fort Union, 200 miles north of Fort Craig, could be a target of a Confederate invasion, and, in 1861, he had ordered the construction of a formidable star-shaped, defensive earthwork. Late on the evening of March 29, the Confederates left Glorieta Pass, passed through Apache Canyon, and, after marching through the night, straggled into Santa Fe. Several days later, Sibley, on April 5, joined his troops in Santa Fe. He realized that his force was not in sufficient condition to assault Fort Union and he also heard news that Colonel Canby, who had left Fort Craig on April 1, was advancing on Albuquerque. That left one option, the Confederates would have to retreat.

Although the historical backdrop of *The Good, the Bad and the Ugly* is clearly Sibley's New Mexico campaign, there are only scant references to any specific historical locations following the Betterville prison camp sequence. After being tortured, Tuco is taken to a railroad station. However, the railroad did not reach New Mexico until around eighteen years after Sibley's campaign, suggesting that the historical setting of the film shifts to the East, where the railroad was expansive (Abdill 1999). All things considered, a remarkable amount of historical research was done to ensure that "the Good," "the Bad," and "the Ugly" seek their fortunes within a plausible historical context.

Scenes and Set Designs Inspired by Historical Books and Photos

Numerous visual elements in *The Good, the Bad and the Ugly* were inspired by historical photos published in books about the American Civil War. Two photographic books, in particular, Alexander Gardner's *Photographic Sketch Book of the Civil War* (hereafter *Gardner's*, 1959) and *Divided We Fought: A Pictorial History of the War 1861–1865* (hereafter *Divided We Fought*, 1956), served as sources for historical photos. The former is a reproduction of *Gardner's Photographic Sketch Book of the War*, published in two volumes in 1866, which collectively contains a hundred albumen prints. The detailed lithograph preceding each volume of photos was used in the design of the Italian (first-release) 18¼-inch × 26½-inch *Fotobuste* for *The Good, the Bad and the Ugly*, as shown on page 129 in Peter J. Hanley's *Behind-the-scenes of Sergio Leone's The Good, the Bad and the Ugly* (2016). On close inspection, both *Gardner's* and *Divided We Fought* can be seen in high-resolution behind-the-scenes stills taken adjacent to the Sad Hill cemetery set. One of these stills (Figure 2.1) shows Sergio Leone directing the positioning of an extra as a dead soldier. Leone is holding a copy of *Gardner's*, and he is using his finger to bookmark a page. Notably, Gardner is renowned for taking the first photographs of dead soldiers lying on an American battlefield. Accordingly, the extras placed as dead soldiers in *The Good, the Bad and the Ugly*, in the scene where Blondie comforts a dying Confederate as he and Tuco near

Figure 2.1 Behind-the-scenes still (Reporters Associati, Rome) showing Sergio Leone positioning an extra as a dead soldier on the Sad Hill cemetery set. Leone is holding a copy of *Gardner's Photographic Sketch Book of the Civil War* in his left hand, and he is marking a page with his forefinger. The inset shows the reverse of the dust cover of *Gardner's Photographic Sketch Book of the Civil War*, part of which is visible in Leone's hand. The dust cover of the book, published by Dover Publications in 1959, had either a green front and orange reverse or vice versa.

Sad Hill cemetery, resemble the images captured by Gardner. Indeed, one of the dead soldiers seen when Blondie and Tuco walk around a cheval-de-frise (a defense consisting of a log with protruding wooden spikes) while approaching the ruin where Blondie gives the dying Confederate a puff on his cigar, is positioned, together with his cap and rifle, in a similar manner to the dead Confederate depicted in Gardner's photo, Plate 40, with the caption: A Sharpshooter's Last Sleep, Gettysburg, July, 1863. Interestingly, Frederic Ray (1961: 19) and William A. Frassanito (1975: 186–92) deduced that Gardner moved the dead soldier to a nearby location to stage his iconic photo titled "Home of a Rebel Sharpshooter, Gettysburg, July, 1863."

In a high-resolution behind-the-scenes still showing Clint Eastwood relaxing with a bottle of El Aguila beer, a historical Civil War book can be identified on the ground. Although the spine is partially obscured by vegetation and a bottle of Okey, a Spanish citrus fruit drink, the text "We F . . . t," as well as part of the date 1861, can be identified (Figure 2.2). The full text on the spine of this book is "Divided We Fought ★ 1861–1865," with Macmillan (the publisher) at the base. Parts of this book were photographed by Leone's assistant director Fabrizio Gianni (e.g., see Fig. 11.59 in Hanley 2016: 366) in order to provide additional copies of selected pages for use by *The Good, the Bad and the Ugly*'s production personnel. Indeed, many of the production designs and sketches made by art director Carlo Simi were copied from archive Civil War photographs found in this book. For example, a technical drawing (Figure 2.3) titled "Batterie Benson" and dated March 3, 1966, closely matches the limbered field gun shown in the foreground of the photo on page 53 (Donald 1956), which has the caption: "Benson's Battery, 2nd U.S. Artillery." All six guns of Benson's field artillery battery can be seen in the photo, taken by Civil War photographer James F. Gibson. In *The Good, the Bad and the Ugly*, several horse-drawn field guns, with cannoneers sitting on the ammunition chest of the limber and drivers riding the left horses, as was customary, can be seen in the scene where Sibley's men are retreating from Santa Fe, New Mexico, just after Blondie has cleaned and inspected the barrel of his revolver. Normally, each gun, attached to a limber, was pulled by six horses, rather than four horses (as in the film), although this is not clear in the Civil War photo of Benson's Battery (Figure 2.3).

In addition to Benson's Battery, Civil War photos of railroad mounted artillery shown in *Divided We Fought* made appearances in the railroad sequence of *The Good, the Bad and the Ugly*, shot at *la Estación de La Calahorra* in Granada, Spain. Page 371 (Donald 1956) depicts a siege mortar mounted on a railroad flatcar with the caption: "Thirteen-Inch Mortar 'Dictator' in Front of Petersburg." Another photo on page 44 (Donald 1956) shows seven 13-inch mortars of Battery No. 4, near Yorktown, Virginia. Carlo Simi made detailed drawings, side and top elevations, of a siege mortar, titled "Il Dittatore" and dated March 10, 1966. The detailed drawings closely match the 13-inch mortars depicted on page 44 (Donald 1956). Another photo of the "Dictator" can be seen on the dust cover, and in the book (Plate 75), of *Gardner's*. In this photo, a group of officers are posing beside the mortar. In *The Good, the Bad and the*

Figure 2.2 Behind-the-scenes still (courtesy © Archivio Fotografico della Cineteca Nazionale [Roma]; photo by Divo Cavicchioli) showing Clint Eastwood relaxing on the Sad Hill cemetery set. On the ground, below his left knee, and partly obscured by shadow, a bottle and shrubs, is a Civil War book (*Divided We Fought: A Pictorial History of the War 1861–1865*) without its dust cover. The inset comparison photo shows the spine of *Divided We Fought* without its dust cover and an antique *Okey* bottle.

Ugly, the 13-inch mortar is not mounted on a railroad flatcar but the railroad sequence does feature a scene in which an actor dressed as the renowned Civil War photographer Mathew Brady is seen taking a photograph of Union officers who are posing beside Simi's reproduction of a 13-inch mortar.

At the start of the railroad sequence, a man can be seen wearing a board with the text: "Thief This Man Benny Dutcher 55th Mass Stole Money from a Wounded Friend." This detail was sourced from a Civil War photo by Haas & Peale which shows a disgraced private wearing a similarly styled board with the text: "Thief.

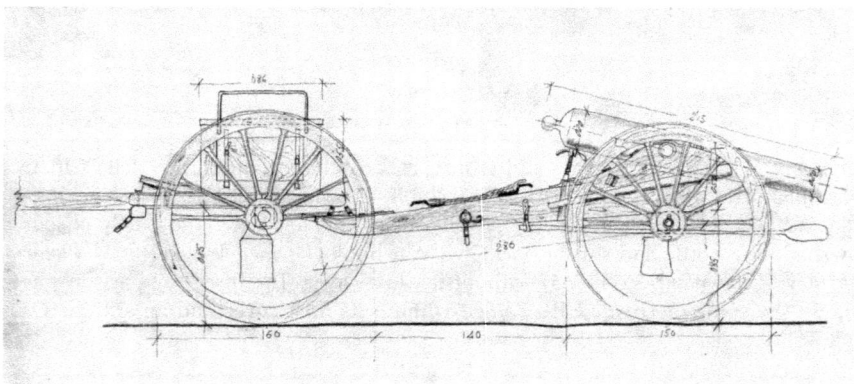

Figure 2.3 Benson's Battery. Top: high-resolution Civil War photo (Library of Congress, Washington, D.C.; reproduction number: LC-DIG-cwpb-00161) of Benson's Battery, which appears in an historical book (*Divided We Fought: A Pictorial History of the War 1861–1865*) used on the set of *The Good, the Bad and the Ugly*. Bottom: side elevation of a limbered field gun drawn by Carlo Simi. The drawing was labeled "Batterie Benson" and dated March 10, 1966. Carlo Simi © VG Bild-Kunst, Bonn 2019. All rights reserved.

This Man Benj. F. Ditcher 55th Mass. Vol's Stole Money from a Wounded Friend." The Haas & Peale photo is not included in either of the production reference books *Divided We Fought* or *Gardner's*. Benny Dutcher duly walks past a breech-loading 12-pounder Whitworth rifled cannon, suspended in a tripod above its carriage. On Dutcher's right is a view of Simi's replica 13-inch mortar, which changes orientation for Mathew Brady's photography exercise later in the scene. Carlo Simi made a detailed drawing of an artillery piece, with side and top elevations, titled "Pezzo Inglese Da 12-Libbre" (translated: twelve-pound English piece) and dated March 10, 1966. This drawing depicts an "English" twelve-pounder (2.75-inch) Whitworth rifle, at least two of which appeared as wooden replicas in the railroad sequence (Figure 2.4), and closely matches the Civil War photo (reproduction number: LC-DIG-cwpb-02744; Library of Congress, Washington, D.C.) shown in Figure 2.4, except one of the two arms (handles) of the breech screw is missing in Simi's drawings. Notably, in the Civil War photograph (Figure 2.4), the hinged breech cap has been swung out to one side. At variance with the Union railroad sequence in *The Good, the Bad and the Ugly*, breech-loading twelve-pounder Whitworth rifles were principally employed by the Confederates during the Civil War (Hazlett, Olmstead, and Parks 2004: 212). However, Union forces used twelve-pounder Whitworth rifles in the Peninsula Campaign (Hazlett, Olmstead, and Parks 2004: 212), a Union offensive in Virginia from March to August 1862, and four Whitworth rifles be seen in a Civil War photograph (reproduction number: LC-DIG-cwpb-01580; Library of Congress, Washington, D.C.), taken in May 1862, of Federal artillery park, Yorktown, Virginia.

At the end of the railroad sequence, an armored railroad car with a mounted gun can be seen at the back of the train which departs with Corporal Wallace (Mario Brega) and his prisoner Tuco inside one of its boxcars. This detail was obtained from a Civil War photograph showing a Parrott rifle mounted on an armored (fourteen-wheel) railroad car, which appears in *Divided We Fought* (Donald 1956: 369), as well as on page 48 of another book that the production used, William H. Price's *The Civil War Centennial Handbook* from 1961 (for more details, see Fig. 4.31 in Hanley 2016). Carlo Simi made a detailed and closely matching drawing of the armored (fourteen-wheel) railroad car, including front, side, and rear elevations. Although Simi's drawings depicted the fourteen wheels, the armored railroad car constructed for *The Good, the Bad and the Ugly* only had four wheels.

Behind the twelve-pounder Whitworth rifle suspended from a tripod, seen in the opening shots of the railroad sequence, wounded soldiers can be observed

Figure 2.4 Twelve-pounder Whitworth rifle. Top: still (Angelo Novi / Cineteca di Bologna) showing the appearances of two replica twelve-pounder Whitworth rifles, one mounted on a tripod above its carriage and the other one (at the center of the image) mounted on its carriage, on the set of *The Good, the Bad and the Ugly*. The inset shows a Civil War photo (reproduction number: LC-DIG-cwpb-02744; Library of Congress, Washington, D.C.) of a Whitworth rifle. Bottom: side elevation of a twelve-pounder (2.75-inch) Whitworth rifle drawn by Carlo Simi. The drawing was labeled PEZZO INGLESE DA 12-LIBBRE and dated March 10, 1966. Carlo Simi © VG Bild-Kunst, Bonn 2019. All rights reserved.

sitting in a horse-drawn ambulance, similar to the one depicted in *The Civil War Centennial Handbook* (Price 1961: 56). This prop would have been more suitable for the Battle of Langstone Bridge sequence, although a similar ambulance is seen while Union soldiers are evacuating a town under artillery bombardment. Like the railroad sequence, the battlefield sequence is also rich in details sourced from archive Civil War photographs. The design of the Union trenches in the Battle of Langstone Bridge sequence, for example, appears to be inspired from a photograph shown in *Gardner's* (Plate 83), which has the caption: "Quarters of Men at Fort Sedgwick, Generally Known As Fort Hell, May, 1865." Simi made a sketch of *quartiere trincea tipico* (typical trench quarters) which resembles this view of Fort Sedgwick (named after Union General John Sedgwick), a large Union fort constructed during the siege of Petersburg, Virginia. This fort provided artillery support for attacks on Confederate lines. In *The Good, the Bad and the Ugly*, the Battle of Langstone Bridge set consisted mainly of deep trenches (breastworks), with little resemblance to Fort Sedgwick. However, similar to the *Gardner's* photograph of Fort Sedgwick, chimneys made of logs and plastered with clay, and extended with a barrel on top, can be seen in *The Good, the Bad and the Ugly*. For example, just after the artillery captain asks whether Blondie and Tuco have "any reason for being around here," smoke can be clearly seen coming out of a chimney barrel. After uttering "Names don't matter," the captain leads the pair along a trench, behind which a wooden rail supported by posts can be identified. This detail can be seen in Gardner's photograph of Fort Sedgwick, as well as in Simi's sketch. Furthermore, as seen in other Civil War photographs, including those of Fort Sedgwick, the earthworks and fortifications on the Battle of Langstone Bridge set incorporated numerous sandbags and gabions, large cylindrical wicker baskets, normally filled with dirt.

Gatling guns make prominent appearances in *The Good, the Bad and the Ugly*. Only thirteen (2nd Model 1862) Gatling guns were ordered by the US government during the Civil War (Hughes 2001: 11). Notably, these guns had six barrels. Gatling guns with ten barrels, first produced after the Civil War, appeared on the Battle of Langstone Bridge set. Behind-the-scenes stills on pages 147 and 158 in Hanley (2016) show ten-barrel Gatling guns fitted with a Bruce cartridge feeder (patented in 1881) and a Broadwell drum (patented in 1870), respectively. Thus, these details, as well as others in the film, are historically inaccurate. The rifle used by Blondie to rescue Tuco in the second foiled hanging ruse resembles a Henry rifle, except that it harbors a loading port on the right-side plate, an improvement (patented in 1866) which was first introduced with the Model 1866 Winchester, the successor of the Henry rifle (see Hanley 2016: 332). Blondie's Model 1851 Colt Navy revolver also shows a post–Civil War modification (for details, see Hanley 2016: 285). His revolver has been converted to a breech-loading cartridge revolver, although it still retains the plunger and loading lever associated with percussion (ball and cap) models. Colt factory conversions from percussion to breech-loading cartridge revolvers were first made after the Civil War, and were stamped with the dates of patents by Charles B. Richards (July 25, 1871) and William Mason (July 2, 1872) (McDowell 1997: 138 and 198). However, Remington, Colt, and other brands of percussion revolvers were privately converted during the Civil War. The various transgressions from historical accuracy may have been due to limited availability, replica Henry rifle versus replica Winchester Model 1866, or intentional embellishments for cinematic effect, in the case of cap and ball versus metal cartridge revolvers or Model 1862 Gatling guns versus later models with more barrels and improved feed mechanisms.

A massive replica 15-inch smooth-bore Rodman gun was used on the Battle of Langstone Bridge set. Carlo Simi made side- and top-view elevation drawings of a 15-inch Rodman gun, which was labeled "Batteria Rodgers." Battery Rodgers was a gun emplacement overlooking the Potomac River and was designed to mount five 8-inch (200-pounder) Parrott rifles and a single 15-inch Rodman gun (Dickman 1980: 23; Cooling and Owen 1988: 47). Originally known as the Water Battery at Alexandria, it was renamed after a naval officer who had died in action, Fleet Captain George W. Rodgers, killed on August 17, 1863 (Dickman 1980: 19). Simi's drawings closely match Civil War photographs of the Rodman gun at Battery Rodgers, including details of the surroundings (e.g., see Hanley 2016: 274). However, Simi's drawings additionally show the elevating mechanism of the 15-inch Rodman gun. A detailed view of this mechanism, showing the ratchet post, elevating bar, and sockets on the breech face, can be seen in *The Civil War Centennial Handbook* (Price 1961: 46). Rodman guns are not depicted in either *Gardner's* or *Divided We Fought*. Simi also made a sketch of a Parrott rifle, including gabions layered with sandbags, which closely matches a Civil War photograph found in *Gardner's* (Plate 12) with the caption: "Battery No. 1, Near Yorktown, Va, May, 1862." Parrott rifles did not make an obvious appearance in *The Good, the Bad and the Ugly*. Instead, various real mortars (e.g., see Hanley 2016: 153) and a genuine Whitworth gun (Hanley 2016: 16) with a hexagonal bore (stamped: "N° 572 Whitworth Trade Mark Manchester 1873"), borrowed from the army museum (*Museo del Ejército*) in Madrid, Spain, made appearances on the set.

In addition to the railroad and battlefield sequences, the Union prison camp sequence showcases many details gleaned from Civil War photographs. After the camp commandant, Captain Harper (Antonio Molino Rojo), has threatened Angel Eyes with a court-martial for the mistreatment of prisoners, Angel Eyes can be seen walking from the commandant's quarters, a blockhouse copied from a Civil War photograph (see Hanley 2016: 366–67), toward his barrack. The panning shot ends with a close-up shot of a brick chimney attended by a man with a floppy hat. The chimney closely matches the prominent brick chimney shown in a Civil War photograph (see Hanley 2016: 369), beside which a man with a floppy hat is standing. The Gatling gun, as well as the wagon (between the chimney and Angel Eyes's barrack), seen in this panning shot reappears in the Battle of Langstone Bridge sequence. In the background of the shot, a water well operated with a large wooden lever, similar to that in a Civil War photograph featured in *Divided We Fought* (Donald 1956: 328), can be seen. In another panning shot, when one of Angel Eyes's gang members (Aldo Sanbrell) walks from Angel Eyes's barrack to an outside table of waiting fellow gang members, further details obtained from Civil War photos can be identified. An outdoor stove can be seen which closely matches a Civil War photo and a sketch made by the set decorator Carlo Leva (for a comparison, see Hanley 2016: 25). Nearby, a pot is also seen, suspended over a fire by means of a small metal tripod. Carlo Simi made a series of sketches, with the legend "Cucine Varie," which included three overlapping tripods with two pots hanging over a log fire, exactly as seen in the Civil War photograph featured in *Divided We Fought* (Donald 1956: 376). A chimney made of logs and clay with a barrel on top, as seen in the aforementioned Civil War photograph of Fort Sedgwick and numerous other historical photographs, appears at the end of the panning shot. There are also macabre tributes to the atrocious conditions which prevailed at Civil War prison camps. In the second panning shot, a carriage full of corpses can be seen being wheeled across the compound by prisoners, and in an earlier shot, when Corporal Wallace walks over to Tuco, a man can be seen in the background hanging from a gallows. The "Dead Line," a wooden rail on posts, of the notorious prison Andersonville also made an appearance in the film (see Hanley 2016: 213). Prison guards had orders to shoot any prisoners which crossed this boundary (Ripple 1996: 19; Futch 2011: 2). Moreover, numerous makeshift tents and an open latrine can be seen when Blondie, Tuco, and the other prisoners are marched into the prison enclosure, as seen in archive photographs of Andersonville prison: for an example see *The Civil War Centennial Handbook* (Price 1961: 59).

Historical sources were not limited to books about the American Civil War. Carlo Simi additionally studied photographs of the American frontier taken by photographer L. A. (Laton Alton) Huffman, published in a book by Brown and Felton (1955; Fig. 1.17 in Hanley 2016: 23). The Western village built by Simi for *For a Few Dollars More* (1965), and used as the Santa Fe set in *The Good, the Bad and the Ugly* (1966), was partially inspired from photos in this book (e.g., see Hanley 2016: 23). In addition, the design of the grave marker for Arch Stanton on the Sad Hill cemetery set was copied from a photo with the caption: "Grave of Colonel Keogh." Indeed, one of the grave designs by Carlo Simi closely matches Colonel Keogh's grave marker, whereas another is explicitly inscribed with Col. Keog (see Hanley 2016: 32). Notably, the H, which was much smaller than the other letters on the original grave marker, was missing in the production design. Colonel Myles Walter Keogh was killed along with General George Armstrong Custer in the Battle of the Little Bighorn on June 25, 1876.

Surprisingly, aside from books, Carlo Simi and Sergio Leone used watercolors by the Civil War illustrator James E. Taylor (1839–1901) as sources of inspiration for different sets and scenes. Taylor worked for Frank Leslie's *Illustrated Newspaper*, founded in 1855, and accompanied General Philip Henry Sheridan during the Shenandoah Valley (Virginia) campaign in 1864. Decades after the war, in the 1890s, Taylor was solicited by Ezra Ripple to illustrate his memoirs about life as a Union prisoner in the stockades of Andersonville and Florence (Ripple 1996). One of the watercolors from Taylor's Florence military prison series, titled "Washing up," inspired an interior monastery scene, in which monks can be seen washing wounded soldiers in large half barrels (Hanley 2016: 356). The original watercolor shows released prisoners, among whom was Ezra Ripple, at Camp Parole in Annapolis, Maryland, being scrubbed by attendants in large tubs before being sent home. In a close-up still of Sergio Leone on the set of *The Good, the Bad and the Ugly*, another watercolor from the Florence military prison series, titled "Our orchestra," can be seen in the foreground (see Hanley 2016: 374–75). The watercolor shows a small orchestra of prisoners playing for the guards in Florence Stockade, a Confederate prison camp in South Carolina. Similarly, in *The Good, the Bad and the Ugly*'s Betterville prison camp sequence, a small orchestra of prisoners play for the guards outside of the stockade, as shown in Taylor's watercolor and documented by the eyewitness account of Ezra Ripple (1996). The band of musicians at Betterville prison camp was used to drown out the cries of prisoners being tortured, whereas the orchestra formed by Ezra Ripple and fellow prisoners, which consisted of two violins, flute, and guitar, played outside of the stockade for Confederate officers' pleasure (Ripple 1996: 107–10).

Conclusion

In summary, close examination reveals that the set decorations and Civil War scenes of *The Good, the Bad and the Ugly*, especially those set at the railroad point, on the battlefield and in the Betterville prison camp, are rich in details directly copied from archive Civil War photos, as well as other nineteenth-century photos and illustrations. In addition, Sibley's 1862 New Mexico campaign, to which there are numerous references in Leone's *The Good, the Bad and the Ugly*, provided a plausible historical setting for a Western with a Civil War backdrop.

Bibliography

Abdill, George B. *Civil War Railroads: A Pictorial Story of the War Between the States, 1861–1865*. Bloomington: Indiana University Press, 1999.

Anon. "Far West. E'Facile." *Vie Nuove*, 25, no. 23, June (1966): 24–25.

Broughton, Lee. "Restoration, Restoration, Restoration: The Changing Appearance of *The Good, the Bad and the Ugly* on British Home Video." In *Cult Media Re-packaged, Re-released and Restored*, edited by Jonathan Wroot and Andy Willis, 67–83. London: Palgrave Macmillan, 2017.

Brown, Mark H. and W. R. Felton. *The Frontier Years: L. A. Huffman, Photographer of the Plains*. New York: Bramhall House, 1955.

Cooling, Benjamin Franklin and Walton H. Owen. *Mr. Lincoln's Forts: A Guide to the Civil War Defenses of Washington*. Shippensburg: White Mane Publishing Company, 1988.

Dickman, William J. *Battery Rodgers at Alexandria, Virginia: A Narrative Report on Battery Rodgers Which, during the Civil War, was One of the Many Fortifications Forming the Defenses of Washington*. Manhattan: Military Affairs, MA/AH Publishing, 1980.

Donald, David. *Divided we Fought: A Pictorial History of the War 1861–1865*. New York: The MacMillan Company, 1956.

Edrington, Thomas S. and John Taylor. *The Battle of Glorieta Pass: A Gettysburg in the West, March 26–28, 1862*. Albuquerque: University of New Mexico Press, 2000.

Frassanito, William A. *Gettysburg: A Journey in Time*. New York: Charles Scribner's Sons, 1975.

Futch, Ovid L. *History of Andersonville Prison*. Gainesville: University Press of Florida (revised edition), 2011.

Gardner, Alexander. *Gardner's Photographic Sketch Book of the Civil War*. New York: Dover Publications, 1959.

Hall, Martin Hardwick. *Sibley's New Mexico Campaign*. Albuquerque: University of New Mexico Press, 2000.

Hanley, Peter J. *Behind-the-scenes of Sergio Leone's The Good, the Bad and the Ugly*. Dulmen: Il buono Publishing, 2016.

Hardesty, H. H. *The Historical and Geographical Encyclopedia: Map of New Mexico*. New York: H. H. Hardesty and Company, 1883.

Hazlett, James C., Edwin Olmstead and Hume M. Parks. *Field Artillery Weapons of the Civil War*. Champaign: University of Illinois Press (revised edition), 2004.

Hughes, James B. *The Gatling Gun Notebook: A Collection of Data and Illustrations*. Lincoln: Andrew Mowbray Publishers, 2001.

Incrocci, Agenore, Furio Scarpelli, Luciano Vincenzoni and Sergio Leone. Unpublished manuscript (screenplay). *Screenplay: Il buono, il brutto, il cattivo*. Rome, 1966.

Ketchum, Richard M. *The American Heritage Picture History of the Civil War*. New York: American Heritage Publishing, 1960.

Macdonald, John. *Great Battles of the American Civil War*. London: Guild Publishing, 1988.

McDowell, R. Bruce. *A Study of Colt Conversions and Other Percussion Revolvers*. Iola: Krause Publications, 1997.

McGilligan, Patrick. *Clint: The Life and Legend*. New York: St. Martin's Press, 2002.

Price, William H. *The Civil War Centennial Handbook*. 1st ed. Arlington: Prince Lithograph Co., 1961.

Ray, Frederic. "The Case of the Rearranged Corpse." *Civil War Times*, 3, no. 6 (1961): 19.

Ripple, Ezra Hoyt. *Dancing Along the Deadline: The Andersonville Memoir of a Prisoner of the Confederacy*. Novato: Presidio Press, 1996.

Schickel Richard. Featurette (Disc 2): The Leone Style. In *The Good, the Bad & the Ugly (Two-Disc Collector's Edition)*. MGM Home Entertainment, 2004.

Slabaugh, Arlie R. *Confederate States Paper Money*. 10th ed. Iola, Wisconsin: Krause Publications, 2001.

Taylor, John. *Bloody Valverde: A Civil War Battle on the Rio Grande, February 21, 1862*. Albuquerque: University of New Mexico Press, 1999.

Thompson, Jerry. *Civil War in the Southwest: Recollections of the Sibley Brigade*. College Station: TAMU (Texas A & M University) Press, 2001.

Wooster, Ralph A. *Lone Star Blue and Gray: Essays on Texas in the Civil War*. Austin: Texas State Historical Association, 1996.

3

Where White Men Dream Out Loud: Robert Altman's West

Cynthia J. Miller

Introduction

Robert Altman's West can be overwhelming at first glance. Sweeping landscapes full of vibrant color and gritty grays are animated by icons and antiheroes, strangers, and stereotypes, all struggling to negotiate their authenticity, make their mark, find their place. Altman's West offers the chance of a lifetime for those with vision and foresight, but devastation for the weak or foolhardy. It is a polestar for progress, yet unyielding and timeless. Here, Native Americans dream of the future in silent moments of sleep, while white men "dream out loud"—carving out those dreams on the land and its inhabitants. More than merely a setting, Altman's West is a constellation of ideas.

Two of Altman's films—*Buffalo Bill and the Indians, or Sitting Bull's History Lesson* (1976) and *McCabe and Mrs. Miller* (1971)—most fully realize these ideas of the West. The two films are utterly dissimilar to the senses: Buffalo Bill's Wild West Show sends a shockwave of color and a blaring of trumpets through the craggy, barren frontier, while *McCabe*'s tiny boomtown of Presbyterian Church is nestled amid drizzly mountain wilderness, awash in hushed grays and browns. The films vastly differ in narrative form and style as well: In one, a shallow, boastful, past-his-prime Buffalo Bill Cody hires Sitting Bull to add spectacular authenticity to his Wild West show, and instead learns a lesson about the West he represents; while in the other, gambler and entrepreneur John McCabe pursues his fortune with the help of an ambitious madam, only to succumb to the grim realities of the frontier life he sought to master. Taken together, the two films speak to the tensions inherent in images and portrayals of the West, as their narratives struggle to achieve authenticity and reconcile lives and landscapes. Each has achieved cult status, in large part, due to its unflinching examination of the dark side of frontier life—notions of which are so central to American history and national identity.

Altman's study in contrast reminds us that the West resists the narrow confines of traditional renderings, and casts a critical eye on the ways that history has been invented and retold, testifying that the West—and our understandings of it—must change with time. This chapter, then, will explore these ideas of the West as they are portrayed in Altman's two iconic works, examining the ways in which each offers its own version of critical commentary on popular notions of the West and the ravages of time on those constructions, as well as the ways in which they respond to and extend beyond earlier revisionist Westerns, such as John Ford's *The Man Who Shot Liberty Valance* (1962).

Buffalo Bill and the Indians, or Sitting Bull's History Lesson

Buffalo Bill and the Indians tells the tongue-in-cheek story of "the man who *is* the Wild West"—Buffalo Bill Cody—and his Wild West show. It is 1885, and the frontier is being pushed back by settlers, adventurers, and railroads. As the actual Wild West vanishes, it is replaced by an overarticulated spectacle of the imagination orchestrated by one of its most ruggedly iconic figures, Buffalo Bill (Paul Newman), and his partner, Nate Salisbury (Joel Grey). Dazzling displays of showmanship thrill and astound, as audiences marvel at the show's cast of cowboys and Indians, including Annie Oakley (Geraldine Chaplin) and Sitting Bull (Frank Kaquitts). The West has been "Cody-fied"—amplified, overwritten, and spit-shined into a garish pretense that lays claim, through Bill, to authenticity.

But Bill has no authenticity to share. When Annie Oakley asks the showman why he doesn't tell the truth in his show, he replies, "I got a better sense of history than that." He cuts a striking figure, but everything about him is inauthentic and disingenuous, right down to his well-known flowing locks, which are really a toupee. Newman interprets Cody as

> the First Star. He was like one of those people in motion pictures who simply cannot live up to their legends. Their legends are created for them. They are simply human beings. Flawed. (McGilligan 1989: 5)

Altman, himself, compares Newman's Buffalo Bill to the character of Willy Loman (Fredric March) in Laszlo Benedek's adaptation of *Death of a Salesman* (1951)—a sad character, trapped in someone else's vision (Sterritt 2000: 39).

Bill dons the Wild West, much as he would his flashy costume or trademark hairpiece, but he is not of the Wild West. The Wild West show is a place betwixt and between, neither the authentic West nor "civilization," and Bill suffers the fate of a man who does not fully belong in either world. With his vanity, false bravado, and weakness of character, Bill and his imported operatic paramours present feminized figures glaringly out of place in stark contrast to the minimalist Western landscape. Sitting Bull, by contrast, is small, unassuming, and silently powerful, in harmony with the rhythms of the terrain that surrounds them: a stereotype, but one, as the film's full title indicates, invoked to retrieve the truth from history.

Buffalo Bill, the living legend, is living a lie, the creation of the man who discovered him, the dime novelist Ned Buntline (Burt Lancaster), who Bill now shuns as he tries to forget that the glorious deeds of his past, like so much history, were invented and refashioned to give audiences what they wanted. When Sitting Bull insists that Cody's show reenact the true events of Custer's Last Stand to show the slaughter of Indian women and children, Buffalo Bill once again refuses to acknowledge the lack of authenticity in representations of things past. When Ned laments that Bill hasn't changed since their parting of the ways, Bill reminds him that "I ain't s'posed to. That's why people pay to see me."

And in this, Altman's Cody speaks an uncomfortable truth about his historical counterpart and real-life representations of the Western frontier. The original, and best known, of the Wild West shows was, of course, founded by Cody, known first in the 1870s as the Buffalo Bill Combination, and then reformed in 1883, as Buffalo Bill's Wild West Show. It was the "gold standard" of Western traveling shows, as the Denver Post lauded: "There never was anything like Buffalo Bill's Wild West show before; there will never be anything like it again" (1913: np). Cody sought, through his Wild West shows, to produce a recreation of border life on a scale grander than the walls of a theater could ever accommodate. Billed as "America's National Entertainment" (Cody 2012: xvi), the show, which included a cast of hundreds, toured the United States, England, and Europe for twenty years, including a landmark performance nearby the 1893 Chicago World's Fair. Its passage required three railway trains of seventy-five cars each.

The promise of authenticity was the lifeblood of Wild West shows such as Cody's, whether presenting feats of extreme skills, such as sharpshooting, roping, or trick riding, or portraying events and occurrences, such as buffalo hunts, Indian raids, or cattle roundups. A key element in making audiences feel as though they had witnessed "the real thing" was the casting of as many Indians as possible in the shows' performances. The Great Chiefs, who were, thanks to the press, household names, were, as theatrical managers would say, "good box office." Sitting Bull participated in Buffalo Bill's show for four months in 1885, appearing for a brief horseback ride through the arena; Geronimo similarly lent his notoriety to Pawnee Bill's show in 1906. They, along with others such as Black Elk and Standing Bear, were showcased as dramatic foils—exhibited as curiosities, and advertised with colorful banners resembling those found in carnival sideshows.

Alongside this emphasis on authenticity, however, entrepreneurs of Wild West extravaganzas frequently thrived on the fascination created by ambiguous pasts in the "real" Old West, and in this, no better example exists than Cody who was already something of a legend, thanks to the dime novels of Ned Buntline. Some called into question Buffalo Bill's heroic history and the realism of his shows, such as a reporter for the Detroit Free Press who quipped "Buffalo Bill has at last found a manager willing to take him to England, but what the public will next want to know is whether he is to be left there or not" (Cody 2012: xvi). Others, however, such as this Londoner visiting New York, reported that the Wild West show he attended was

> an entertainment in which the whole of the most interesting episodes of life on the extreme frontier of civilization in America are represented with the most graphic vividness and scrupulous detail . . . no one can exaggerate the extreme excitement and "go" of the whole performance. (Burke 2012: 214–15)

As historian Louis S. Warren observes, these contemporary arguments about the truthfulness or fabrication of Buffalo Bill's heroics were commonplace and "mirrored much wider debates about the meaning of the Far West and the trustworthiness of the organs of popular culture through which most Americans learned about it: newspapers, advertising, literature, painting, and theater" (2005: xiii). Warren explains that Cody, a showman on par with P. T. Barnum, mingled his real-life adventures with "colorful fictions," creating for himself an image that was the embodiment of public fantasy—indistinguishable from the very myths created by his Wild West shows (2005: xiii). And, while Cody, like his fellow showmen, had his detractors, others were steadfast in their faith in the man behind the spectacle:

> To see him in his trimmins, he can't hardly look the same,
> With laundered shirt and diamonds, as if "he run a game."
> He didn't wear biled linen then, or flash up diamond rings;

The royalties he dreamed of then were only pasteboard kings;
But those who sat behind the queens were apt to get their fill,
In the days when Cody was a scout and all the men knew Bill. (Annin 1891: np)

Buffalo Bill's "trimmins"—along with the show's headliners and cast, horses and buffalo, wagons and tents, weapons, and banners—became such potent icons of the Wild West that for many, particularly audiences in Eastern cities and across the Atlantic, they *were* the American West. And as the Wild West, along with the men and women who became synonymous with it, made its way into film, that legacy would persist and deepen.

McCabe and Mrs. Miller

Altman fashions another figure whose pretensions strain at the Western landscape in John McCabe (Warren Beatty), antihero of *McCabe and Mrs. Miller*. While in the original screenplay by Brian McKay, "McCabe was more of a cocky gunfighter than an antihero playing a shell game of life or death"—an image that is transformed in the film's final version—echoes of that earlier persona have a significant impact on the trajectory of the narrative that is unmistakable (McGilligan 1989: 339).

Paul Arthur observes that while the film offers no shift away from the "familiar lineup of characters, situations, settings, and themes" of the traditional Western, the genre's conventions are presented from "unfamiliar angles" that lack the usual "romanticized, dualistic luster" (2003: 19). When a rain-soaked McCabe makes his way into the tiny mining town of Presbyterian Church and is mistaken for a gunslinger, he offers no objection, taking advantage of his newfound notoriety. He makes no bones about his disdain for the town's grit, harshness, and lack of refinement, all displayed to the fullest in Altman's naturalistic vision. The town, at the farthest edge of habitable frontier, barely hangs on, thanks to a fleabag hotel, a saloon, and steady work from the mining company. It is a fine setting for a traditional Western, but Altman bends and complicates those expectations with a cast of fallible, contradictory characters who struggle toward some form of community, as both nature and corporate greed threaten to overtake them (McGee 2007: 203). Robert Kolker argues that the film "mourns . . . the lost possibility of community and the enforced isolation of its members" (2000: 341), but as Patrick McGee counters, that isolation is bridged by the townspeople's shared exploitation by the Harrison Shaughnessy Mining Company—they are bound together in a set of relationships that leave them economically and existentially impoverished (2007: 208).

When McCabe arrives, he holds himself apart from the townsfolk as he establishes his own means of exploitation. A true American entrepreneur, he is too clever by half. He introduces gambling and prostitution to the town, and the squalid shacks and lack of women spell opportunity to the gambler-turned-businessman. With three small tents and three sorry women, he opens a makeshift whorehouse, where the sex is as isolating and lackluster as the wilderness on the other side of the canvas flap. Enter, Mrs. Miller (Julie Christie), who knows her way around a bordello and convinces McCabe that they should partner. She is a woman of vision, who aims to make the West safe for a "proper sportin' house" featuring "class girls, clean linen, and proper hygiene," and under her watchful and insistent eye, that "proper" whorehouse is constructed. Mrs. Miller persuades McCabe that the trappings of "civilization" matter, and that a more refined pursuit of pleasure will loosen the purses of the men of Presbyterian Church and make them both rich. She does, in fact, bring class to McCabe's frontier whorehouse, with not only clean linens but mandatory baths, and higher rates than McCabe thought possible. As Hoberman observes, their "casino-bordello is a virtual hippie commune of music and dancing, birthday parties and hot-tub frolics" (2003: 309). And while Mrs. Miller and her ladies are archetypal characters in service of the template of the Wild West, she succeeds in taming some of that wildness and in domesticating male space (at least within limitations of her profession and the confines of the bordello). As Altman relates:

> This was the way the West really was. There were no other women out there, because they couldn't handle the hardships. So the whores came along and made the men take baths, put on suits and clean up. They said, "You can drink in here, but you can't come in drunk and start fights." Now you have the beginnings of protocol. (Demby 1977: 49)

In Altman's muted Western landscape, its puddles of mud gently blended with evergreen and snow, McCabe's establishment provides glimmers of vibrant color and warmth uncharacteristic of the world outside: lingering images of playfulness and laughing faces, lit by warm, yellow lamplight. These visuals evoke what Robert Self calls "the beauty of a painterly West" (2007: 76). As McGee notes:

Altman's images are not the gorgeous, intensely illuminated landscapes that one associates with the Technicolor Westerns of the fifties and early sixties. He intentionally subordinates the visual image to an expressive intention that subverts the classical value of a landscape as a utopian image of the freedom that the West is supposed to signify. (2007: 210)

Arthur points out that Presbyterian Church, "the archetypal Western town—or in this case, a bleakly soggy Northwest mining outpost in 1902—is adorned with a grubby miserableness we tend to call 'realistic'" (2003: 19). Critic J. Hoberman agrees, but reads the film more as a product of its era than of the region's history, describing the setting not only as "provocatively naturalistic" but also as "hippified" (2003: 308). Both of these observations are, in many ways, true, but while considering the film's place within the body of cult Westerns of its era, such as *El Topo* (Alejandro Jodorowsky, 1970), *The Hired Hand* (Peter Fonda, 1971), and *Doc* (Frank Perry, 1971), Hoberman fails to consider *McCabe and Mrs. Miller* in relation to Altman's own work, and specifically, in the context of his other Westerns for film and television, particularly *Buffalo Bill and the Indians* (Altman's televisual West includes episodes of *Sugarfoot, Bronco, Maverick, U.S. Marshal, Bonanza*, and *The Lawman*, all of which aired between 1959 and 1961). McCabe's whorehouse shares the liminal quality of Buffalo Bill's Wild West Show: one, a spectacle of women, and the other, a spectacle of Indians, both playing to the imagination, betwixt and between frontier and "civilization," but containing bits of each. McCabe, like Buffalo Bill, also contains bits of each and, like Cody, his flawed character wrestles with inner demons, struggling between hero and antihero: "There's poetry in me, Constance," he argues to the absent Mrs. Miller. Poetry, honor, truth—a hero trying too late to emerge. He seeks, as McGee suggests, "a redeemer and some kind of redemption" (2007: 205), but all he finds is a town in which self-interest is the main organizing principle. There is a consistency of vision here that moves beyond simply the zeitgeist of an era and speaks of Altman's imprint on the genre.

But the power of frontier nihilism overtakes the pair full force when the mining company tries to buy out McCabe. His vanity and bravado lead him to arrogantly reject their offers, until the company stops negotiating and sends hired guns to do their talking. Desperate panic grips McCabe, but his foolishness cannot be undone. He consults a lawyer (William Devane), who convinces him to take a stand against the corporation and become an icon for the frontier spirit: "If men stop dying for freedom, freedom itself will be dead." McCabe is trapped in a deadly game of cat-and-mouse with the gunmen while the local church burns, the townspeople unaware of his plight as they salvage their icon of civilization and redemption. As he dies alone from his wounds, McCabe is silently covered by drifting snow, the gentlest act the harsh wilderness landscape can offer.

The Man Who Shot Liberty Valance

In many ways, Altman uses these two films to deliver a sharp response from the next generation to director John Ford's revisionist Western *The Man Who Shot Liberty Valance*—a reminder that those in the early 1960s who thought they were disillusioned with the Great American Myth had not seen anything yet. Seen by some as a "poignant tribute to the passing of the Old West" (Aquila 2015: 190), Ford's film exhibits a lack of sentimentality toward the myth of the frontier that is apparent from the outset. The film begins with elderly senator Ransom Stoddard (James Stewart) and his wife Hallie (Vera Miles) returning to their hometown of Shinbone for the funeral of an old friend, Tom Doniphon (John Wayne). When the editor of the local newspaper presses him about his relationship with Doniphon, the senator reluctantly tells his story.

Twenty-five years earlier, Stoddard is a young Eastern lawyer making the journey west, when his stagecoach is held up by outlaw Liberty Valance (Lee Marvin). When Valance forces a widow to surrender a brooch given to her by her late husband, Stoddard intervenes. His gallantry earns him a brutal beating, and he is left for dead. When Doniphon finds him the next day and brings him to town to be nursed back to health, the pair embark on a complex relationship that will forever change the trajectories of their lives. As the narrative unfolds, the two men's diametrically opposed worldviews and masculinities are drawn into focus. On the one hand, Doniphon stands as an icon of rugged Western masculinity—a character type vital to notions of taming the wilderness of the frontier, who admonishes the green lawyer that "out here, due process is a bullet." On the other hand, Stoddard is a civilized, well-educated character who rejects the doctrines of the Old West, and whose weapons are thoughts and words. He is a "gentrifier"—an outsider with plenty of ideas about change—who relies on those like Doniphon to get the hard work done. Patrick McGee elaborates:

> Ultimately, Ranse and Tom represent the two sides of a social identity that, within the frame of the film, can never be unified. Ranse imagines a legal system that would [represent the common good] through its dis-identification with the

agents of social violence. . . . Tom, by contrast, almost completely identifies with the use of force that Ranse opposes. (2007: 136)

And yet, the world that Stoddard both envisions and represents cannot be achieved without the social violence and personal action embodied in Doniphon. The film represents, as Richard Aquila observes, a transitional time for the West and the Western, a time when old-fashioned Western cowboys yield to those for whom they have paved the way (2015: 190). Stanley Corkin further discusses the transitional moment in films such as *Liberty Valance*, which problematize the glorification of the gunfighter and the use of guns as a means of solving broader social issues, arguing that they

> dwell explicitly on *whether* violence is an appropriate means of resolving the various crises defined in their plots. . . . These films question whether a social system defined by its ability and tendency to deal with disruptive elements by annihilating them may be flawed; they also probe the prospect that characters will become physically and morally marred beyond repair if they engage in gunplay. (2004: 95)

The pair enacts this ideological shift on multiple levels: Hallie, the woman Doniphon loves and intends to marry, falls in love with Stoddard and, in doing so, chooses brains and refinement over the rough-and-tumble physicality of the cowboy hero; when Stoddard and Valance meet for a showdown, it is Doniphon's frontier prowess that kills Valance, not his counterpart's helpless good fortune, yet he remains silent and allows Stoddard to believe himself a hero and bask in the limelight; and finally, when Stoddard learns the truth, Doniphon urges him to accept his good fortune and live the lie that he has created, saying: "Go back in there and take that nomination. You taught [Hallie] how to read and write. Now give her something to read and write about." Meanwhile Doniphon, the real frontier hero, the man who *truly* shot Liberty Valance, yields to the forces of progress and time. He walks sadly away as the world moves on without him, broken, alone, and soon, forgotten. This scene adds particular poignance to singer Gene Pitney's 1962 lyric "The man who shot Liberty Valance, he was the bravest of them all" (Bacharach 1962: np). Doniphon knowingly walks off into irrelevance—the most heroic act of the film.

Shot on sets, in muted grays and lacking Ford's signature vistas, even the beauty of the Western landscape is strikingly absent. The West, Ford tells us, is dead, but the mythic West lives on. As the newspaper editor explains to Stoddard when he refuses to print his story, "This is the West, sir. When the legend becomes fact, print the legend." Ford's elegiac film was thus intended as a complex farewell to the wild frontier. It signals the power of the mythic West to address the problems of a postwar world, yet at the same time, as Brandon Soderberg argues, subtly damns those who believe the legend (2015: np). While Ford's film is generally considered to be a watershed in portrayals of the frontier, the tension it foregrounds permeates the films of its era. In *The Dream Life: Movies, Media, And The Mythology Of The Sixties*, critic J. Hoberman suggests even larger implications to its message, arguing that *The Man Who Shot Liberty Valance* is a movie based upon "the astounding statement that American history was founded on a necessary lie" (2003: 105).

The Western as History, Myth, or Zeitgeist?

The ideological tension foregrounded in Ford's *Liberty Valance* follows the Western genre forward and settles firmly in Altman's two cult Westerns. Each takes on the myth of the West and the question of historical "truth," damning not only those who believe the legend but also those characters who, like Ford's Doniphon, perpetuate it. This is one of the central problems of the genre: The Western is always about history and the "real"—its realization, representation, authenticity, illusion—and of course, its significance (Self 2007: 15). From the silent classics to the present day, genre films strive to make the past come alive. From ranching to railroading and sheriffs to schoolmarms, "the western provides history lessons in all these matters, constantly revising them to get it right" (Self 2007: 16).

If we examine Altman's Westerns as historiography—as creating a way of thinking about history, and of selecting and displaying particular historical icons, objects, and events as denoting historicity (Self 2007: 15)—it quickly becomes apparent how each, in its own way, reveals the ideological underpinnings of the myth of the frontier, and highlights the ways in which "imagination and presence come up against each other," allowing viewers to "test the strength of each against the claims of the other" (Lavine 1991: 5). Both of these films strip the veneer from the imagined West and its characters, and lay bare the realities of being in and of a frontier where legend is hollow and pain is real.

In an interesting intertwining of fiction and history, the Gene Autry Western Heritage Museum deemed *Buffalo Bill and the Indians* "the richest and most interesting interpretation of this historical character that we have found on film" (Dauber 1987: np), finding resonance in Altman's caustic portrayal that juxtaposed the showman's public image—"brave, considerate, and handsome"— with an unflattering behind-the-scenes image of an aging man who was bitter, prejudiced, drunk, and unfaithful (Sagala 2013: 162). Returning to *Liberty Valance*, the lineage of Altman's flawed version of Cody may be seen. Cody is, perhaps, a more emotionally honest version of Ransom Stoddard, given form after the senator's return to Shinbone forces him to confront the haunting truth that he has suppressed for decades. Everything that the voting public thinks he is, everything that they think makes him a hero, is a lie—a legend that he is complicit in promoting.

In 1962, Ford lets Stoddard off with a saddened shake of the head. The narrative events suggest that, while he is complicit in the lie on which his career has been built, it was not *his* lie. The legend of the man who shot Liberty Valance emerged spontaneously among the townspeople who believed that they saw the unlikely event with their own eyes, and for a while, Stoddard believed it to be the truth, as well. His true complicity rests in not correcting the lie once he knew the truth, and subsequently reaping the benefits. Still, by the time of his confession, he has been an upstanding politician and a forthright and just agent of justice, nationhood, and the taming of the frontier. In the end, his sins are absolved by an editor who believes in the power of the Legend, and elects to compromise the truth in order to perpetuate it for the greater good.

In 1976, however, Altman has no such inclination. The years that have passed since Ford's film have assaulted American national identity with the Gulf of Tonkin Incident and the country's amplified involvement in Vietnam, a controversial bombing campaign in Cambodia, and the Watergate scandal— all of which have left the country divided and reeling with uncertainty about the integrity of public figures. Unlike Stoddard, who while benefiting from the legend is troubled by guilt and seeks absolution, Cody merely seeks to excuse himself, content with the excuse that he is simply giving his audiences (and the nation at large) what they need and want. He tries, as actor Newman suggests, to see his authenticity as a casualty of the Legend, but Altman is having none of it. The architect of the Myth of the West is not absolved simply because the spectacle he has created now substitutes for history.

Filmed almost a decade after Ford's man of letters survives the shoot-out, John McCabe may be seen as the younger version of Stoddard—the naive, idealistic young man with a vision, who believes that simply having a vision is enough. Ford suggests that, for the "gentrifiers"—the educated, refined visionaries of the

East—that may be true. The luxury of naivete still exists in 1962 in the mythic West. When Stoddard—inept in the ways of the frontier—squares off against Valance, Doniphon exhibits the mastery of personal violence for which the West is known and ensures that the right man wins. Thus, while a decidedly revisionist Western, nostalgia for romantic ideals and the greater good prevails in Ford's film. Doniphon, made from the same dirt as Alan Ladd's eponymous character from George Stevens' *Shane* (1953), portrays a backhanded heroism by sacrificing his honor for the life of his friend. Altman's film, however, illustrates that in the absence of traditional Western values and traditional Western heroes, idealism has no protector. There is no Tom Doniphon to save the day, and unlike Stoddard, McCabe meets his end at the hand of the mining company's hired gunmen. The company's thugs possess the same frontier prowess as Ford's cowboy antihero, but lack his moral compass. They calmly track down McCabe and, because he's no more the gunfighter than Stoddard, effortlessly shoot him down, leaving him and his idealism to die in the snow.

Conclusion

John Ford, at the end of the day, is a romantic, and his lament for the West-that-wasn't in *Liberty Valance* is an elegy for the values, lifeways, characters, and events of the Legend. In Ford's West, ideals matter. Stoddard's belief in the civilizing power of the law, Doniphon's belief that Hallie deserves "better" than the rough-around-the-edges life he could offer her, and even the newspaper editor's choice to "print the legend" all give testimony to Ford's belief in a moral order that adapts to survive the challenges posed by changing times. Altman's West, however, filmed after icons of American ideals such as John F. Kennedy, Medgar Evers, Malcolm X, and Martin Luther King, Jr. have been gunned down either actually or metaphorically "in the street," sees ideals meeting a different fate.

As Patrick McGee argues, however, while neither of Altman's films "postulates a romanticized dualism between the good guys and the bad guys," even the dismal *McCabe and Mrs. Miller* foregrounds a conflict between marginalized, exploited individuals, and an economic system that "subordinates human desires to abstract wealth" (2007: 203). In that sense, there is, as he notes, no transcendence of the traditional Western binary oppositions of good and evil—and the evil that exists is one familiar to Western audiences: the brutality of the capitalist system, and the impersonal corporations that exploited human labor and left scars on the land.

In the end, then, Altman's West amounts to a complex landscape of the mind. It is not one idea, but a cluster of closely held, sometimes conflicting, values, and beliefs, often perpetuated at great cost. It draws together the imagined and the real, the familiar and the unfamiliar, hope and disillusionment—not Western dualities in the traditional sense, and yet perhaps just more nuanced, jaded versions of the kind of oppositions on which Jim Kitses (1969) suggests the Western genre has always turned. Through both *Buffalo Bill and the Indians* and *McCabe and Mrs. Miller*, Altman reminds us that the West resists the narrow confines of traditional renderings, yet never fully escapes the confines of convention. His films cast a critical eye on the ways that history has been invented and reinvented, yet remind us that just as the mythic West is unchanging, its renderings must change with time. His retort to Ford's nostalgia echoes Buffalo Bill as he chides Sitting Bull's ghost: "Look at ya! You want to stay the same! Well, that's going backwards!"

Bibliography

Annin, William E. "Bill Cody." Omaha Bee, February 28 (1891).

Aquila, Richard. *The Sagebrush Trail*. Tucson: University of Arizona Press, 2015.

Arthur, Paul. "How the West Was Spun: *McCabe and Mrs. Miller* and Genre Revisionism." *Cineaste* 28, no. 3 (2003): 18–20.

Bacharach, Burt and Hal David. *The Man Who Shot Liberty Valance*. New York: Musicor, 1962.

Burke, John M. *Buffalo Bill from Prairie to Palace*. Lincoln: University of Nebraska Press, 2012.

Cody, William F. *The Wild West in England*. Lincoln: University of Nebraska Press, 2012.

Corkin, Stanley. *Cowboys as Cold Warriors: The Western and US History*. Philadelphia: Temple University Press, 2004.

Dauber, Roslyn. Letter to Robert Altman, September 21, 1987. University of Michigan Libraries, Altman Archive. Available online at: https://www.lib.umich.edu/online-exhibits/exhibits/show/altman/altman---genres/the-western#the-western (accessed February 8, 2019).

Demby, Betty Jeffries. "Robert Altman Talks About His Life and His Art." *New York Times*, June 19 (1977): 49.

Denver Post, July 13 (1913).

Hoberman, J. *The Dream Life: Movies, Media, and the Mythology of the Sixties*. New York: The New Press, 2003.

Kitses, Jim. *Horizons West: Anthony Mann, Budd Boettcher, Sam Peckinpah: Studies of Authorship Within the Western*. London: Secker & Warburg, 1969.

Kolker, Robert. *A Cinema of Loneliness: Third Edition*. Oxford: Oxford University Press, 2000.

Lavine, Steven D. "Introduction: Museums and Multiculturalism." In *Exhibiting Cultures: The Poetics and Politics of Museum Display*, edited by Ivan Karp and Steven D. Lavine, 5. Washington: Smithsonian Institution Press, 1991.

McGee, Patrick. *From Shane to Kill Bill: Rethinking the Western*. Malden: Blackwell Publishing, 2007.

McGilligan, Patrick. *Robert Altman Jumping Off the Cliff*. New York: St. Martin's Press, 1989.

Olderman, Murray. "The Making of Buffalo Bill, Superstar." *Oswego Palladium Times*, July 17 (1976): 5.

Sagala, Sandra K. *Buffalo Bill on the Silver Screen*. Norman: University of Oklahoma Press, 2013.

Self, Robert T. *Robert Altman's McCabe & Mrs. Miller: Reframing the American West*. Lawrence: University of Kansas Press, 2007.

Soderberg, Brandon. "Subversive Western 'The Man Who Shot Liberty Valance' at the Senator." April 8, 2015. Available online at: https://www.citypaper.com/film/bcp news-subversive-western-the-man-who-shot-liberty-valance-at-the-senator-2015 0407-story.html (accessed February 2, 2019).

Sterritt, David (ed.). *Robert Altman, Interviews*. Jackson: University Press of Mississippi, 2000.

Warren, Louis S. *Buffalo Bill's America*. New York: Knopf First Edition, 2005.

4

The Gold Rush:
The New Right and the Westerns of 1980

Craig Ian Mann

Introduction: This Town Isn't Big Enough

The year 1980 was pivotal for both the American Western and America itself. With regard to the Western, it is often characterized as the year in which one of America's most enduring cinematic genres went into a period of hibernation, not to return for a decade. While such claims are not strictly accurate—for that to be true we would have to forget the likes of *Barbarosa* (Frank Schepisi, 1982), *Silverado* (Lawrence Kasdan, 1985), *Pale Rider* (Clint Eastwood, 1985), and *Young Guns* (Christopher Cain, 1988)—it is certainly fair to say that the 1980s mark the period in which the genre was at its least popular or prolific up to that point. Having all but disappeared for ten years, it did not experience a true revival until a new cycle of big-budget and often critically lauded Westerns, which included *Dances with Wolves* (Kevin Costner, 1990), *Unforgiven* (Clint Eastwood, 1992), *Tombstone* (George P. Cosmatos, 1993), *Wyatt Earp* (Lawrence Kasdan, 1994), and *The Quick and the Dead* (Sam Raimi, 1995), arrived at the dawn of the 1990s.

For the country, 1980 was a year of profound change: the electorate rejected Jimmy Carter's bid for a second term as the president of the United States and instead turned to Ronald Reagan, a back-to-basics Republican (and representative of a conservative movement popularly termed the "New Right") who stood for traditional values and promised to reinvigorate an unstable economy with his pro-business policies. Reagan remained in office until 1989, his departure correlating with the arrival of a new Western cycle. Here I intend to investigate the three most notable American Westerns released in 1980: William Wiard's *Tom Horn*, Walter Hill's *The Long Riders*, and Michael Cimino's

Heaven's Gate, all of which met with varying degrees of commercial failure. I will explore their thematic preoccupation with social injustice, class warfare, and a corrupt establishment, and consider whether the failure of these films—and the Western's decline—might be attributed to the fact that they were ideologically opposed to America's swiftly changing social, cultural, and political climate as the 1970s came to a close.

Before all three of these films floundered at the box office, the industry press was anticipating a Western revival. Andrew Patrick Nelson draws attention to a *New York Times* article published in June 1980, which predicted that "the future of the Western was bright" (2015: 191). This piece by Miles Beller (1980) cites *Tom Horn* and particularly *The Long Riders* as examples of the genre's apparent return to form before going on to express high hopes for *Heaven's Gate*, due for release later that year. It draws on the opinions of several commentators—as Beller describes them, "psychologists, filmmakers, actors and [Western] experts" (1980: D15)—who largely come to the conclusion that, after the politicized introspection of revisionist Westerns like *Little Big Man* (Arthur Penn, 1970), the genre's return could be attributed to America's longing for a return to the traditional values of classic frontier movies such as *Stagecoach* (John Ford, 1939) and *Red River* (Howard Hawks, 1948).

Nelson eventually comes to reject cultural explanations for any apparent "revival." He acknowledges that the *New York Times* article is a "fascinating historical document" (2015: 191), but only for what it can tell us about scholarly and popular discourses on the genre. Even for a culturalist, the suggestion that the Westerns of 1980 revive the "classic" Western—as Beller and his respondents imply—by adopting a regressive pro-American stance (or even an escapist apolitical one) seems absurd and is directly contradicted by the films themselves, all of which tackle the nation's failure to foster an equal society. However, while the article's findings cannot be considered an accurate representation of *Tom Horn*, *The Long Riders*, or *Heaven's Gate*, they can tell us a great deal about American society at the time of their release. Despite Nelson's reservations, Beller's focus on the relationship between these films and the larger culture that produced them makes clear that it is important to consider the contemporary political climate in any discussion of the Western's fortunes at the turn of the decade. Shortly before deferring to commentary from his interviewees, Beller asks a telling rhetorical question and evokes many of the political frustrations of the day:

> Why, in the [1980s], is the Western staging a comeback? Does the answer lie deep in the national psyche, where the gall of dependency on Arab oil, the ebbing

strength of the once mighty dollar, the debacle in Vietnam and the inability to resolve the hostage crisis in Iran have combined to create a yearning for the return of America's mythic hero, the cowboy? (1980: D1–D15).

These were all concerns at the forefront of the national consciousness ahead of the presidential election. Of particular importance was "the ebbing strength of the once mighty dollar." Of course, the circumstances surrounding America's weak currency were largely beyond Carter's control; when he was elected in 1977, he inherited an already floundering economy from Gerald Ford and Richard Nixon. America's troubles had truly begun not with Carter but with the 1973 oil crisis, which saw a trade embargo placed on nations—chiefly the United States—that supported Israel during the Yom Kippur War. As a result, the price of oil in America quadrupled. The crisis had disastrous effects for the nation's economy long after it ended, establishing "a general price inflation that persisted throughout the remainder of the decade" (Howison 2014: 91).

America's financial troubles continued throughout Carter's presidency, and his government failed to bring the economy under control. The United States endured high levels of inflation in tandem with a stagnant economy and high unemployment rates, or "stagflation." A second crisis worsened the situation in 1979 as the price of oil doubled. With Americans panic-buying at gas stations all over the country (amid the economic troubles that had been ongoing for over half a decade), Carter delivered his famous "crisis of confidence" speech, in which he lamented the nation's inability to come together for the common good—and then attacked the increasing greediness and materialism he saw growing in the American people:

In a nation that was proud of hard work, strong families, close-knit communities, and our faith in God, too many of us now tend to worship self-indulgence and consumption. Human identity is no longer defined by what one does, but by what one owns. But we've discovered that owning things and consuming things does not satisfy our longing for meaning. (Carter in Kaufman 2006: 583)

Reagan exploited these consumerist impulses in his campaigns for the Republican nomination and the presidency. While "Carter was calling for national sacrifice . . . Reagan, on the other hand, neither blamed the American people nor advocated policies prescribing pain and discipline" (Skinner et al. 2007: 142). His rhetoric—based on the idea that the American economy could be brought under control using tax reforms and deregulatory legislation—was based on the thinking of the New Right movement. As Michael Schaller suggests, "New Right economic theorists rejected the system of social welfare and business regulation that prevailed since the New Deal" and "maintained that a minimalist government that provided few services and levied lower taxes would cure most economic ills" (1992: 25–26). As Reagan pushed this agenda in his bid for the White House, Carter failed to respond: "His economic speeches and plans appeared to be reactions to economic shocks rather than innovative measures" (Skinner et al. 2007: 143). And Reagan pounced on Carter's mistakes; when his opponent used the term "depression" instead of "recession," Reagan retorted: "A recession is when your neighbor loses his job. A depression is when you lose yours. And recovery is when Jimmy Carter loses his" (Broussard 2014: 98).

Jimmy Carter lost his job when Reagan won a landslide victory on November 4, 1980, winning the nation over with the promise of a prosperous future. In this context, Beller's article takes on a new and interesting meaning. The author and his respondents expected (and given Beller's exasperated comments on Carter's latter years in office, even wanted) the Westerns of 1980 and beyond to embrace the patriotic optimism and individualist spirit associated with the New Right— and to reject Carter's frank assessment of a country riding into a corporate abyss. Ultimately, though, not one of them is the "classic" Western that Beller—and, clearly, the American public—desired. Instead, they offer a bleak view of a West blighted by greed, corruption, and inequality. These are imaginings of America's past that are closely aligned with Carter's grave concern for the nation's future.

It's Getting Dangerous to Be Poor

Heaven's Gate was the final Western to be released in 1980, but its reputation is such that it is necessary to address it before discussing *Tom Horn* and *The Long Riders*. For many commentators on the Western, including Jim Kitses (2004: 5), Stephen McVeigh (2007: 193) and Howard Hughes (2008: 228), the commercial failure of *Heaven's Gate* is the sole reason for the genre's decline. An epic retelling of the Johnson County War, it was Michael Cimino's third film as director after *Thunderbolt and Lightfoot* (1974) and *The Deer Hunter* (1978). Given the success of his two previous features, Cimino was granted the go-ahead to make *Heaven's Gate* by United Artists in 1979, with an initial budget of roughly $12 million. He demanded unprecedented terms in his negotiations and secured open-ended financing for the project (Prince 2000: 35).

The film's production was famously blighted by delays and overspending; on August 15, 1979, *Variety* reported: "Originally planned for a 17-week shoot, the epic western is currently wrapping its 16th week of shooting with no definitive end in sight" (Anon. 1979: 30). When Cimino finally reached the end of production (having spent $30 million), the film received a critical mauling. *Variety* suggested that Cimino's film "fails to work at almost every level" (Geri. 1980: 14), while Vincent Canby penned a vicious review for the *New York Times* in which he called *Heaven's Gate* "an unqualified disaster" (1980a: C29). Poor box office and scathing reviews led UA to withdraw it from theatres within a week, and soon critics were far more interested in the making of the film than the film itself; Canby quickly wrote a second piece reflecting on the film's failure (1980b: D1, D17).

The critics felt that *Heaven's Gate* failed simply because it was a "bad" movie. The film has since enjoyed a significant critical reappraisal, but this remained the prevailing view for over twenty years. Strangely, though, many contemporary analyses of the film and its fortunes had very little to say about *Heaven's Gate* itself; in his second piece, Canby admitted his intention to discuss "the phenomenon not the movie" (1980b: D17). Ironically, given its thematic preoccupation with class divides, much of the critics' ire was concentrated on the financial excess that *Heaven's Gate* represented rather than its narrative, style, or themes. For example, Canby opened his article with an attack on the film's lavish premiere, a symbol of "Money and power" (1980b: D1), without ever acknowledging that *Heaven's Gate*—the movie, not the phenomenon—is thematically concerned with exactly those two things: money and power.

Loosely based on a bloody conflict between cattle barons and homesteaders that occurred between 1889 and 1893, *Heaven's Gate* follows Jim Averill (Kris Kristofferson), a wealthy Harvard graduate who becomes a marshal in Wyoming at the beginning of the Johnson County War. The film chronicles Averill's efforts to aid the county's immigrant community against a band of mercenaries hired to kill over a hundred of their number by the Wyoming Stock Growers Association—ostensibly for the crimes of theft and cattle rustling, though in truth the stockmen simply want to remove the farmers from their land. Averill becomes embroiled in a love triangle with Ella Watson (Isabelle Huppert)—the proprietor of a local brothel—and Nate Champion (Christopher Walken), an enforcer for the ranchers, as tensions build to a gruesome standoff in which many of the homesteaders are slaughtered before the stockmen are rescued by army forces.

Heaven's Gate attacks America's penchant for corruption and greed, making villains of men who value land more than human life; as Jeff Bridges's bartender tells Averill in the film's first act, "It's getting dangerous to be poor in this country." In fact, given how obvious this theme is throughout the film, it is odd that contemporary critics had very little to say about it. That is not to say that Canby did not note the film's anti-capitalist message in his original review: he observes that "the point of *Heaven's Gate* is that the rich will murder for the earth they don't inherit" (1980a: C29). Likewise, *Variety* acknowledges that the film's aim is to reveal "the evils suffered by the poor" (Geri. 1980: 14). Unfortunately, neither reviewer has much more to say on this point. Clearly—as America turned from Carter to Reagan—such ideas did not require a great deal of thought.

Scholars have since noted the film's radicalism. Robin Wood was one of its earliest defenders, and described its final battle as being "on a symbolic level for an American identity centered on equality" (1986: 313). He goes on to summarize the film as "an elegy for a possible alternative America destroyed before it could properly exist" that supplants the individualism traditionally at the center of Western narratives with an "emphasis on the communal action of the common people" (1986: 314). The film certainly romanticizes images of solidarity and togetherness: in one scene a group of farmers are seen pushing a plough through a field; when one falters—falling exhausted to the ground—another dutifully takes her place. One of the film's most famous sequences sees the citizens of Johnson County dancing and playing music together in a roller-skating rink in an attenuated celebration of working-class culture. Later, the community is united in anguish when they gather in that same space to hear the names of those marked for murder by the ranchers.

Of course, these images of unity precede the community's destruction; as Patrick McGee suggests, "In this movie, the multitude is something we can only glimpse as a social possibility" (2007: 233). McGee expands on Wood's conceit, pointing out that even the film's protagonist is designed to emphasize its plea for cooperation. McGee deconstructs Averill's character: a rich man who is seemingly desperate to help the impoverished citizens of Johnson County, his privilege prevents him from ever becoming one of them. As a final confrontation grows nearer, he reveals himself to be ineffectual and unwilling to take "responsibility for the current social order that has produced the conflict" (2007: 223). And while McGee concentrates much of his analysis on Averill, Nate Champion is equally interesting in this regard. While Averill is a rich man motivated by an apparent desire to help the poor, Champion is a poor man with a thirst for wealth. In an attempt to escape poverty, he has become a mercenary, murdering those accused of rustling by the cattle barons. When Averill questions him on what he wants to get out of his line of work, he replies: "Get rich, like you."

Champion is motivated solely by class mobility: when he brings Ella to his home, a humble wooden house on the range, he tells her with pride that he has decorated the interior with wallpaper. When they go inside, she observes that his wallpaper is in fact newspaper: a pathetic image of Champion's selfish desire for material wealth. He eventually turns his back on the ranchers as he comes to be disgusted by their lawless brutality, but he still has no interest in fighting for the greater good; he just retreats to his home, which the stockmen swiftly burn to the ground in an effort to drive Champion out. The camera lingers on the newspaper as it goes up in flames, Champion visibly pained to watch it burn. As that performative status symbol is destroyed, it becomes clear that his efforts to "get rich" have been for nothing, his comfortable life built on his participation in the oppression of the poor (and his willful ignorance of their suffering). In this, Nate comes to represent the capitalist values that Carter bemoaned in 1979: he is a man so driven by greed, self-interest, and materialism that he is blinded to the fact that while the stockmen he emulates might be monetarily wealthy, they are morally bankrupt.

Heaven's Gate, then, is clearly aligned with Carter's "crisis of confidence." As many scholars have noted, it is a film about a socialist path that America chose not to tread; but what they have not observed is that this was the same path that Carter urged America to take. *Heaven's Gate* pleads with Americans, just as Carter did, to put aside their individual drives and work together for the common good—to "have faith in each other" (Carter in Kaufman: 584). Released two weeks after Carter's defeat, *Heaven's Gate* was rendered irrelevant before it even arrived in theatres. American society had embraced Reagan's individualist rhetoric and would soon come to be defined by the pursuit of material wealth. These drives are apparent even in the commentary surrounding *Heaven's Gate*. Canby's dissection of the film's failure begins with an account of his arrival at the premiere. He muses: "To someone who has just emerged from a ratty old BMT subway, limousines are awe-inspiring. They represent expense accounts and momentous decisions" (1980b: D1). Canby's aim is to highlight the decadence of the event, but his choice of words ("awe-inspiring") is telling; this was the beginning of a decade in which America would make idols of the rich and ruthless.

I Said I'd Earn My Keep

Tom Horn, the first major Western of the new decade when it was released on March 28, 1980, is now relatively unknown, having been overshadowed by the *Heaven's Gate* affair. But *Tom Horn* had its own problems; its commercial performance was poor enough that—at around the same time that the *New York Times* was anticipating a Western revival—Todd McCarthy penned an article for *Variety* asking whether Western plots amounted to box office poison, using both *Tom Horn* and *The Long Riders* as evidence that frontier movies had become a "liability" (1980: 7). The critical consensus was not wholly negative, but the film was certainly not well received. The *Boston Globe's* Bruce McCabe glibly opined that "the kindest thing one can say is that the film doesn't conclusively prove that the Western is dead" (1980: 18). Unlike *Heaven's Gate*, mainstream critics did not recognize its anti-capitalist subtext even in passing.

Loosely based on the last years of scout and tracker Tom Horn, the film follows its title character (Steve McQueen) as he drifts into Wyoming in 1901. There he falls into the employ of rancher John Coble (Richard Farnsworth), initially working as a farmhand before he is enlisted by a marshal, Joe Belle (Billy Green Bush), to track and kill cow thieves on behalf of Coble and the local Cattlemen Association. When bystanders witness a gunfight between Horn and a vengeful rustler, the stockmen become concerned that Tom's illegal activities might be traced to them, and set him up for the killing of a young sheep farmer. He is imprisoned in the town jail and, following a rigged trial, hanged for murder.

Many contemporary critics framed *Tom Horn* as being primarily about the death of the frontier, and characterized its flawed protagonist as a relic from a bygone age who is confronted with the approach of modern civilization. For example, Janet Maslin characterized Horn as "a former frontiersman who can't make his peace with the new gentility of the old West" (1980a: C8). But *Tom Horn* is not really about a man struggling to come to terms with the arrival of civilization as such, but specifically with the coming of capitalism. From the moment Horn arrives in Wyoming, he finds himself in conflict with the wealthy elite. After leaving his horse in a livery, he walks through a humble town, mud beneath his feet and mountains on the horizon. As he approaches a saloon, we hear a distant voice from within making a request that seems completely incongruous with the landscape: "Harry, pass the champagne."

This disparity between sound and image is soon reflected in the striking visual contrast between Horn and the customers dining inside the saloon. While

Horn wears chaps, spurred boots, a woolen shirt, and brown jacket, the kind of practical clothes that clearly mark him as a working man, the excited patrons are identified as men of wealth by their spotless black suits, silk ties, and bowler hats. They are toasting the boxer "Gentleman Jim" Corbett (Steve Oliver), who is soon to contend for the heavyweight championship. Horn insults Corbett and his companions twice in quick succession: first by refusing their offer of champagne and then by comparing the boxer to the Apache leader Geronimo (in rather an unflattering manner) when he opines: "Corbett there would have to stand on his mother's shoulders to kiss his ass." As Corbett stands to defend his honor, he removes his coat and jacket to reveal a garish golden waistcoat: an obnoxious symbol of his status. Horn, however, clearly has little appreciation for champagne or fine suits. His reverence for Geronimo reveals that his respect is earned only through struggle and hard work, and his conflict with Corbett illustrates that those values will not stand in a West increasingly ruled by privilege.

This opening scene is soon echoed in Horn's first meeting with the Cattlemen Association at a lavish dinner served on a ranch. Again, the mise-en-scène creates a striking disparity between Horn and the other attendants that visualizes the class divide between them: he arrives in the simple and functional attire of a cowhand, while the diners are dressed in formal wear. Horn is then presented with a boiled lobster and is unimpressed ("I've never eaten a bug that big before"), struggling to eat it while the camera lingers on the ranchers and their wives relishing the decadent feast. These scenes establish that Horn is not just out of place in the capitalist West; he has utter contempt for it.

It is during the lobster dinner that Horn falls into the employ of the Cattlemen Association, and agrees to run cow thieves off their land by any means necessary. (Belle heavily implies that he should disregard the law and shoot any rustlers he encounters). He thus becomes a character not unlike Nate Champion in *Heaven's Gate*: a poor man doing the dirty work of his rich employers. But unlike Champion, Horn is not at all interested in material wealth. In the film's very first scene, he tells a stable owner that thieves are welcome to steal his belongings if they can get past his ill-tempered horse, and he later relays to Belle that he refused the opportunity to join the cast of *Buffalo Bill's Wild West* show, clearly illustrating that fame and fortune mean nothing to him. His distaste for champagne and lobster further reveal that he has no interest in the finer things in life; he even states to the ranchers gathered at the dinner that he accepted Coble's offer of work for a place to stay rather than money ("I said I'd earn my keep").

It is clear that Horn views his role as a stock detective in the same terms: having been convinced to take the job by Coble, he believes he is simply earning his keep. Horn takes no joy in shooting rustlers, and uses lethal violence only in self-defense; his first two kills are cow thieves who ride toward him with pistols drawn. McQueen, wide-eyed, exhales deeply, swallows and nervously looks away from the bodies lying on the ground, subtly revealing Horn's deep regret. He only shows genuine malice once in the entire film, when dealing with the rustler who killed his prized horse. Horn's clear discomfort with death is contrasted with the joy he derives from the other half of his working life; McQueen has Horn come alive when working the land and breaking horses, revealing that tracking rustlers is nothing more than a way to keep a roof above his head.

Horn, then, is not a violent mercenary or even just a relic of a bygone age: he is a working man manipulated by corrupt businessmen desperate both to maintain their wealth and to distance themselves from blame. In his brief discussion of the film, Philip French suggests that Horn is eventually betrayed by the Cattlemen because his role is "executed with too great a thoroughness for his hypocritical employers" (2005: 212), but this is not entirely true. After he has negotiated his labor for the Association, Coble reassures Horn: "I want to tell you, any means you have to take to eliminate this rustling problem, we're all behind you one hundred percent." Horn simply replies, "Well, I'll just have to take your word on that, John." As Coble later tells his partners, Horn only does what he is hired to do.

Coble himself comes to represent the utter ruthlessness of capitalism. French characterizes him as a "deeply sympathetic" man "trapped between the lethal duplicity of his fellow cattlemen and his friendship for Tom Horn" (2005: 212), but in fact Coble is the embodiment of that "lethal duplicity." Once Horn has been set up, Coble tells him that he had no idea what the Association was planning, but this is directly contradicted by earlier scenes. Coble tells Belle that Horn is expendable following the Cattlemen's dinner, and later he is present when the Association agrees to get rid of their stock detective. And, aside from a few performative displays of anger and apparent regret in the film's final act, he does nothing to prevent Horn from going to the gallows. Coble's turncoat nature and quiet inaction reveal that he is motivated entirely by capitalist self-interest. Ralph Lamar Turner characterizes the stockmen's actions as a "deliberate and systematic betrayal" (1999: 49), and Coble is just as culpable as any of his associates.

Although he does not expand on this point, French suggests that *Tom Horn* might be seen as "a companion piece to *Heaven's Gate*" (2005: 212). This is clearly true in that both films are based on real-life cases of injustice, and both failed to find favor with either critics or audiences. But the two are also aligned by Carter-era politics, and share thematic concerns with unchecked capitalism and the failure of individualism. Horn is a man who despises privilege and believes in self-reliance, but he is easily crushed by the wealthy elite that uses and manipulates him: individual effort means nothing when the system is rigged. *Tom Horn* stands in direct opposition to the New Right's capitalist rhetoric, which would prove so influential in the presidential election later in the year. The New Right promised a bright future in a country centered on capital, where free-market economics would ensure prosperity for all citizens who are willing to work hard. In contrast, *Tom Horn* illustrates the consequences of a society led by business, where individual achievement is only valued for as long as it benefits those at the top—and all but the elite are expendable.

Take Everything He Has

On paper, *The Long Riders* was the most successful period Western of 1980. Produced by United Artists on a budget of $8 million, it earned $5,891,149 in rentals before the end of the year, indicating moderate box office (Anon. 1980: 29). However, Michael Coyne is justified when he characterizes the film as a "flop" (1997: 185). Accounting for the costs of distribution, prints, and marketing, it is unlikely that the film was profitable for UA, and it would be difficult to frame the film's box office as a success—especially considering that it was heralded as the film that would breathe new life into the Western. And while the reviews for the film were generally better than those for *Tom Horn* and *Heaven's Gate*, reaction was decidedly mixed.

The Long Riders concerns brothers Jesse and Frank James (James and Stacy Keach), Cole, Jim, and Bob Younger (David, Keith, and Robert Carradine), and Ed and Clell Miller (Dennis and Randy Quaid), the members of the infamous James-Younger gang. The film follows the outlaws' exploits as they are pursued by Jacob Rixley (James Whitmore Jr.) and several other Pinkerton agents working on behalf of the Union Pacific Railroad. The agents kill members of the James and Younger families before finally catching up to the gang during a raid on a bank in Northfield, Minnesota. With Clell dead and all three Youngers wounded, the James brothers escape and form a second gang, only to be betrayed by new recruits Charley and Robert Ford (Christopher Guest and Nicolas Guest).

In their reviews of the film, several critics drew attention to one apparent flaw: its refusal to characterize its outlaws. The *Boston Globe*'s Michael Blowen attested that the film fails "to tell the entire history of seven men" (1980: 33); writing for the *New York Times*, Maslin suggested its central roles "are barely distinguishable from one another" (1980b: C14); and *Variety* commented that director Walter Hill "refuses to investigate the psychology or motivations of his characters" (Cart. 1980: 10). There is some truth to these claims. Early in the film, Clell explains—or, rather, fails to explain—why the gang robbed its first bank: "seemed like a good idea at the time." But *The Long Riders* is not a film about individuals, represented here as fallible and unsure of their own motivations. As French asserts, it is about "family obligations and the rootedness of a threatened clan" (2005: 170). The individual members of the gang are not as important as what they collectively represent to the community that surrounds them: revolutionary defiance.

Like *Heaven's Gate*, *The Long Riders* is far more interested in the bonds of community than in individualist heroes. As French observes, "When they're not robbing trains and banks, the gang are involved in domestic and community activities" (2005: 170). After their first robbery, half of the group retreats to the farm that is home to Zee Mimms (Savannah Smith), who will soon become Jesse's wife. Here, the outlaws are reframed in a domestic setting: Jesse and Jim speak tenderly to the women they love, while Frank dutifully chops firewood. Jesse's wedding then follows the film's second holdup, and presages the dance sequence in *Heaven's Gate*: the camera lingers on the guests playing music and dancing together, celebrating the bonds that exist between them. The fact that these scenes of domestic and communal harmony directly follow the sequences in which the outlaws commit their crimes creates an implicit association between the two, suggesting that it is the financial aid provided by the gang that ensures the survival of the entire community. As the *Washington Post*'s Gary Arnold stated in his positive review, it depicts "the James Brothers, the Younger Brothers and their outlaw associates as an integral, albeit criminal, part of the rural American society of a particular time and place" (1980: D1).

Of course, by a "particular time and place," Arnold is referring to Missouri in the aftermath of the Civil War. In this regard, an uncomfortable aspect of the film is that the members of the gang—and their community—are ex-confederates. But while it is troubling that the film fails to question the gang's support for the

Confederacy, it must be noted that it reconfigures the basis of the conflict between North and South for its own thematic needs. There is only one direct allusion to slavery in the film: a scene in which Clell intimidates a band performing a traditional Unionist song. Otherwise, animosity between Dixies and Yankees is redrawn as a conflict based on class divides. *The Long Riders*, then, taps into one of the central myths surrounding Jesse James: that "those who robbed from the rich were often assumed to be redistributing from the rich North to the poor South" (Parker 2011: 357).

This binary opposition of the wealthy North and the impoverished South is revealed in the film's second robbery scene, which sees the gang hold up a stagecoach. Two of the passengers are clearly contrasted with each other through costume and performance: one, a bearded and disheveled older man with a Southern accent, wears a crumpled cap and a creased gray jacket; the other, eloquent and sporting well-tended sideburns, wears a bowler hat, a pressed suit, and a pocket watch. When questioned by Bob on their allegiances, the younger man is revealed to be a Unionist, creating a clear visual distinction between North and South, rich and poor. Jesse then orders Bob to "take everything he has," and the older man zealously joins in as the gang strips the Yankee of all that symbolizes his wealth. Later this visual distinction is echoed in the contrast between the costuming of the gang and the Pinkerton agents sent to eradicate them. The gang is characterized through its uniform duster coats, a piece of clothing associated with working life on the range. On the other hand, the Pinkertons—some Yankees, others Southern men employed by the agency— wear expensive suits and ties that align them with the rich North.

Regardless of their individual motivations, it is clear that together the gang members form a revolutionary force: an underclass revolting against the wealthy establishment. And it is notable that they are given a clear moral code; they are all opposed to unnecessary violence. Only two innocents are killed by the gang: the first is murdered by Ed in the film's opening scene, resulting in his immediate exile from the group. The second is shot by Clell in a moment of panic during the Northfield raid (and even then Frank rebukes him for the killing). By contrast, the Pinkertons are depicted as the dishonorable invaders of a peaceful community: they force their way into the James household; murder the Youngers' innocent brother; and cause the death of the youngest member of the James family—a disabled boy of only fifteen. They become violent enforcers of capitalist ideology, willing to sacrifice life in order to protect the profits of their employers. And while Rixley is depicted as a principled man—often seen to reprimand his agents—even he is revealed to be corrupt by the film's end, when he coldly hires the Fords to assassinate the James brothers.

The Pinkertons' actions do nothing but strengthen support for the gang, rendering it not just a means of survival for the community but also a symbol of rebellion. As the agents intensify their violent campaign, the society surrounding the group presents a united front in a scene that underlines a need for communal resistance: as huge numbers gather to mourn the youngest James brother, every man carries a firearm in case they will need to repel a Pinkerton ambush. Later, the bandits are given refuge by a farmer, McCorkindale (West Buchanan), who gives his life to protect them. Importantly, the outlaws are shown to care as much about their community as their community cares about them; as McCorkindale lies dead, Frank risks his life by leaving cover in the hope that the farmer can be saved.

Like *Heaven's Gate*, then, *The Long Riders* is aligned to Carter's concerns through its plea for unity. It depicts communal resistance as the only way to combat capitalist ideologies, whether represented by the Union Pacific Railroad or the New Right. Even Hill, who denied that the film contains any specific social commentary, evoked Carter's anti-capitalist sentiments in reflecting on the gang's importance to its community: "They robbed and stole from the railroads and banks, which the Missouri farmers hated more than we hate the oil companies today" (Hill in Greco 1980: 15). In fact, the James-Younger gang collapses because Jesse loses sight of the importance of community and chooses to act in his own self-interest. Following the disastrous Northfield raid, he convinces Frank to abandon their wounded comrades. The film indicts individualism by illustrating how Jesse's selfishness leads to the group's destruction: Clell dies shortly after the James brothers leave; the Youngers, unable to escape, are arrested; Jesse is betrayed by his new associates; and Frank, with no allies left, turns himself in.

At the film's end, the Ford brothers come to cement its critique of the capitalist impulses central to the New Right's rhetoric. They meet with Rixley in a darkened saloon, dressed in simple attire that associates them with the Southern underclass: wide-brimmed hats, worn jackets, and faded patterned shirts. After negotiating their terms for killing Jesse James, they appear totally transformed in the next scene: clean-shaven, hair slicked, and parted, they are wearing brand-new tailored three-piece suits when they assassinate a man they once admired. Their deal with Rixley has allowed them to transcend their class—but in doing so they have chosen to betray their community.

Conclusion: How the West Was Lost

Many commentators on the Western have linked the genre's waning fortunes to Reagan. For example, Alexandra Keller notes that the Western's decline and resurgence "coincide with the seismic shift in American culture" that his presidency represented. However, Keller suggests that its hibernation is ultimately traceable to the revisionist films of the 1970s: "By 1980, the Western, having become the counter-Western . . . for the duration of the Vietnam War, itself was experiencing a momentary and not unusual fatigue" (2005: 240). What Keller overlooks is that 1980's genre offerings were in fact counter-Westerns, albeit ones that moved beyond the horrors of Vietnam and attacked America for its increasingly materialistic and corporate society. I would argue that it is for that very reason that they failed to resonate at a time when the countercultural spirit of the preceding decades was fading away in favor of a capitalist future.

Admittedly, a handful of scholars have recognized that a popular rejection of radical themes may have at least played a part in the failure of *Heaven's Gate*. Nelson admits that it was "out of step with contemporary cinema not only artistically but ideologically as well" (2015: 193) and suggests that part of its failure is attributable to its criticism of capitalism "at a time when capitalism was on the comeback" (2015: 194). Nelson echoes French, who suggests that critics rejected "a movie of such an obviously left wing, quasi-Marxist character" in a manner that embodied "the changing mood of a nation that was turning its back on the spirit of the 1960s" (2005: 139–40). It is not surprising that contemporary reviewers noted the film's radical themes but neglected to acknowledge their cultural significance; released during the year that witnessed the New Right's ascent to office, it was doomed to fail.

Coyne, too, has noted that the politics of *Heaven's Gate* undoubtedly contributed to its catastrophic reception. However, none of these scholars considers the thematic connections between *Heaven's Gate* and its most notable contemporaries. Coyne suggests that *The Long Riders* failed to find success because it is "gimmicky" and "yet another Jesse James movie," while *Tom Horn* is "unremittingly bleak." And while he goes on to observe that Westerns "had no solid resonance in the era of Ronald Reagan" (1997: 185), Coyne does not recognize that the major American Westerns of 1980 uniformly rally against the capitalist ideologies that the New Right embodied during the latter years of the 1970s—ideologies that would firmly take hold in America at the beginning of the next decade.

During his "crisis of confidence" speech, Carter issued a grave warning against the New Right's promise of future prosperity: "There are two paths to choose. One is a path I've warned about tonight, the path that leads to fragmentation and self-interest. Down that road lies a mistaken idea of freedom, the right to grasp for ourselves some advantage over others" (Carter in Kaufman 2006: 584). *The Long Riders, Tom Horn,* and *Heaven's Gate* are thematically aligned to one another by a concern that America might choose the path of "fragmentation and self-interest": *Tom Horn* sees its title character manipulated, betrayed, and murdered by the businessmen who hire him to do their dirty work; *The Long Riders* imagines the James-Younger gang as revolutionaries fighting back against the wealthy elite that threatens to destroy their impoverished community; and *Heaven's Gate* sees innocent homesteaders targeted for extermination by the cattle barons who value the land they live on more than their actual lives. In short, these films steadfastly belong to both the Carter-era (in their depiction of a nation in which business runs amok) and Carter's politics (in their lamentation of a society that values material wealth above all else and has forgotten the virtues of equality and community). These films failed in part, then, because America yearned for Westerns that embraced the New Right's vision for America—and instead they clung to ideals that, by 1980, already belonged to the past.

Bibliography

Anon. "Big Rental Films of 1980." *Variety* 301, no. 11 (1980): 29, 50.

Anon. "Cimino's 'Heaven's Gate' Costs Alarming UA on Top of Coppola." *Variety* 296, no. 2 (1979): 30.

Arnold, Gary. "Easy 'Riders': An Elegant Entry in the Western Genre." *Washington Post*, May 16 (1980): D1, D4.

Beller, Miles. "The Hollywood Western Rides Into Favor Again." *New York Times*, June 8 (1980): D1, D15.

Blowen, Michael. "Western Almost Returns with 'The Long Riders'." *Boston Globe*, May 16 (1980): 33.

Broussard, James H. *Ronald Reagan: Champion of Conservative America*. London: Routledge, 2014.

Canby, Vincent. "Movie: 'Heaven's Gate,' a Western by Cimino." *New York Times*, November 19 (1980a): C29.

Canby, Vincent. "The System that Let 'Heaven's Gate' Run Wild." *New York Times*, November 30 (1980b): D1, D17.

Cart. "*The Long Riders*." *Variety* 299, no. 1 (1980): 10.

Coyne, Michael. *The Crowded Prairie: American National Identity in the Hollywood Western*. London: I.B. Tauris, 1997.

French, Philip. *Westerns*, exp. ed. Manchester: Carcanet, 2005.

Geri. "*Heaven's Gate*." *Variety* 301, no. 4 (1980): 14.

Greco, Mike. "Hard Riding." *Film Comment* 16, no. 3 (1980): 13–19.

Howison, Jeffrey D. *The 1980 Presidential Election: Ronald Reagan and the Shaping of the American Conservative Movement*. London: Routledge, 2014.

Hughes, Howard. *Stagecoach to Tombstone: The Filmgoers' Guide to the Great Westerns*. London: I.B. Tauris, 2008.

Kaufman, Burton I. *Presidential Profiles: The Carter Years*. New York: Facts on File, 2006.

Keller, Alexandra. "Historical Discourse and American Identity in Westerns since the Reagan Era." In *Hollywood's West: The American Frontier in Film, Television, and History*, edited by Peter C. Rollins and John E. O'Connor, 239–60. Lexington: The University Press of Kentucky, 2005.

Kitses, Jim. *Horizons West: Directing the Western from John Ford to Clint Eastwood*, new ed. London: BFI, 2004.

Maslin, Janet. "Film: '*The Long Riders*,' With Gangs of the West." *New York Times*, May 16 (1980b): C14.

Maslin, Janet. "Movie: McQueen Stars in '*Tom Horn*'." *New York Times* May 23 (1980a): C8.

McCabe, Bruce. "McQueen Misses with *Tom Horn*." *Boston Globe*, June 7 (1980): 18.

McCarthy, Todd. "Is 'Western' Plot Now A B.O. Liability?." *Variety* 299, no. 8 (1980): 7, 28.

McGee, Patrick. *From Shane to Kill Bill: Rethinking the Western*. Oxford: Blackwell, 2007.

McVeigh, Stephen. *The American Western*. Edinburgh: Edinburgh University Press, 2007.

Nelson, Andrew Patrick. *Still in the Saddle: The Hollywood Western, 1969–1980*. Norman: University of Oklahoma Press, 2015.

Parker, Martin. "The Wild West, the Industrial East and the Outlaw." *Culture and Organization* 17, no. 4 (2011): 347–65.

Prince, Stephen. *A New Pot of Gold: Hollywood under the Electric Rainbow, 1980–1989*. Berkeley: University of California Press, 2000.

Schaller, Michael. *Reckoning with Reagan: America and Its President in the 1980s*. Oxford: Oxford University Press, 1992.

Skinner, Kiron, Serhiy Kudella, Bruce Bueno de Mesquita, and Condoleezza Rice. *The Strategy of Campaigning: Lessons from Ronald Reagan and Boris Yeltsin*. Ann Arbor: The University of Michigan Press, 2007.

Turner, Ralph Lamar, and Robert. J. Higgs. *The Cowboy Way: The Western Leader in Film, 1945–1995*. Westport: Greenwood Press, 1999.

Wood, Robin. *Hollywood from Vietnam to Reagan*. New York: Columbia University Press, 1986.

Part Two

Charting New Frontiers and Mapping Identity and Politics in International Cult Westerns

5

Landscape, Imagery, and Symbolism in Alejandro Jodorowsky's *El Topo*

Matt Melia

Introduction

The *Guardian* critic Steve Rose attempts to sum up and define the Chilean director Alejandro Jodorowsky's strange, complex, transgressive, and provocative oeuvre via a roll call of diverse cultural and religious reference points:

> If you have never seen one of his movies, they are difficult to explain. You could start by throwing together Sergio Leone, Luis Bunuel, Hieronymus Bosch and Buddha, and perhaps start by spiking their Kool-Aid for good measure. They're filled with Wild Beasts, cosmic symbolism, freaks, naked women and spiritual masters. Where else, for example, would you see a re-enactment of the conquest of Latin America with costumed frogs and chameleons? Or a geriatric hermaphrodite squirting milk from breasts that appear to be the head of ocelots. (2009)

Jodorowsky's cinema is not merely "difficult to explain" but it consciously evades explanation, easy critical definition, or generic categorization. It deliberately misdirects the viewer via a complex bricolage of disparate sources, symbols, and cultural markers. The director offers an alchemical mix of artistic influences and high and low cultural points of reference (from Antonin Artaud and the Theatre of Cruelty, Samuel Beckett and Salvador Dali to the slapstick comedy of Buster Keaton and George Romero's *Night of the Living Dead* [1968]); popular genre and exploitation cinemas (not only the Western but also the horror, religious drama, and even the Samurai films); and esoteric spiritual symbolism (drawing heavily and imagistically on the Tarot in films such as *El Topo* [1970] and *The Holy Mountain* [1973]).

Textually and meta-textually, Jodorowsky's cinema is also one of displacement. His films not only present narratives of displacement and journeys/quests (a signifying trope of the Western), they are themselves displaced entities (or may be read as such) existing on the extreme margins of the global paracinema. Victoria Ruetalo and Dolores Tierney (2009) include *El Topo* as a significant moment within the canon of "Latsploitation Cinema" (the exploitation cinema of Latin America: a "displaced" cinema which they define in opposition to the exploitation cinema of North America as having its own particular cultural and industrial criteria and practices).

This chapter will present a discussion of *El Topo* as a transgressive, violent, displaced Western and examine how the film's presentation of the scorched, surrealist, mountainous, and desert landscapes of Mexico as spaces of displacement, metamorphosis, apocalypse, and extinction recall and deliberately appropriate the absurdist landscapes and imagery of Irish writer and dramatist Samuel Beckett's early dramas. *El Topo* does employ the thematic and iconographic tropes of the Hollywood Western. However, here the iconic figure of the black-leather-clad gunfighter, "El Topo" ("The Mole," played by Jodorowsky), is propelled on a violent, absurdist, picaresque, and ultimately cyclical spiritual journey of enlightenment through an abstract and carnivalesque landscape of deformed and grotesque bodies, spiritual masters, and transgressive sexual experiences that subvert the Fordian or Hawksian landscapes of the Hollywood Western. Similarly, *El Topo* is also cloaked in the mantle of a Sergio Leone-esque visual aesthetic but Jodorowsky invites the viewer to gaze beyond this facade by increasingly subverting the film's generic identity as it moves inexorably toward its third and final act.

Both Foster Hirsh (1972) and J. Hoberman and Jonathan Rosenbaum (1983) have examined *El Topo*'s three-act structure. Hoberman and Rosenbaum present a topographical view of the film's structure, narrative, and (counter) cultural context while noting how the film is broken into three "movements," each of which untethers the film more and more from the generic anchor of the Western. They describe the first of these movements as "a kind of Spaghetti Western with crudely Buñuelian overtones" (1983: 82). This movement ends with the gunfighter's visceral castration of the Colonel (David Silva) and the abandonment of his son (Brontis Jodorowsky) to the monastic care of the monks he has rescued. In the second movement, Jodorowsky "broadens his range to let fly with a nonstop barrage of Tao, Sufi, Tarot, Nietzschean, Zen Buddhist, and biblical references" (1983: 82) while El Topo defeats three spiritual masters. The third movement

> concerns El Topo's penitent reincarnation. In tight close up, the hero is shown as
> a frizzy-haired blond, sitting in the lotus position and holding a flower. He has

just woken up from a twenty-year sleep, during which the dwarfs and cripples
have cared for him. (1983: 86)

As the gunfighter sheds his iconic costume in favor of the robes of enlightenment,
the film itself gradually sheds its costume and the visual aesthetic of the Western
genre (although as we shall see, not entirely).

By focusing on the visual aesthetics that Jodorowsky's employs, this chapter
will initially explore the presentation of landscape in *El Topo*. In the next section
I will explore how *El Topo* "displaces" the Western by examining the film's
contextual cultural landscapes and its engagement with cultural imagery. In the
final section I will note how (certainly in the first two movements) Jodorowsky
deliberately scatters the visual iconography of Samuel Beckett's work across the
cinematic landscapes of his film. While Hoberman and Rosenbaum, Benn Cobb
(2007) and Doyle Greene (2007) have all noted and explored the influence of
Antonin Artaud and the Theatre of Cruelty (a "total" theater of purely visceral-
gestural attack and physical-metaphysical experience) on *El Topo*, the pervasive
influence of Beckett's work has been less well noted (despite the director's own
personal experience of it in the immediate postwar years in France). I will
explore how Beckett's influence works to further distance the film from its
outward Western identity.

Cultural Landscapes: (Dis)Placing *El Topo*

The Landscape of Mexico

Wimal Dissanayake proposes that

> the relationship between cinema and landscape is a complex and multifaceted
> one, generating issues of ontology, epistemology, aesthetics and forms of cultural
> representation. Most often, we tend to think of landscape in films as a provider
> of the requisite background for the unfolding of the narrative and a giver of
> greater visual density and cogency. This is indeed true so far as it goes: however,
> landscapes in cinema perform numerous other functions that are more subtle
> and more complex which invest the filmic experience with greater meaning and
> significance. (2010: 191)

The landscape of *El Topo* has a much broader function than simply serving as
a backdrop to an unfolding narrative. Jodorowsky uses the evocative deserts,

caves, and mountain ranges of Mexico as a canvas to explore and deconstruct cinematic Hollywood myths and their cultural imposition on the cinema of Latin and South America (which has its own indigenous "cowboy" or Gaucho culture). The Brazilian director Glauber Rocha explained that

> Hollywood films have had a tremendous meaning for Latin Americans, they colonized a culture. They kill our culture. Things I saw in Westerns come back in my films in other forms. One of the things that characterized the New Wave was a nostalgia for the old Hollywood. The first films of Truffaut and Godard where an attempt to read these symbols. Hollywood is the major influence in colonizing the minds and culture of Latin America. . . . The Myths of the West are very appealing to Latin American masses because they are historical. When they think of film they think of Westerns, it is a fundamental myth in films for them. (Glenn O'Brien 1970: 37)

One might hypothesize here that if, as Rocha claims, the Hollywood Western and its myths are fundamentally ingrained in the DNA of contemporaneous Latin American Cinema then Jodorowsky's intent is to destabilize and subvert this cultural colonization by deconstructing it, lampooning it (notably in the third act's presentation of the grotesque whorehouse and the Wild West town's ritual fetishization of the gun) and remythologizing it through the imposition of arcane religious iconography and *Eastern* spirituality while presenting a landscape that is at once familiar and also utterly alien.

One might also hypothesize that the landscape of Mexico had the same appeal to Jodorowsky as it did to his greatest influence: the founder of the Theatre of Cruelty, Antonin Artaud, who traveled to the Sierra Tarahumaras to engage in Peyote rituals with the Tarahumaras Indians. Stephen Barber notes that

> Artaud anticipated that he would discover a revolutionary society in Mexico, and that it would conform to his vision of a kind of anatomical revolution which would dispense with its own history. He believed that the Mexican revolution of 1910-11 had signaled a return to the mythological concerns of the imperial civilizations which had existed before the Spanish conquest of Mexico in 1519. He would be the instrument that could catalyse and focus these revolutionary forces. . . . Although Artaud was disappointed in his attempt to break utterly from European society, he nevertheless found in Mexico a tenable image of revolution, which fed into his work until his death. He discovered revolution inscribed into the Mexican landscape itself, as a perpetually self-cancelling and self-creative force. (2003: 96)

For Jodorowsky this primal backdrop is integral to his cinematic revolution, and the creation of a new revolutionary cinematic aesthetic. Like Artaud, Jodorowsky aims to break away from and oppose a dominant colonial (cultural ideology). Jodorowsky's landscapes are complex and mythic spaces. If, for Artaud, this experience of the Mexican landscape was part of an ongoing project of personal, ritualistic, metaphysical, and theatrical liberation, we might consider that for Jodorowsky it has a similar function in liberating and freeing cinema and reimagining the cinematic image. Karl Smith once asked Jodorowsky:

> Mythology was a necessary tool in interpreting the landscape—geography, meteorology, astronomy—but how can myth work, continue to fulfill its function, when as a society we know these myths not to be true?

Jodorowsky responded:

> We need to study myth to be a wise person. A normal person is living just like an animal or a plant and if we want to develop, to grow inside, we need myths— old knowledge, traditional knowledge, these are looking for something that is lost: alchemy was searching for that, magic was searching for that, religion was searching for that. "Where is the centre of the universe?," "How do I find the centre?": some persons, they say the centre is the heart. In addition, the centre of the heart is love. Love is beauty. We cannot know the truth but we can know love and beauty. (Smith 2015)

This idea is the key to understanding *El Topo*: the landscape is a space or canvas where the idea of myths and symbols themselves may be explored (this includes cinematic, religious, and spiritual mythologies, symbols, and iconographies). That the incorporation of Beckettian imagery, with its connotations of spiritual emptiness, corporeal evanescence, existential anxiety, and the God-shaped hole at the heart of the twentieth century, presents a counterpoint to the diverse religious imagery and spiritual richness found in *El Topo*. In recognizing and incorporating Beckett's influence into the visual DNA and iconography of the film, I would suggest that Jodorowsky was seeking to engage with a fully comprehensive array of belief systems which included imagery suggestive of the existential *absence* of belief. The arid landscape of the film is presented as a spiritual void (note the grotesque hypocrisy, cruelty, and spiritual emptiness of the frontier town at the third "movement") which Jodorowsky fills with a barrage of spiritual and religious imagery. Similarly, in suggesting that Jodorowsky was attempting to repurpose cinema itself, Roger Ebert observes that *El Topo*'s diverse mix of "symbols and mythologies" creates an effect that resembles that of T. S. Eliot's stream-of-consciousness poem "The Waste Land" (1922), "especially Eliot's notion of shoring up fragments of mythologies against the ruins of the post-Christian era. . . . What is El Topo seeking in the desert? Why, he is seeking symbols, images, bizarre people and events with which to fill the film?" (Ebert 2007 [1970]).

Displacing the Western

Graeme Harper and Jonathan Rayner note that

> the role of the film director could be seen as similar to the role of an individual map-maker. Both maps and films assume and position audiences ideologically as much as geographically. The interaction between map-makers and film makers and audiences can be akin to a shared pilgrimage in which the individual, the group, or a culture moves through a familiar or newly discovered landscape. (2010: 16)

This is an appropriate filter through which to discuss *El Topo*, whose blasted and scorched desert landscapes recall those of the avant-garde cultural preoccupations of its director as well as those of Artaud and Beckett. Jodorowsky is a cinematic "map maker": not only does his central character navigate a reimagined "Western" space that is simultaneously familiar and alien (reflecting the cultural and geographical differences between Latin and North America), his cinema is an experimental and experiential one where the viewer is invited not merely to witness but also to experience and share this "pilgrimage" or journey. Furthermore, the landscape is an open space in which the viewer is "positioned" (both consciously and unconsciously) in relation to an array of high and low cultural markers.

Here, with regard to El Topo's own physical and metaphysical journey across the film's landscape, we may also note a further degree of self-reflexivity. Jodorowsky who plays the central role of El Topo had, himself, traversed a series of international and cultural spaces and landscapes. Jodorowsky has described his own itinerant journey thus:

> My parents were Russian. I was born in Iquique, a small town of 2000 people in Chile near Bolivia. I lived in the desert for 10 years. The children didn't accept me because I was Russian. I moved to Santiago, the capital of Chile where I studied Philosophy and Psychology. I worked as a circus clown. I

acted in several plays and formed my own marionette theatre. I created a theatre of mime. I lived in Santiago for 10 years. The young men did not accept me because I was a Jew. I went to Europe and lived in Paris. During that time I worked with Marcel Marceau. . . . I directed Maurice Chevalier. I founded "The Panic Movement" with Arrabal and Topor. I realised a 4 hour happening which has been acclaimed as the best happening ever made. I lived in Paris for 10 years. The French did not accept me because I was Chilean. I moved to Mexico where I directed 100 plays (Ionesco, Strindberg, Arrabal, and Beckett). . . . The Mexicans didn't accept me because I was French. Now I live in the United States where I am finishing my film *The Holy Mountain.* The Americans think I am Mexican. After 10 years, I will move to another planet. They won't accept me because they think I am American! (Cerdán and Labayan 2009: 103)

Just as the director describes himself as emerging from the desert, his cinematic counterpart, El Topo – The Gunfighter, is depicted in the film's opening sequence emerging out of the burning desert sand on horseback with his young naked son in tow. Throughout the film Jodorowsky presents characters who merge with, emerge out of, or are encased by the surrounding landscape. For example, in the film's second movement El Topo is depicted as almost physically merging with a rock face while Maria (Mara Lorenzio) bathes in a desert pool. This approach is also indicative of the pervasive influence of Beckett, whose own characters are contained or imprisoned both literally and metaphorically by their environments. For example, Winnie in *Happy Days* (1961) is presented buried up to her waist in sand beneath the burning sun in Act 1 and then buried up to her neck in Act 2.

Stephen Barber further notes the theme of displacement in Jodorowsky's films, observing that "with Jodorowsky, everything is pushed to the extreme, with the result that his audiences experience the impact of his films from a uniquely sensitised, unforeseeably displaced viewing position" before adding that "Jodorowsky has inhabited deliriously outlandish and wayward territory, often staking claims in the pre-occupations and locations of his films, to terrains that at first sight nobody else would want to approach" (2007: 9). The burning and surrealist desert landscapes of *El Topo* are filled with grotesque, deformed figures (dwarfs, hermaphrodites, amputees), shocking violence (e.g., the charnel house of the village massacre stumbled upon by El Topo and his son and the visceral castration of the Colonel), and mystical esotericism which works to defamiliarize any viewer accustomed to the more recognizable imagery and locales of the Hollywood Western. As Barber notes, "It is evident that Jodorowsky and the Hollywood industry work according to two irreconcilably different conceptions of time and myth" (2007: 11).

Indeed, *El Topo* is the maleficent double of the classical Hollywood Western, a genre itself built on a set of frontier, colonialist, and masculine myths played out against the mythologized space of the American West and which through a director like John Ford offered a romanticized version of America's violent history. In *El Topo*'s third movement we find a parody of a Wild West town peopled by what Foster Hirsh describes as "grotesque parodies of acquisitive, rapacious, hypocritical capitalists. Putrefying everything they touch, the towns people force El Topo and his midget-teacher-companion to perform public intercourse for the public amusement" (1972: 13).

In this "Wild West Town," churchgoers fetishize and worship the gun, taking part in a ritual of Russian Roulette which ends with the brutal physical death of a young boy and the spiritual death of the, now adult, son of El Topo. While *El Topo* is the maleficent double of the Hollywood Western, it also contains interesting "doubled" imagery, the most obvious being the mirroring of the village massacre and the massacre of the rabbits later in the film. Interestingly, the white uniforms of the massacred villagers are not only visually mirrored in the overhead shot of the massacred white rabbits. The uniforms are also suggestive of a cult—a prescient image in the wake of the Manson family's crimes. This detail supports Hoberman and Rosenbaum's suggestion that *El Topo* is linked to the "wasteland of the counterculture" (1983: 77). Indeed, at the film's finale, the now grown up son of El Topo has rejected the spiritual vestments of the monk and has adopted the earlier dark costume of his father—the fetishistic black leather of the gunfighter. This provides a contrast to *El Topo* himself, who in the final movement has rejected such a costume in favor of the garb of a Buddhist monk.

When comparing *El Topo* with Arrabal's Spanish Civil War drama *Viva La Muerte* (1971), Hirsch observes that *El Topo* is "built on the same general themes: the tortuous discovery and acquisition of manhood" (1972: 11). The film opens with El Topo instructing his young son to dispose of childish things by burying his toy and a photograph of his mother in the burning desert sand, in a series of images that resonate with both Beckett's *Waiting for Godot* (1953) and *Happy Days* (1961).

Richard Slotkin notes the transition between what he terms the "Town Tamer" Westerns of the classical Hollywood (see *Dodge City* [Michael Curtiz,

1939] and *My Darling Clementine* [John Ford, 1946]) and the "Outlaw" or "Revenger" Westerns of the postwar years (see *The True Story of Jesse James* [Nicholas Ray, 1957]), and suggests that the later "psychological Westerns" appealed to "film makers and artists who sought to make the genre a vehicle for works of 'literary' seriousness" (1992: 380). This elevation of the genre is present in Jodorowsky's film via the visual references to Beckett and other absurdist writers and dramatists. Indeed, Hirsch observes that

> Jodorowsky wants every bit as much as Arrabal or Artaud to dazzle and purge us, he is as alert to the exorcising potential of Cruelty and Panic, he is as conscious of myth and ritual as Beck and Grotowski, he is as attuned to the absurd as Ionesco or Beckett. (1972: 12)

Slotkin notes the festishization of the gunfighter in the Western: an isolated, existential, and mythic figure, apposite to the genre as it developed post–Second World War and later exemplified by Alan Ladd's eponymous character in *Shane* (George Stevens, 1953), when observing that

> ideological clichés of the historical Western give way to a new view of the Western myth in which the difference between lawman and outlaw is obscured by their kindred gift for violence and is rendered problematic by their characterological difference or alienation from their communities. . . . The Gunfighter is psychologically troubled, isolated from normal society by something dark in his nature / his past. That darkness is bound up with and expressed by his highly specialised social function: he is a killer by profession. (1992: 383)

El Topo is a pastiche of that figure and while the character incorporates elements of this trope, we are given no information about his background, identity, or his purpose: he emerges fully formed from the sands of the desert. In this way El Topo is more akin to the Western characters that are commonly played by Clint Eastwood.

Jodorowsky, also replaces the romantic mythos of the North American Western with a set of cosmic, esoteric myths and Jewish, Latin American and Eastern belief systems which appear discordant with the mythic space of the specifically Christian Hollywood Western. One may also question the extent to which *El Topo* navigates the contemporary revisionism of the Western, as exemplified by the films of New Hollywood. Despite its non-American origins, Rosenbaum (2018) notes how *El Topo* was central in the formation of the subgenre of the "Acid Western."

El Topo and the Countercultural Cinematic Landscape

El Topo is frequently recognized and discussed by commentators as the prototypical cult midnight movie and the apotheosis of the paracinematic: an iconic moment of countercultural cinema. Roger Greenspun observes that

> during its months of midnight screenings at the Elgin, Alexandro Jodorowsky's *El Topo* became a secret rite of some importance in New York City. . . . During the time of its midnight screenings I asked someone who had seen it what *El Topo* was all about. He responded "Everything" and now I've seen it I know what he meant. (1971)

El Topo's countercultural contexts and aesthetics have been much discussed elsewhere (Cobb [2007]; Hoberman and Rosenbaum [1983]; Greene [2007]), so there is no need to recycle the history of its run as a "midnight movie" in New York City here. Similarly, *El Topo*'s status as an "Acid Western" has been well documented by Rumsey Taylor (2013).

Indeed, the film was a fixed point in the countercultural cinematic landscape of North America. While *Easy Rider* (Dennis Hopper, 1969) might outwardly anticipate *El Topo* in the way that it mythologizes the landscape, foregrounds themes of cultural isolation and displacement, and presents characters on an abstract quest for subjectivity and identity, a more comparable film is one which lies outside the Western genre altogether but which was still absorbed into the countercultural cinematic zeitgeist: *2001: A Space Odyssey* (Stanley Kubrick, 1968). Indeed, Hoberman and Rosenbaum opine that *El Topo* "captured the countercultural imagination like no movie since Stanley Kubrick's *2001*" (1983: 94). The countercultural context and identity of *2001*, its presentation of a spiritual journey or odyssey and its emphasis on cycles, set Kubrick's film up as an intriguing comparison piece. Just like *El Topo*, *2001* redrew the parameters of its genre and demanded to be received as an immersive "total" experience rather than a classical exercise in narrative storytelling. Christopher Frayling reports that Jodorowsky acknowledged that the "'duel of destiny' [set] in a circular *corrida*" in *El Topo* was a "small homage" to Sergio Leone's Italian Westerns (1981: 285). However, it is the atypical, violent and surreal Spaghetti Western *Django Kill* (*Se sei vivo spara*, Giulio Questi, 1967) that *El Topo* usually gets compared to. Mark Goodall asserts that *Django Kill* exists "in close artistic proximity" to *El Topo* while also functioning in a similar way (2016: 202, 208). Although *Django Kill* is ostensibly a Spaghetti Western, Goodall finds genre-bending cinematic strategies relating to Italian *mondo* shockumentaries, *giallo* thrillers, and gothic horror films at play too (2016: 204–9).

Similarly, both *2001* and *El Topo* collapse a variety of cinematic frontiers and boundaries and reimagine the role and purpose of cinematic landscape. *2001* moves beyond the generic parameters of science fiction while *El Topo* does likewise in relation to the Western genre. While science fiction elements are visibly present in *2001* (spaceships, dangerous artificial intelligences, alien consciousnesses, and so on), Kubrick's use of these genre tropes ultimately results in the film as a whole transcending its genre identity. In *El Topo* Jodorowsky anchors the viewer to the Western by employing common genre tropes (horses, guns, the wilderness, and so on) and then moves them beyond the Western via his incorporation of mystical, spiritual, and biblical imagery and allusion. This is something that the marketing for the film was keen to point out since the trailer advised potential viewers to "be prepared to live the most wonderful experience of your life. . . . *El Topo* Is NOT a Western, it goes far beyond any Western. . . . *El Topo* is not a religious film . . . it contains all religions."

There are parallels as well between El Topo's transcendent journey and the transcendent journey that *2001*'s astronaut Dave Bowman (Keir Dullea) and, in a broader sense, humanity itself experiences—a journey which begins within the primal desert landscape of the "dawn of man" sequence where man is necessarily depicted in his hominid state and ends with the birth of the Star Child at the film's conclusion. Cobb notes *El Topo*'s allusions to Friedrich Nietzsche when he notes that Nietzsche's

> *Thus Spoke Zarathustra* [1883] is an account of a cave dwelling prophet who emerges from his mountain solitude to preach to the people. This is directly referenced in *El Topo* at the beginning of the third act, when the spiritually reborn El Topo awakes in a cave of inbred cripples and travels down to the people (living in this case in a Wild West Sodom). Zarathustra announces the death of God and argues for man to master himself and harness his own power, to be reborn as "Ultimate Man" or "Superman." (2007: 73)

Hence both Jodorowsky and Kubrick present the emergence and rebirth of man from the literal and metaphorical cave, using primal and primitive landscapes. *2001* actually opens with Richard Strauss's "Thus Spake Zarathustra" (1896) actually playing on the soundtrack as the sun comes up during the "dawn of man" sequence. Similarly, while Kubrick took the cosmic void of space—the "landscape" of his film—and filled it with evasive symbolic meaning, Jodorowsky took *El Topo*'s desert void and filled it with myths and symbols of all kinds. Indeed, rather than being a space odyssey, Cobb suggests that El Topo is "a desert odyssey" (2007: 74). Significantly, both *El Topo* and *2001* end ambiguously and cyclically with the birth or imminent arrival of a child. El Topo's son rides off with his late father's pregnant lover, and their baby, like the Star Child, offers hope for the future. However, El Topo's son's appropriation of his father's black costume suggests the cycle of violence and self-discovery will begin again— something also suggestive in the ambiguity of the Star Child's gaze (which is matched at the start of Kubrick's next film, *A Clockwork Orange* [1971] by the malevolent stare of Alex [Malcolm McDowell]).

Alejandro Jodorowsky, Samuel Beckett, and *El Topo*

If the surface of *El Topo* offers a pastiche of Western imagery, symbols, and mythologies, at a deeper level the film is informed by Jodorowsky's time in Paris during the early 1950s. At this time he mixed with the postwar liberal intellectual elite (Andre Breton, the "Pope of Surrealism"; Samuel Beckett; Marcel Marceau et al.) and collaborated with Fernando Arrabal in the Panic Movement (through which emerge the influence of Artaud and Beckett). Jodorowsky told Klaus Bisenbach:

> In '53 I left for Paris. I wanted to know Andre Breton because of surrealism and Marcel [Marceau] because I wanted to be a mime. Marcel was a genius mime, but not so intelligent. Myself, I was not so good a mime, but I was very intelligent. I say to him, "You are making an imitation of Charlie Chaplin. Why don't you make a metaphysical pantomime?" And then I composed *The Mask Maker* and *The Cage* [two mime routines] for him. I was a writer for him. But I did what I wanted. I also studied philosophy at the Sorbonne. Then I saw Samuel Beckett's *Waiting for Godot* and I wanted to do theatre. (2012)

We might speculate that this interest in mime, masks, and pantomime lays a foundation for the way Jodorowsky uses the framework of the Western and its aesthetic as a costume for his film, and for the array of grotesques and carnival imagery he confronts the audience with. Jodorowsky had lived in postwar Paris in the early 1950s and had been exposed to changing cultural landscape of the city scarred not only by occupation but also by the violence of liberation, and by the creative voices which this landscape had provoked and over which hung the legacy of Antonin Artaud (who had died in 1948 at the clinic of Ivry-Sur-Seine after having experienced nine years of asylum internment, insulin therapy, withdrawal from laudanum, and over fifty sessions of electro shock therapy) and the Theatre of Cruelty, Jean Genet and Samuel Beckett. The influence of this milieu and zeitgeist in *El Topo* results in the concerns of two separate countercultural traditions—those of postwar Europe and the transgressive Theatres of Cruelty and the Absurd and the acid soaked countercultural landscape of the late 1960s and early 1970s (during which period Artaud was undergoing a cultural renaissance amid contemporary creative and experimental voices of the underground)—being drawn together in one cinematic landscape.

Jodorowsky had formed a creative theatrical partnership with dramatist Fernando Arrabal (he had relocated to Mexico in the late 1950s) as cofounder of the Panic Movement in 1962, which as Doyle Greene reminds us:

> Was a deliberate effort to put Antonin Artaud's theories of the Theatre of Cruelty into practice. . . . The Theatre of Cruelty had demolished the conventions of Western Theatre—characterization, dialogue, realism, narrative and good taste in favour of intense spectacle that assaulted and bombarded the viewer's senses with disorienting, provocative, often violent and sexual imagery. . . . However Artaud's conception of the Theatre of Cruelty was not merely intended to simply batter and bewilder and offend the viewers with images of sex and violence, it was a deliberate attempt to stir and awaken all that was hidden and forbidden in the spectator's consciousness—a cathartic, even ceremonial spectacle intended to drastically and permanently transform the viewer's psyche. (2007: 8)

Jodorowsky's cinematic output is an attempt to succeed where Artaud had failed, in transferring this project to the realm of the cinematic (where Artaud had envisioned his project heading). Arrabal had struck up a close friendship with Beckett in the late 1950s after the latter had garnered fame with *Waiting for Godot*. Furthermore, as Greene also reminds us, in-between relocating to Mexico in the late 1950s and returning to France to work with Arrabal in 1962, Jodorowsky "established himself as a force in avant garde theatre" (2007: 8), which included staging Beckett's *Waiting for Godot*. Greene proposes that

> it was in this cultural context, the "shift towards post-modern consciousness and cultural fusion" that the nomad-hippie-artist-philosopher par excellence, Alejandro Jodorowsky began his filmmaking career. His debut film *Fernando Y Lis* (1967), was a loose adaptation of a play by Arrabal first staged and directed by Jodorowsky in the days of the Parisian Panic Movement. *Fernando Y Lis*

chronicled the aimless journey of Fando and his paralysed lover *Lis,* in search of the mythological city of Tar, a place they never locate, replacing Beckett's absurdist comedy with the patented and provocative scenes of sex and violent characterisation of both Jodorowsky and Arrabal's work. (2007: 9)

Beckett's early dramas *Waiting for Godot, Endgame* (1958), and *Happy Days* are distinguished by the presentation of imprisoning, empty, desolate spaces and environments. In *Waiting for Godot,* two tramps, Vladimir and Estragon, interminably wait on a lonely road for a figure who may or may not arrive; *Endgame* takes place inside a shelter. What has happened outside remains a mystery—a possibly apocalyptic space. The blind, tyrannical, wheelchair bound Hamm exerts his control over his servant Clov, on whom he depends for food and survival, while his two aging parents, Nagg and Nell, live in dustbins. And as discussed earlier, *Happy Days* depicts the character of Winnie buried up to her waist in sand under the burning sun. Beckett's plays deal with postwar space and the annihilated landscape of Europe. Beckett himself had worked for a resistance cell during the war, which had been infiltrated and decimated by the Nazis; his comrades had been rounded up and executed or sent to internment or concentration camps while Beckett himself had escaped to Roussillon—an area with distinctive desert like sand dunes—in the unoccupied zone of Southern France (Knowlson 1996: 319). Characters in his later plays, such as *Not I* (1973), evanesce into nothingness in their search for personal subjectivity, identity, and self-determination within the empty void of the stage. In *El Topo* Jodorowsky deliberately intersperses the film's landscape with image taken from Beckett's plays.

The film opens with a series of images that recall both *Waiting for Godot* and *Happy Days. El Topo* emerges from the desert on horseback carrying a black parasol á la Winnie from *Happy Days* (whose parasol catches fire beneath the burning sun). Greene further links this image to the cultural space of postwar Europe when he observes that

> despite all of Jodorowsky's avant-garde window dressing, *El Topo* is very much within certain traditions of the Western: a figure riding a horse in expansive landscape. However one is immediately struck by the incongruities between the image and the Western proper, not the least of which being that the figure inexplicably and humorously totes an umbrella in the desert—a Western depicted by Rene Magritte or Luis Buñuel. (2007: 13)

The empty space of this arid desert contains a single post (upon which El Topo hangs his hat) which deliberately recalls the desolate dead tree which stands at the center of *Waiting for Godot*'s mise-en-scène (and which had been sculpturally designed for the original performance of the play the artist Alberto Giacometti). El Topo instructs his young son, Brontis, to enter manhood by burying a toy and a picture of the mother beneath the sand (the boy begins the film naked but will end the film in the iconic clothes his father wore in this scene). This is the first instance in the film where we see a body encased, submerged in, and emerging out of the landscape: as *El Topo* and his son ride away, the photograph of the mother is pushed to the fore of the frame, her head emerging from the hot sand, just as Winnie's does in Act 2 of *Happy Days*.

Later in the first movement of the film Beckett is recalled during the sequence in which we are introduced to the Colonel and Maria. The sequence takes place in a desert "mission": a conical structure (which recalls the shelter in *Endgame*). A chapter of monks have been displaced from the mission, which has been colonized by Colonel. (The monks are subsequently tortured and sexually abused by the Colonel's three grotesque gunfighters.) Within this architectural structure Maria and the Colonel exist in a power dynamic of master and servant which also recalls Hamm and Clov's relationship in *Endgame* and the dynamic of Pozzo and Lucky's relationship in *Waiting for Godot*. This power dynamic will eventually be reversed when El Topo castrates the Colonel, just as it is in *Endgame*—which ends with Clov about to leave the shelter, therefore condemning the previously dominant Hamm to certain death—and in Act 2 of *Waiting for Godot* which sees Pozzo and Lucky's return and the reversal of their own cruel master and servant relationship.

If Beckett's plays are (in part) defined through characters who are anchored to or unable to escape their environments, then in *El Topo*, the environment is a similarly imprisoning void. The film's landscape is frequently allowed to fill the screen; in his framing of the landscape, Jodorowsky presents a prominent frontier via the presence of strong horizon lines between the land and the sky, which bisect the screen. And characters are repeatedly shown emerging from the landscape: later in the film we are shown El Topo and others buried beneath the desert and in the film's finale the exiled cripples and deformed persons submerged underground escape from their cave and descend upon the "Wild West Town," presented like the zombies in George A. Romero's *Night of the Living Dead* (1968). If *El Topo* incorporates Beckettian imagery into the Western genre, then one might argue that it does so to elevate the genre and give it "literary resonance." Jodorowsky recognizes the inherent Beckettian existential isolation implicit particularly in later postwar Westerns, and we may note here briefly a set of contemporary Western texts which pay homage not only to Beckett but also to Jodorowsky.

Bone Tomahawk (S. Craig Zahler, 2015), a film which also combines the Western with the exploitation horror/cannibal film, opens with a conscious reference to *Waiting for Godot* as two violent drifters, murderous Vladimir and Estragon types (they wear similar hats), occupy a quiet desert clearing, at the center of which is a dead tree, as they loot the belongings of their victims. The writings of Cormac McCarthy present a series of apocalyptic and dystopic representations of the American landscape, and the 2006 novel *The Road* (made into a film in 2009 by John Hillcoat) is of particular interest. In his review of the novel, Ron Charles observes that

> in Cormac McCarthy's new novel, *The Road*, the bloodbath is finally complete. The violence that animated his great Western novels has been superseded by a flash of nuclear annihilation, which also blasts away some of what we expect from the reclusive author's work. With this apocalyptic tale, McCarthy has moved into the allegorical realm of Samuel Beckett and José Saramago—and, weirdly, George Romero (2006).

Furthermore cultish TV megahits *Westworld* (HBO, 2016–) and *The Walking Dead* (AMC, 2010–) both allude to *El Topo*: the former in its presentation of a violent black clad gunslinger and the latter in which its two central characters, Sherriff Rick Grimes (Andrew Lincoln) and his young son Carl (Chandler Riggs) wander a bleak and apocalyptic landscape, encountering in picaresque fashion, various desolate fighters, survivors, and grotesques. Echoing events depicted in *El Topo*, young Carl dons his father's wide-brimmed hat and after the death of his mother, he must learn to put away childish things and modes of behavior (a key test being the ability to kill a man).

Conclusion

This chapter has provided a critical reading of the cultural and contextual landscapes found in Alejandro Jodorowsky's cult Western *El Topo*. I have argued that the film's landscape is actually an empty interpretive space that Jodorowsky invites the viewer to fill with meaning. The viewer is aided in this task by the diverse mythological and religious symbolism that Jodorowsky loaded the landscape with. It is a landscape as informed by Beckett, Eliot, and Artaud as much as it is by the landscape of the Western genre. Ultimately, Jodorowsky's appropriation of the genre's cinematic tropes presents a space that is ripe for exploring and deconstructing a set of real, imagined, cosmic, and cinematic myths that are embodied through El Topo's own picaresque, metamorphosing, and ultimately cyclical journey of discovery.

Bibliography

Barber, Stephen. *Antonin Artaud: Blows and Bombs*. London: Creation Books, 2003.

Barber, Stephen. "Introduction." In *Anarchy and Alchemy: The Films of Alejandro Jodorowsky*, edited by Ben Cobb, 9. London: Creation Books, 2007.

Bisenbach, Klaus. "Alejandro Jodorowsky." *Interview*, February 14 (2012). Available online at: https://www.interviewmagazine.com/film/alejandro-jodorowsky (accessed December 2, 2018).

Cerdán, Josetxo, and Miguel Fernández Labayan. "Art, Exploitation, Cool Cult and the Cinema of Alejandro Jodorowsky." In *Latsploitation, Exploitation Cinemas, and Latin America*, edited by Victoria Ruetalo and Dolores Tierney, 102–14. New York: Routledge, 2009.

Charles, Ron. "Apocalypse Now In Cormac McCarthy's new novel, The Road, the blood bath is finally complete." *The Washington Post*, October 1 (2006). Available online at: https://www.washingtonpost.com/archive/entertainment/books/2006/10/01/apoca lypse-now-span-classbankheadin-cormac-mccarthys-new-novel-span-classitalthe -roadspan-the-bloodbath-is-finally-completespan/e996bc8d-8942-49b4-ae9b-1e3 8e16d5965/?noredirect=on&utm_term=.d10ee07efec1 (accessed December 2, 2018).

Cobb, Ben. *Anarchy and Alchemy: The Films of Alejandro Jodorowsky*. London: Creation Books, 2007.

Dissanayake, Wimal. "Landscapes and Meaning in Cinema: Two Indian Examples." In *Cinema and Landscape*, edited by Graeme Harper and Jonathan Rayner, 189–202. Chicago: Intellect, 2010.

Ebert, Roger. "El Topo." *RogerEbert.Com*, October 6, (2007 [1970]). Available online at: https://www.rogerebert.com/reviews/great-movie-el-topo-1970 (accessed December 17, 2018).

Frayling, Christopher. *Spaghetti Westerns: Cowboys and Europeans from Karl May to Sergio Leone*. London: Routledge & Kegan Paul, 1981.

Goodall, Mark. "'Spaghetti Savages': Cinematic Perversions of *Django Kill*." In *Critical Perspectives on the Western: From A Fistful of Dollars to Django Unchained*, edited by Lee Broughton, 199–212. Lanham: Rowman & Littlefield, 2016.

Greene, Doyle. *The Mexican Cinema of Madness: A Study of Six Landmark Horror and Exploitation Films*. London: McFarland & Co, 2007.

Greenspun, Roger. "*El Topo* Emerges: Jodorowsky's Feature Begins Regular Run." *New York Times*, November 5, (1971). Available online at: https://www.nytimes.com/1971/11/05/archives/el-topo-emergesjodorowskys-feature-begins-regular-run.html (accessed December 17, 2018).

Hirsch, Foster. "Viva La Muerte and El Topo." *Cinema* 7, no. 2, Spring (1972): 8–13.

Hoberman, J., and Jonathan Rosenbaum. *Midnight Movies*. New York: Harper and Row, 1983.

Knowlson, James. *Damned to Fame: The Life of Samuel Beckett*. London: Bloomsbury, 1996.

Love, Damian. "The Mole Man: Going Underground with Alejandro Jodorowsky." *Bright LightsFilm*, July 31, (2008). Available online at: https://brightlightsfilm.com/wp-content/cache/all/the-mole-man-going-underground-with-alejandro-jodorowsky/#.XBwNLmj7TIU (accessed December 17, 2018).

Marsden, Michael. "*El Topo*: Cult Film Phenomenon or Epic Western?" In *International Westerns: Re-Locating the Frontier*, edited by Cynthia J. Miller and A. Bowdoin Van Riper, 185–202. Plymouth: Scarecrow Press, 2014.

O'Brien, Glenn. "Glauber Rocha." *Inter/View* 2, no. 3 (1970): 37.

Rose, Steve. "Lennon, Manson and Me: The Psychedelic Cinema of Alejandro Jodorowsky." *The Guardian*, November 14, (2009). Available online at: https://www.theguardian.com/film/2009/nov/14/alejandro-jodorowosky-el-topo (accessed December 14, 2018).

Rosenbaum, Jonathan. "Responding to some questions about Acid Westerns and Dead Man," *Jonathan Rosenbaum.Net*, November 27, (2018). Available online at: https://www.jonathanrosenbaum.net/2018/11/responding-to-some-questions-about-acid-westerns-and-dead-man/ (accessed December 18, 2018).

Slotkin, Richard. *Gunfighter Nation: The Myth of the Frontier in Twentieth-Century America*. New York: University of Oklahoma Press, 1992.

Smith, Karl Thomas. "Alejandro Jodorowsky—The Quietus, 2015." *KarlThomasSmith.com*, October 8, (2015). Available online at: http://karlthomassmith.com/home/alejandro-jodorowsky-interview (accessed December 16, 2018).

Taylor, Rumsey. "Acid Westerns." *Not Coming to a Theatre Near You*, April 1, (2013). Available online at: http://www.notcoming.com/features/acidwesterns/ (accessed December 12, 2018).

6

Dancing with Death:
Whity, a Singular Western

Hamish Ford

Introduction

Set in late-nineteenth-century Southern United States, Rainer Werner Fassbinder's *Whity* (1971) is a very unusual Western. Featuring risky investigations and essaying of race, explored via an overdetermined mise-en-scène featuring self-consciously theatrical sets and actors wearing ethnically coded makeup as they move through almost entirely interior spaces, this is clearly a non-"classical" Western. But the film is also hard to square with "revisionist" takes on the genre. This chapter will position *Whity* as a singularly "outré" contribution to what is often seen as the most conservative Hollywood-derived film genre, featuring hybrid "low" sources mixed with a modernist approach to form and aesthetics while also offering a radical political outlook.

Whity applies an idiosyncratic, operatic-yet-intimate blowtorch to the Western's mythic foundations, violently framing, revealing, and exploding its traditional concern with white, heteronormative masculine power. The film does not, however, isolate or imagine a more human reality and potential community beneath or beyond the prevailing bigoted ideologies that are so familiar to the genre. Nor does it offer a glib or simply violent apocalyptic vision. Instead, Fassbinder provides us with an intricately patterned and radical yet ultimately far from romantic-outsider critique of race as played out in the context of the Western. The result is a film of queer genre intervention that explores contradictory elements found at the Western's core, and pushes them to their logical and destructive limit points.

Framing Genre and Form

Fassbinder's most expensive and least financially successful production to date, *Whity* was booed at its Berlinale premiere. Failing to find theatrical distribution, the film remained unavailable until an early 1980s West German television broadcast, after which it disappeared again (Spaich 1992, cited in Layne 2011: 262; Sieg 2014). Until its 2001 appearance on DVD, *Whity* was therefore one of the most difficult Fassbinder films to see, and has received less sustained critical attention than most of his other work. On the surface at least, *Whity* does not fit neatly within the director's oeuvre and the grand thematic-historical prism through which we have long been encouraged by scholars (and often the filmmaker himself) to understand it: as a sustained critical cinematic essaying of West Germany that confronts ugly truths beneath the country's prehistory, emergence, and economic success. Another potential reason for scholars' avoidance of the film, Katrin Sieg (2014) suggests, is its rather extreme and controversial treatment of race, even by Fassbinder's standards. In addition to the lack of German setting and "risky" charting of race, and a treatment of sexuality more in keeping with the director's better-known cinema, the film's other challenges and potential interests include its unusual articulation of the Western combined with other generic, formal, and aesthetic elements. In addition to the Western, watched today, *Whity* also incorporates the family and historical melodrama, gothic, and horror literature and cinema, the then-nascent Blaxploitation cycle and more broadly what we often categorize as "cult" or "exploitation" cinema, as well as the "art film" at its more formally, aesthetically, and politically radical end.

Appropriating the mixed cinematic languages of popular genre cinema and the modernist art film—and, in the process, enhancing rather than dulling the challenging aspects of each—*Whity*'s critical interrogation can be perplexing to viewers and critics favoring one of these modes, despite "high/low" hybrid forms having now enjoyed lengthy scholarly attention. Nevertheless, it can be situated as Fassbinder's key transitional work wherein the director concurrently perfects the Brecht-influenced political modernism of the earlier films and inaugurates his famous "conversion" to melodrama's subversive potential. There also remain questions over the film's generic identity. In a rare sustained scholarly account of the film, Priscilla Layne, for example, asserts that *Whity* is "often considered a mere exercise in melodrama" (2011: 261). While it certainly engages with this important and much-discussed genre, the film remains rather different to Fassbinder's much more celebrated subsequent work that uses melodrama to approach specific German social realities, locations, and historical settings. Here, for once, the protagonists and location are notionally "American," but the spoken language remains German.

Writing of *Whity's* unusual foreign setting, Layne cites German scholars Peter Jansen and Wolfgang Schutte's view that the film does not thereby directly reflect on German identity or life in West Germany (2011: 262). Sieg suggests part of the problem is that *Whity's* potential impact and critique is easily blunted through its US location, denuding the film of Fassbinder's usual sociopolitical, close-to-home knowledge, and contextual richness. Yet its clear internationalism, despite or in fact due to the film's notional setting, should allow us to make broader connections, such as Layne (2011) pursues. At the same time, Sieg worries that the

> critique of a racial imaginary that Layne . . . characterizes as transnational, however, could too easily be subsumed under the common vilification of American racism and imperialism, which allowed Germans to avoid facing their own racial fantasies and practice. (2014)

Suggesting that the film's main potential interest lies in contributing to the sustained essaying of West German identity characterizing much of Fassbinder's work, the above criticism would also be more efficacious if *Whity's* setting and performative elements (including language) were remotely convincing as realism. Rather, its fundamentally non-realist agenda, still very "Brechtian" artifice and lack of believable setting or characters, enables the portrayal of race and racism in particular to resonate across spatial and historical barriers while avoiding bland universalist prescriptions.

Race is certainly impossible to ignore in *Whity*. Played by Günther Kaufmann, the film's titular character (we eventually learn his real name is Samuel King) initially seems so enamored of being a slave that his investment in the ideology of whiteness and slave-owner privilege is apparently—and literally—self-defining. Rather than simply delusional or mad, this bad case of "false consciousness" comes across as the logical result of living in a world in which whiteness is inextricably linked to power as the ultimate reality and identity generator. At the heart of *Whity's* formal and thematic radicalism is its most notorious aspect: the use of theatrical makeup as a signifier of race, class, and power. While the comparably "real" Hanna (Hanna Schygulla), the film's local singer and prostitute, wears "normal" beautifying feminine makeup, and Whity's skin is left natural except for white lip-gloss, his mother, Marpessa (Elaine Baker), is made up with extreme "blackface" despite being played by a black actor. Meanwhile, the white Nicholson family (played by white actors) wears similarly exaggerated "white face" that is later strongly tinged with nauseous green, while other pasty Germans performing bullet belt-clad barflies appear with absurd fake "brown face" tans.

The risky hyper-reflexive device whereby the actors wear ethnically coded makeup, in addition to the film's other scandalous aspects—ultra racism (a Ku Klux Klan hood makes an oblique, fetishistic appearance as worn by one of Whity's white half-brothers, Frank), both queer and S&M sexuality, incestuous liaisons and schemes, interfamily murder plots, and finally an assassination spree—demonstrates how in addition to the Western, family melodrama and political fable, we can chart additional generic, thematic, and aesthetic ingredients associated with gothic horror and contemporaneous "exploitation" cinema. Exploiting and fusing these elements for their identity-undermining potential, *Whity* essays the absolutely regressive historical and inherently political power of class, gender, sexuality, and especially race, as played out in a particular national context via grotesque and ritualized extremes of identity, neurosis, and performance. The family patriarch, Ben Nicholson (Ron Randall), laments near the film's end that both of his white male heirs, Davie and Frank, are "sick" in the mind—thereby incapable of carrying on his property- and slave-owning legacy. In fact, apart from the uniquely lucid and rational Hanna, everyone in this film is sick.

With Hanna again as the one exception, all the figures on screen behave or perform as if under a kind of hypnosis. "Fassbinder places emphasis on the process," writes Lisa Thatcher (2013) of *Whity's* deliberate style and approach to form: "His sensuous camera moves around the action (or emphatic lack of it) revealing over and over the various prisons and treadmills each character finds themselves trapped in." The film delivers the majority of its narrative and thematic material via long, often wordless sequences, occasionally peppered by minimalist, glacially delivered dialogue. Throughout, elaborately staged tracking shots reveal, almost in slow motion, an overwhelming mise-en-scène comprising human and nonhuman elements that evoke in exaggerated, and decaying, form the world of the Western.

Western Elements

Shifting presentations of both gender and ethnicity were often important to the Hollywood Western's gradual and in many ways palimpsestic transformation out of its "classical" mode, a process largely complete when *Whity* emerged. While Fassbinder's film can certainly be seen as a radically post- or anti-classical Western, some contextualizing reveals important links. For example, in being set almost entirely indoors, the film is less a total break than an extension of the "town Western" tradition, which includes classical 1950s exemplars of the genre such as *High Noon* (Fred Zinnemann, 1952) and *Buchannan Rides Alone* (Budd Boetticher, 1958). Some similar connections can be seen when it comes to critically examining the genre's central mythos. Most famously, perhaps, John Ford had already shown the internal contradictions and psychological schisms at the heart of the United States' enabling national *histoire* in films like *The Searchers* (1957) and *The Man Who Shot Liberty Valance* (1962). *Whity* extends the notion of a crisis-ridden central human figure to a point now beyond character and psychology.

If now-venerated "revisionist" Westerns emerging at the same time as *Whity*, such as Robert Altman's *McCabe and Mrs. Miller* (1971), get credited in part for voicing suspicions about the corporate men in suits' obsession with money and the violent ends to which they will go in furthering what would become the fundamental religion of the United States—business—we should remember that many "traditional" Westerns offer variously trenchant critiques of nascent US capitalism and its errant "civilizing"—and thereby, in the logic of the films, enslaving—aspects. Certainly *Whity* emerged at the moment when a new generation of far less formally and politically conservative US directors had taken the Western's reins. Their work foregrounded more overt critiques and unambiguous mythic revisions, variously showing how the imperial westward expansion of the United States might look from the point of view of its "others."

The other relevant, much-discussed, and in fact more fundamental, break in the genre's development came via the European Westerns spearheaded by the success of Sergio Leone's *A Fistful of Dollars* (*Per un pugno di dollari*, 1964). *Whity*'s European origins, and more specifically actual production context, situate Leone's work as its closest connection to the broader world of the genre, not only borrowing the Italian director's Andalucían locations and sets but also including very brief moments that openly reference the overdetermined compositional elements strongly associated with his enormously successful *Dollars* trilogy. Writing about European Westerns in general, Lee Broughton (2016) notes that German filmmakers typically employ the figure of the "Native American" when making political points about race, while Italian filmmakers more usually feature African Americans in a similar manner. Fassbinder reverses this national tendency in *Whity*. But while the film appeared at the height of the Spaghetti Western's decade-and-a-half-long run, beyond differences of language and national culture, this closest ancestry still remains rather distant.

While it is useful to situate *Whity* in terms of the Western's complex worldwide history, such contextualization also has its limits. Featuring almost no action sequences, the film's narrative and scenes move slower even than Leone at his most leisurely. Rather perversely, *Whity* features only one shot that properly utilizes the recognizable exteriors and visual style characterizing the Italian's famed "spaghetti" productions. Indeed, Fassbinder could have made nearly the entire film using sets in Germany. The above exception—a single exterior tracking shot showing the film's powerful white male characters as they move through the small town center—is just one of three brief sequences unambiguously set outdoors. The second is the extremely sadomasochistic scene set on stone steps when Whity volunteers to replace his half-brother, Davie, being whipped by the family patriarch. The third, *Whity*'s final image, is so theatrical in set up, framing, and lighting, that it could have been shot in the studio against a fake, back-lit horizon. The remainder of the film stays indoors, resulting in a very claustrophobic and recognizably Fassbinderian on-screen world a long way from the landscape-heavy function of most Westerns.

Fassbinder's film does nonetheless substantively evoke and contribute to the Western's already diverse history. The genre's imperial, frontier world supplies crucial context for *Whity*'s operations, but played out on a both shockingly literal and figurative interior canvass. "So rarely does a scene take place outside," writes Jake Cole (2014), "yet the frontier weighs heavily over everything, a means of cutting people off and forcing them to fend for themselves." But in case this sounds like fairly familiar Western territory and mythology after all, Cole concludes his point: "Individualism is bypassed for solipsism." Ben Nicholson's rather sclerotic efforts and already domesticated ways notwithstanding, the Western's famous white masculinity and obsession with masculine freedom is nowhere to be found outside the cartoonish secondary characters occasionally seen in the saloon. In fact, no remotely convincing "individual" exists on screen, least of all a familiar white male agent. However, to invoke a binary argument whereby Fassbinder simply undermines regimes of identity and the ideology associated with the lone hero otherwise secure in "classical" Westerns, is much too simple. Rather, *Whity* examines and lays bare to an unusually heightened degree, thanks to its foregrounded expressive cinematic form, the dysfunction, neurosis, and vertiginousness that drives the genre from its most conservative through to its liberal, revisionist, leftist, and exploitation incarnations.

Layne (2011: 265) compares *Whity* to revisionist Hollywood Westerns such as *Hombre* (Martin Ritt, 1967), to which we could add contemporary productions such as *Little Big Man* (Arthur Penn, 1970) and *A Man Called Horse* (Elliot Silverstein, 1970), or much later entries like *Dances with Wolves* (Kevin Costner, 1990). Such avowedly liberal productions feature supposedly "mixed race" protagonists (usually played by white actors), or those who willfully adopt the ways and position of a subaltern, indigenous identity. In these films "Whitey"—here meaning both white "Yankees" and "Southerners"— is the bad guy while the protagonist, who is placed "in-between" cultures, ultimately becomes the hero by leading an actual indigenous group out of trouble—a narrative contrivance exercising the overtly imperial and ultimately racist values surviving within, and often driving, such liberal fantasies. Unlike most Hollywood Westerns tagged as revisionist, *Whity* starkly frames white and black identities, their co-reliant relationship, and the truly "in-between" status of the protagonist (rather than actual or feigned indigenous subjectivity). The film is instead concerned with two vastly unequal classes of dysfunctional immigrants or descendants thereof. And the "in-between" role is not played by a white actor, but an African-German.

Just as importantly, *Whity*'s belated rebellion is a solo effort. Although encouraged by Hanna to stand up to his oppressors, Whity's definitive, violent killing spree is undertaken without her. But perhaps most significantly, it is hard to take a liberal conciliatory politics from the film, for reasons I have already suggested. Layne cites German Fassbinder commentator Herbert Spaich (1992), who is surely correct in writing:

> Fassbinder takes the rituals [of the Western] and the sentiment implied in the genre and exaggerates them into the realm of the grotesque: the protagonists, caricatures of human existence, are made up like clowns. Günther Kaufmann is at times reminiscent of Al Jolson. (cited in Layne, 2011: 268)

This is clearly far from a classical film, but it goes much further—into more radical, concurrently modernist and also more "lowbrow" territory. *Whity* may well be an "anti-Western" but its interest for the genre is not superficial, merely instrumental, or glibly oppositional. Rather, the film takes seriously and reaches into the core of the Western's central interest in racialized identity, presented here in sepulchral form.

Theatrical Race

In addition to the melodrama and Hollywood-via-Italy Western, Layne (2011) suggests that *Whity* can also be linked to what is often, if somewhat problematically, seen as the earliest Blaxploitation film, Melvin Van Peebles's *Sweet Sweetback's Baadasssss Song* (1971). Shot almost simultaneously, these two singular, renegade and in their own ways radical productions invoke and comment on myths associated with the Western. Fassbinder more explicitly situates his film in direct relation to the genre while Van Peebles only suggests this connection. Both films feature initially passive, almost-silent black heroes that share a kind of hyper-sexualization and suggested queerness, both desired and exploited by multiple characters to different ends.

Is there a more precise relationship between these two films when it comes to race and politics? The Black Panther Party (which famously endorsed *Sweetback*) was a cited influence for West Germany's most notorious far-left organization, the Red Army Faction (AKA the Baader-Meinhof Group). The radical wing of the German Socialist German Student Union also explicitly cited the Panthers as models. Yet Sieg (2002) argues that the broad German and European New Left were often unprepared to directly tackle race, and neglected to include it as an analytical category in their antifascist polemics. Discussing Fassbinder's earlier film *Katzelmacher* (1969)—in which he himself plays a Greek guest worker experiencing terrible, casual racism at the hands of young Munich residents— as a partial exception and potential comment thereon, Sieg suggests that Fassbinder's approach to race in that film (with obvious connections to *Whity*) is to emphasize social construction, thereby declining to ascribe any sense of character or subject to the "foreigner" and instead positioning such a figure as "a bodily surface on which the German mobs project their racial fears and desires" (2002: 156–60). Critique of race, Sieg concludes, can easily lead to abandoning its discussion in favor of presumed, "normal" whiteness. She argues that for the contemporary German Left, racial Otherness is always positioned from the viewpoint of white activists and radicals, thanks to "the universal performability of the white body" (2002: 165), thereby sidestepping whiteness itself and its own artifice.

Neither whiteness nor blackness are sidestepped in *Whity*, while retaining an overall stress on constructedness with no sense of "authentic" ethnic identity— whether conservative, liberal, or left-wing in orientation—on offer. In addition to being marked in different, far from simple, ways as black without "ontologizing" such a position, both *Whity* and *Sweetback*'s titular characters share more specific characteristics. As well as being handsome, virile, yet also sexually passive, and almost mute, both men are initially unenlightened as to the political and ethical debasement in which they live, only eventually rebelling thanks to being shown the enslaved nature of their existence by more aware characters (a young Panther activist in *Sweetback*, Hanna in *Whity*). Both also end up facing likely death in the desert. Rather than being able to ride away into nature and ongoing freedom, these appropriated Western heroes are most likely doomed. Within currently existing social reality, there is literally nowhere outside the desert to go where our freedom-seeking protagonists will not likely be re-enslaved.

There are also important differences between Van Peebles's and Fassbinder's films when it comes to Western appropriation and beyond. The rebellion and discovery of agency occurs early in *Sweetback*, generating the film's forward movement played out against the urban spaces of Watts and greater Los Angeles, replacing the Western's usual picturesque wilderness. Yet despite literally being on the run for most of the film, heading south to freedom in Mexico, the almost-silent Sweetback's near-constant movement is essentially reactive. In *Whity*, the rebellion is far more delayed in coming, its protagonist not only almost entirely passive and taciturn but occupying a position of virtual stasis—a mode painted as the logical culmination of narrative events and racist ideology authored by others. The film is also rather bleaker in its final outcome. While large concluding on-screen text assures Van Peebles's audience that Sweetback is "coming back to collect some Whitey dues," even as his actual fate remains unknown and potentially fairly grim, Fassbinder's *Whity* ends in the almost certain failure of its titular character and Hanna to survive. West, south, or east of the country, there is nowhere to call home and attain a basic level of freedom for anyone outside the Western's white male heterosexual hero.

A "persistent dualism" marks the scholarly field of Whiteness Studies, writes Peter Kolchin:

> At times, race—and more specifically, whiteness—is treated as an artificial construct with no real meaning aside from its particular social setting; at other times it becomes not only real, but omnipresent and unchanging, deserving attention as an independent force. . . . If we see whiteness as omnipresent we lose sight of the fact of its social constructedness. (2002: 160)

What can make many people uncomfortable about Fassbinder's films is that they chart how subaltern subjects—defined by a mix of race, gender, sexual orientation, and socioeconomic class—can come to take on the regressive ontological and ethical markers that have been the source of such characters' oppression, reinforcing their reality and thereby, in effect, legitimacy. In addition to *Whity* and *Katzelmacher*, Fassbinder's *Fear Eats the Soul* (*Angst essen Seele auf*, 1973), *Fox and His Friends* (*Faustrecht der Freiheit*, 1975), and *In a Year with 13 Moons* (*In einem Jahr mit 13 Monden*, 1978) encapsulate Germany's pre- and postwar "others" (black, Jewish, queer, and working-class characters) in this way. *Whity* marks the lesser-known limit-point exploration of this thematic territory in Fassbinder's work, whereby oppressor and oppressed "need" each other, a horrible co-reliant relationship that Thomas Elsaesser (1996) sees as tragically marking intertwined German-Jewish identities since at least the 1930s.

Whity's presentation of the ideological "sustaining" power of whiteness and blackness alike, through the constant and concurrently alienating presence of their clearly unequal binary other, can come across as enforcing a decidedly "hopeless" conclusion. Yet the film offers an urgent, enlivening, and confronting provocation to both "conservative" and "progressive" discourses of race and ethnicity alike as rendered in the Western. Retaining its radical power, the film works as a sober reminder of the risks of not looking at "race" the way it actually works, as a constructed category, rather than how it should or could be in a theoretically better world that a liberal gaze often misidentifies as our own, whereby identity can somehow be reappropriated and proclaimed (often involving a retreat into ontology) in the name of self-assertion and liberation.

Race—more exactly, its performance and representation—is clearly at the deceptive, crucial heart of both Whity and *Whity*. But the film does not stake any claims about its protagonist and his identity, so overdetermined as to be historically contingent artifice. Rather, no matter the ethnically coded presentation on screen at any given time, Fassbinder's real project is to offer a very particular vision not of blackness but of whiteness as it performs and maintains identity and power. What emerges is a specific, guilty and irredeemable, figuration that does not speak its own name, a truly neurotic hegemony that resonates with the still-raw history of this filmmaker's national culture. In his better-known films dealing with ethnic "others," Fassbinder focused on the extremely unflattering white German response to designated outsiders, exaggerating linguistic and other differences. With *Whity*, he approaches the horrible story of race in its loosely US version via Hollywood's most central and revealing genre. It is up to the viewer whether she or he joins the dots connecting this context and the German experience, and the particular psychological dysfunction and dreadful violence defining and inflicted by these powerful nations' respective histories upon their copious "others." Despite—or due to—its foreign setting, *Whity* is Fassbinder's clearest and most operatically laid out reflection on whiteness: the starkest and most basic yet also most radical, and one of his most sustained meditations on power. The story, as typical for this filmmaker, features an intermingled essaying of race, sex, and class. If race is foregrounded, the concept is meaningless without the other two. The film's primary setting and generic vehicle is ideal to frame this material, thanks to the literal history of slavery and the ongoing struggles over race in the United States.

The epicenter of *Whity*'s controversial essaying of race remains its singular use of theatrical makeup. Playing Whity's mother, Elaine Baker is made up with exaggerated "blackface" and wears what appears to be a large "afro" wig. In the film's first shot, she is filmed with extreme backlighting so that all we can occasionally see of the human figure in front of us is the whites of eyes and teeth. Despite his nickname, Whity does not attempt to pass as white. Rather, he quintessentially "knows his place" in an irrevocably racist ideological context that generates his very identity and purpose. With the white actors' makeup similarly exaggerated, race is theatricalized and made unnatural, its ideological effects enlarged and also blocked, starkly foregrounded yet "smudged." What is the purpose and effect of this hyper-threatricalization concurrently highlighting and deconstructing racially coded identities?

In one sense, Fassbinder treats race as he does other inscribed markers of identity such as gender and sexual orientation, effectively "queering" it, or treating often assumed identity markings as socially enforced "drag" in a way that resonates with some Whiteness Studies work. Summarizing the latter's central claims, Gregory Jay writes:

> Race is a reality in the sense that people experience it as real and base much of their behaviour on it. Race is real in the same way that a building or a religion or a political ideology is real as each is the result of human effort, not a prescription from nature or God. Thus the concept of race can have little or no foundation, yet it can still be the force that makes or breaks someone's life, or the life of a people or a nation. (2007: 101)

Whity offers a devastating deconstruction of whiteness while also—as with most of Fassbinder's films—problematizing attempts to progressively appropriate identity markers such as race in the name of liberation. Its artifice is laid bare, but the ingrained power of race seems impossible to transcend in the social reality presented. One of the key thinkers influencing Whiteness Studies' development, bell hooks, threw out this challenge thirty years ago:

> One change in direction that would be real cool would be the production of a discourse on race that interrogates whiteness. It would just be so interesting for all those white folks who are giving blacks their take on blackness to let them know what's going on with whiteness. In far too much contemporary writing— though there are some outstanding exceptions—race is always an issue of Otherness that is not white. (1989: 902)

Whity effectively carries out such a move two decades earlier. But it also positions such an interrogation as utterly vertiginous for all involved, highlighting the price paid for both black and white identities upon seeing theatrical artifice where there was supposed to be meaningful—even biologically determined— identity-providing difference.

This film, like so many by its director, essays and dissects the horrors of identity. But there is little sense that overthrowing such a regime, which administers extremely and irrevocably unequal social and interpersonal relations, will lead to liberation rather than a different kind of suffering as we glimpse the intimate and social void beneath identity-generating mechanisms. The cost of both identity and its obliteration is extensive for both the powerful and subjugated, with confronting ramifications for liberatory or revolutionary discourses, just as much as for rearguard conservative ones.

Identity Inside Out

Whity's main effect is not to represent difference, define it, or prescribe how oppressed subjects could be liberated in a less hierarchical social reality, but rather to show how such regimes of identity inevitably behave in accordance with the framework set out for them: that of dominant identities and social groups. Identity mechanisms have been almost entirely constructed and controlled by people other than those being positioned as "different." Yet Fassbinder's work strongly argues for the uncomfortable, often even taboo idea that despite not having authored the systems and ideologies that oppress them, "others" nonetheless often present as having a certain stake and role in sustaining the status quo because it ascribes some form of identity no matter how prescriptive, humiliating, and denuded of power. More significantly and by way of partial explanation, perhaps, their subaltern position often means that such figures have no way of envisioning, let alone bringing about, any alternative reality or way of life. But while Fassbinder's various disenfranchised "victim" characters may initially seem to be his cinema's focus, the subjects with the most power ultimately occupy the central grounds for critique. More precisely, the reality they administer is the films' main concern, forensically examined on screen through processes of construction and maintenance. Whiteness, masculinity, heterosexuality, and a bourgeois socioeconomic class therefore comprise this cinema's primary interest and target. *Whity* concerns how a dominant culture's necessary "others" are imagined, invented, and systematically limited, while also ultimately being impossible to know or permanently control. The notionally conservative genre of the Western provides the perfect vehicle for such inside-out identity rendering and critique.

In this film, race is made to appear a truly horrific kind of masquerade or "drag," essayed through "white face" as a means of rendering the dominant class's inbred dysfunction. The sensitive, almost erotic scene between Whity and Davie (the overtly "underdeveloped" Nicholson son) in the stables when the former shows his half-brother how to gently groom a horse, offers a true mini-essay on the notion—here, racially coded—that workers know how to do everything while the "inbred" white upper class, especially its primary offspring, are utterly hopeless, even mentally incapable. The scene also offers a brief, rare glimmer of fraternal affection, with slight incestuous overtones, marked by true pathos between two very different products and unequal victims of the social and psychic patriarchal reality violently authored and maintained by the father.

With Davie's exaggerated, infantilized state seeming to draw him to the servants, he is twice shown in the kitchen helping Marpessa. When Whity reprimands his mother for "letting a Nicholson peel potatoes," she immediately reminds him: "Don't forget, you're a Nicholson, too." Soon, Davie will accompany our protagonist as he murders his white family. The former's final pathetic act is to offer a small suicidal nod, licensing his half-brother to kill him. In addition to having two sons designated "sick" by their father and his young wife (not the mother to Ben's various children), the white Nicholsons are all revealed to have nothing beneath their thinly layered personas or shells: they are ready to turn on each other at a moment's notice by trying to seduce Whity into doing murderous dirty work as part of their power-grabbing schemes.

Whity's initial investment in his own oppression remains an important element of the film and the key to his striking, pathetic yet also attractive and gradually intimidating, passivity. As the other "other," Hanna feels sorry for Whity after he is beaten up in the saloon while attempting to behave like the white/brown-face cowboys. She tries to convince him they should both escape. But Hanna also chastises Whity for not feeling a sense of rebellion against his oppressors and later for seeking to buy her love by trying to "be a (white) man." He is eventually convinced that his "family" is bad—not so much for political or ethical reasons but because Whity finally learns of their duplicity, the hatred each family member feels for the others, and the truth behind their various seductions and entreaties toward him. However, the result of this rebellion is not only death for the Nicholsons but also almost certainly for Hanna and Whity as well. The film's final image is a minute-long shot of the two outcasts at dusk in the desert after their last drop of water is gone, as they perform a romantic dance that is also ultimately a quiet dance of death. "You know we'll die of thirst now," she says. There is no escape from the identity authored by the regime that controls you—no liberation, at least not on the screen.

While possessing his own anarchist-leftist views, Fassbinder remained skeptical about revolutionary claims, mindful of how easily they can feed an oppressive status quo that is supposedly the enemy. This is possibly why the filmmaker was so drawn to notionally conservative genres—the melodrama, and here the Western—that, on the surface at least, were incompatible both with his own politics and modernist formal-aesthetic tendencies. Fassbinder said of his peers in the radical political and terrorist movements of the 1970s that while he understands and shares such groups' anger, they achieve nothing but their own destruction and that of others, ultimately reinforcing and further legitimating conservative structures and power. In *The Third Generation* (*Die dritte Generation*, 1979), the director portrays far-left terrorists aiding the corporate-security state they purport to oppose, by helping justify ever more draconian measures as a result of their actions, even being directly funded by such forces for this explicit purpose. The more aggressive the violent resistance, the more the system lives on, strengthened and re-legitimized. Elsaesser describes the difficult relationship Fassbinder had with his radical fellow travelers, quoting the filmmaker:

> Fassbinder refuses the solidarity discourse of the group and the utopian programme of the anti-authoritarian generation: "Whenever I can imagine a counter-model, I know it must be wrong. . . . A counter-model always contains within itself that which it opposes." (1996: 34)

This is a central clue as to why *Whity* and other Fassbinder films cannot supply a happy ending. Or where they do, the effect is that of a lie so starkly out of step with the preceding narrative and the society it sketches that the dramatic effect is the same or even worse. If a film concludes with the hint of a hopeful conclusion, it is also very much undermined by the protagonists using the very means to attempt liberation that their oppressors employ in maintaining an unequal status quo. This is put into even sharper relief by *Whity*'s ending thanks in large part to its setting and gender presentation.

On the importance in *Whity* and Fassbinder's work of the way desire is always intimately linked to power, resulting in inherently sadomasochistic relationships, Thatcher writes:

> Mention must be made of the sadomasochistic underpinnings of the film, which is obviously Fassbinder's "reasoning" behind the Western genre and our passion for it. Fassbinder sees sadomasochism in slavery as well as in the desires to shoot an enemy dead in the street and he relates it powerfully to sex and sexual perversions such as incest, sadomasochistic domination and submission and economic power. Money is never far behind in a Fassbinder film, as capitalism is the ultimate sadomasochistic dominant. Whity and his lovers, male and female, are all controlled economically, forcing them perpetually into new levels of depravity and self-loathing. (2013)

Hanna tells Whity with equal parts frustration and bemusement, disdain and affection, before his turn to violent rebellion: "I don't understand you. You don't want to be free. You like it when they beat you. You swine. Servile and dependent. You don't deserve any better." But once he discovers the moral degeneracy at the very heart of his "family"—not in fact their treatment of him so much as of each other—Whity carries out his murderous spree exhibiting no hint of vitalization caused by the cathartic exorcizing of false consciousness, instead wearing his now familiar impassive expression mixed with muted melancholia.

Fassbinder's politics were endlessly debated upon his films' release. Especially disappointing for those on the left was his failure to provide "positive" portrayals of oppressed characters, or any real solution to their oppression. In its place, we see played out a terrible mutual co-reliance or co-dependence: the sexual, sadomasochistic (masochism for Whity, sadism for the powerful white characters) desire for reaffirming an identity that is the only one seemingly available, "given" and sustained by the ideological order of the day. This operation plays out in most of his films, but is staged in uncommonly striking and enlarged form throughout *Whity*. Without the articulation and setting made possible by the Western, we could not have the ultimate expression of this sadomasochistic desire at the heart of such dysfunctional, codependent, and ultimately auto-destructive identity regimes.

All this is made quite literal by the darkly comical whipping scene. In addition to close-ups of both master and slave in action and a soundtrack comprising the recipient's grunts followed by his father's delirious approvals, repeating "That's good, Whity!" as the whip cracks down hard, the camera cuts away to show a fainting on-screen spectator—Ben's wife, herself erotically taken aback that Whity would "take a beating for Davie." Right before collapsing, she tells Frank—as the two (who seem to have a sexual relationship) look down with fascination on the whipping spectacle from a balcony—the initial reason for Davie's punishment was sheer patriarchal humiliation and emasculation: He had walked in on husband and wife failing to have sex, as the estate master "couldn't get it up."

Conclusion: A Dance of Death

"Hanna and Whity end in California's Death Valley, like two flowers whose destiny is to die immediately after flowering," Victor-Katia writes of *Whity*'s final movement. "Maybe it's the best they could do in their circumstances" (2018). The film is apparently bleaker still when we realize our two notional heroes are only able to leave thanks to bribe money Ben had given Hanna for lying about witnessing him commit a murder. Victor-Katia (2018) continues that Whity's white

> relatives, including his father, wanted to use him against each other with hope that . . . because of [his] love for them [he] will participate in their schemes. . . . When he really understood how ugly they are in their immorality he felt that he must punish them, but pay for it with his own life, because this punishment includes a crime, and in this sense it makes him similar to them. . . . When he realized that human civilization as it is uses evil to punish evil—for example, in trying to be stronger in destruction during the war than the enemy, or teaching people how to be ahead of one's rivals in wealth-appropriating, he felt that he cannot be part of this civilization because it's a form of barbarism.

If viewer reactions to Whity's apparently passive, even accepting, attitude to the class and race representatives and associated ideology that defines him up until his late murderous turn, are likely frustration and anger, where does the film leave our hopes for the slave and the prostitute finding some kind of freedom?

Rather than positive signs of liberating—let alone revolutionary—energy, *Whity* ends on what can be seen as a very "German" and certainly "Fassbinderian" note. In a world defined by rigid oppression and seemingly insurmountable regimes of identity, freedom, and the expressing of genuine desire can only be marked by a sublime, ephemeral, tragic, and here entirely secular eschatological gesture—a brief dance in the face of impending death against an almost perversely beautiful dusk horizon. Now reduced to silhouettes, our protagonists' racial and gendered identities are at last erased. In the face of their demise, they are finally, if very briefly, free. However, this doomed beauty, this freedom in death, can only be suggested within a space, the nature and lighting of which, is even more theatrical and artificial than the rest of this already highly non-realist film.

This very unusual Western's presentation of the ideological sustaining power of whiteness can come across as offering a decidedly "hopeless" conclusion. Such an apparently "depressing" story, however, is only seemingly so because it refrains from repeating and accepting the way things are in a violent social reality that is deeply unfree for the majority of its occupants. Rather than the kind of film that we may initially see as "optimistic," *Whity* potentially offers genuine hope due to its honesty and respect for the audience in presenting an oppressive on-screen reality and challenging us to do better. This is the true gift of an intensely reflexive, self-critical, modernist cinema that doubts the medium's ability to represent reality itself but does not doubt that terrible reality exists beyond the frame, demanding urgent attention and direct engagement by filmmakers and viewers alike (Ford 2012).

Whity offers a still-urgent provocation to both "conservative" and would-be "progressive" discourses of race and ethnicity within and well beyond the usual framework associated with the genre it notionally inhabits. To be prescriptive about positive change not only is arrogant but frequently results in at best a soft and illusory liberalism that does not challenge the overall system in which it operates, resulting, in fact, in a textbook "small-c" conservative or at best modestly reformist vision. Fassbinder asks us why we expect films to tell us how to live when we are so rightfully skeptical of politicians or other human figures offering similar advice. He serves up something decidedly more with this singular, queer, modernist Western: a hard look at the way patriarchal whiteness continues to construct itself and its others without acknowledging the process.

This movement applies not just to *Whity* itself, but doubles back to countless Westerns no matter their surface ideology, as well as other kinds of films, and beyond the screen. That the on-screen "others" do not end up looking especially inspirational, or their brief self-liberation is from the start intricately corrupted through its enabling cost (Hanna's bribe money, Whity's murder spree), and doomed to fail due to literally lacking any reality within which to conceivably thrive, is hardly their fault.

While the world as visualized on screen may seem without hope, surely its rendering is enough to make us feel the urgency of the need for change, no matter how limited, contingent, or ephemeral our agency may be. With *Whity's* final, lingering image, the essential tragedy is enforced: There is no viable escape from the social regime that defines the "other" and through which they maintain some sense of identity within the overdetermined, diverse, and always generatively contradictory genre of the Western—certainly no "liberation" on the horizon, let alone revolutionary overthrow. Only death. But even this sublime, tragic conclusion is itself undermined through being set within an even more fundamentally artificial space. Sieg (2014) writes:

> Given that *Whity* was produced in the wake of the student and anti-war protests waged in major western and eastern European cities, Priscilla Layne's (2011) reading of the film as a historically and geographically displaced reflection on the possibility and failure of revolutionary change seems fully justified.

Precisely because of its inbuilt restrictions and overdetermined (if always complex and frequently contradictory) conservatism, the Western is the perfect, partially disguised means of generating a more genuinely, radically sober vision— paradoxically, in light of its mythic investment in an ideologically loaded, highly selective white, male, heterosexual subject and his sacred individuation and liberty—demonstrating how true freedom remains, for now at least, impossible when it comes to the plight of those placed outside the usual story.

Bibliography

Broughton, Lee. *The Euro-Western: Reframing Gender, Race and the "Other" in Film.* London: I.B. Tauris, 2016.

Cole, Jake. "*Whity.*" *Letterboxed* (2014). Available online at: https://letterboxd.com/jakepcole/film/whity/ (accessed September 18, 2018).

Elsaesser, Thomas. *Fassbinder's Germany: History, Identity, Subject*. Amsterdam: Amsterdam University Press, 1996.

Ford, Hamish. *Post-War Modernist Cinema and Philosophy: Confronting Negativity and Time*. New York: Palgrave Macmillan, 2012.

hooks, bell. "Critical Interrogation: Talking Race, Resisting Racism," *Inscriptions*, 5 (1989). Available online at: https://culturalstudies.ucsc.edu/inscriptions/volume-5/bell-hooks/ (accessed July 2, 2018).

Jay, Gregory. "Who Invented White People?" In *The Thompson Reader: Conversations in Context*, edited by Robert Yagelski, 96–102. Belmont: Wadsworth Publishing, 2007.

Kolchin, Peter. "Whiteness Studies: The New History of Race in America." *The Journal of American History*, 89, no. 1, June (2002): 154–73.

Layne, Priscilla. "Fassbinder's *Whity* at the Crossroads of Hollywood Melodrama and Blaxploitation." In *A Companion to German Cinema*, edited by Terri Ginsberg and Andrea Mensch, 260–86. Malden: John Wiley and Sons, 2011.

Sieg, Katrin. *Ethnic Drag: Performing Race, Nation, Sexuality in West Germany*. Ann Arbor: University of Michigan Press, 2002.

Sieg, Katrin. "Remediating Fassbinder in Video Installations by Ming Wong and Branwen Okpako." *Transit*, 9, no. 2 (2014). Available online at: http://transit.berkeley.edu/2014/sieg/ (accessed July 9, 2018).

Thatcher, Lisa. "*Whity*—Fassbinder and the Dark Side of the Western." *LisaThatcher.com* [blog]. February 12, (2013). Available online at: https://lisathatcher.com/2013/02/12/whity-fassbinder-and-the-dark-side-of-the-western-film-review/ (accessed September 4, 2018).

Victor-Katia. "Rainer Werner Fassbinder's *Whity* (1970)." *Acting Out Politics* [blog]. March (2018). Available online at: http://www.actingoutpolitics.com/rainer-werner-fassbinders-whity-1972/ (accessed September 4, 2018).

7

Man of the West:
Dean Reed's (Cinematic) Frontier Personas in
Blood Brothers and *Sing, Cowboy, Sing!*

Sonja Simonyi

Introduction

The Western is a quintessentially performative genre in which iconic visual elements and a distinct set of generic motifs, gestures, dress codes, and actions emphasize the spectacle of the frontier. Scholars of Wild West shows such as those produced by Buffalo Bill Cody have investigated the ways in which the spectacularized frontier created by showmen allowed "national identity" to be "performed" (Kasson 2000) and "essentially invented the Western as a performative genre" (Rebhorn 2012: 1). Their work thus highlights the centrality of performance, artifice, and showmanship in the narrativization of national history and identity within a popular US frontier context.

With regards to the cinematic Western, this performative element has been taken up within a wide range of genre studies. Richard Dyer has notably identified different ways in which performativity as self-reflexivity and self-consciousness permeates the genre, for instance through iconic Western actors being cast in roles that critique the myth of the West and draw attention to its constructed nature, *The Man Who Shot Liberty Valance* (John Ford, 1962) being a foremost example (2007: 95). Attached to these gestures of self-conscious performativity are the various ways in which celebrity and the broadly perceived public identity of actors closely associated with a given genre can intertextually and self-reflexively interact with the ideological as well as cultural meaning of a film text, as Nahuel Ribke's (2015) analysis of the political careers of John Wayne and Clint Eastwood highlights.

This chapter draws on various intersecting understandings of the Western as performance in order to explore the on-screen frontier persona of American singer-performer Dean Reed in two films made in East Germany during the late socialist period. Reed was a vocal supporter of leftist ideology and moved to East Germany in the early 1970s. He became a celebrated, state-sanctioned public personality across the Soviet Bloc and the Soviet Union. Reed, known across the region as the Red Elvis, often performed an American national imaginary expressed through frontier tropes in various media, from print publications to concerts, television appearances, and roles in fiction films. Yet he persistently entwined this fantasy of Americanism with an internationalist message of solidarity that vocally celebrated the promises of state socialist ideology. Reed's performative Americanness represents the crucial paradox of his celebrity, which squarely evolved around the exotic nature of his leftist political activism and wholesome, rather uncomplicated, appropriation of cowboy motifs.

This chapter addresses how questions of celebrity, musical performance, genre, race, ideology, and national identity intersected and were negotiated through Reed's on-screen appearances in two East German Westerns: *Blood Brothers* (*Blutsbrüder*, Werner Wallroth, 1975) and *Sing, Cowboy, Sing* (Dean Reed, 1981). As I argue, Reed's performances self-reflexively referenced his American cowboy identity and celebrity singing cowboy persona and as such complicated the straightforward ideological appropriation of the Western in these socialist productions. In studying the ways in which frontier tropes inform his multilayered on-screen performances, my study considers Reed's image primarily within a Western genre context alongside the East German sociopolitical and cultural framework within which it functioned.

Setting the Stage: The Origins of Dean Reed's Transnational Celebrity Persona

Popular biographies of Reed's life (see, for example, Nadelson [2006]) habitually stress his astonishing trajectory from all-American youth to international communist rock star. Born in 1938 on the outskirts of Denver, Colorado, Reed's initially modest career as a singer started in the late 1950s in Los Angeles. Although he only attained limited success in his native country, his song "Our Summer Romance" became a hit across South America in 1959–60, turning Reed into a hugely popular singer there (Mularski 2014). Reed's South American experiences in the 1960s resulted in his political awakening and he became an outspoken leftist, partaking in demonstrations and turning his musical performances into vocal acts of political resistance. His explicit rejection of US capitalism, military imperialism, and American foreign policy considerably alienated him from his native country as well as right-wing governments worldwide (notably Argentina), which drew him to explore new career opportunities in Europe.

Before becoming the quintessential American communist behind the Iron Curtain, Reed lived in Rome and appeared as an actor in popular Italian films. These included Westerns such as *Winchester Does Not Forgive* (*Buckaroo: il winchester che non perdona*, Adelchi Bianchi, 1967) and *Adiós, Sabata* (*Indio Black*, Gianfranco Parolini, 1970). Though lacking in both charisma and impressive acting skills, Reed featured as a serviceable presence in these films, which used his conventional good looks to present him as a reliable young male protagonist. So even before his move to the GDR, it is clear that Reed's political activism already coexisted with a desire for uncomplicated stardom, whether achieved through music or movie appearances.

Reed and other American actors performed their "authentic" national identity to playfully enrich Italian constructions of the US frontier on film, resulting in often ironic presentations of their national-cultural identities. Reed's career in Italy was clearly self-consciously constructed through his identity as an American singer-actor-performer. So while his celebrity persona within a state socialist context evidently functioned as a unique phenomenon, its origins cannot be separated from his experience with the Western genre in a distinctly European context. His GDR career must be understood not as a direct transposition of his American (cultural) identity into a state socialist realm but as an extension of his already artificial American cowboy performances in Italian Westerns.

Performing the American West in East Germany

Reed ultimately settled in East Germany in 1973. For the East German government, he became a crucial spokesperson of leftist ideals. His popularity in the GDR, the Eastern Bloc and the Soviet Union relied largely on the mythology of an American superstar willfully seeking to live on the more just side of the ideologically divided world. Seán Allan (2016) usefully outlines the parameters of Reed's star persona in the context of his film career with the state-owned East German DEFA Studios, where he made several films. Allan's (2016) analysis foregrounds the ways in which the studio negotiated Reed's contradictory public image, caught between cultivating his ideologically aligned socialist celebrity and controlling his at times undeniably idiosyncratic and individualistic performance as a conventional American star. Central to this precarious construction was his exotic image as the "Man from Colorado." As Allan explains, publicity at DEFA "homed in on what, at least in their imagination, was typically American about Reed: rodeos, cowboy hats and horsemanship all set against a quasi-Wild West setting" (2016: 180). Allan's study ultimately follows Dyer's influential understanding of the "star image" as an "intertextual construct produced across a range of media and cultural practices, capable of intervening in the working of particular films" (Dyer cited in Allan 2016: 184). Applying this idea to Reed as a celebrity construct, Allan argues that the American's image was meant to primarily "demonstrate a congruence between his on- and off screen personalities" (2016: 184) and as such portray him as a fighter for the freedom of oppressed peoples around the globe across various media.

This chapter expands the notion of the interconnectedness of Reed's various public personas and the markedly interdisciplinary status of his celebrity as an American abroad to explore how it interacts with cinematic frontier tropes. Before turning to a close reading of *Blood Brothers*, I will outline how the notion of performativity has been understood in relation to Native American culture through the East German subgenre of *Indianerfilms* of which this 1975 production is a notable example. As I argue, Reed's own performativity as an American cowboy importantly shifts the habitual focus on Indians found in these films.

Indianerfilms: Performing German Cowboys and Indians

The *Indianerfilms* presents the most quintessential appropriation of the Western in the Soviet Bloc. After the launch of its first installment, *The Sons of Great Bear* (*Die Söhne der großen Bärin*, Josef Mach, 1966), the series became a huge success for DEFA. As scholars have noted, *Indianerfilms*, as frontier narratives habitually set in the American West of the nineteenth century, aimed to revise America's official historiography and the ways in which its frontier mythology had been constructed in US popular culture, including classical Hollywood Westerns (see, for example, Dika [2008]; Gemünden, [2002]). It is also for this reason that the East Germans sought to give their regional genre a new name that fundamentally obscured any connection with the American genre. As revisionist examples, *Indianerfilms* restaged the classical civilization-wilderness binary from a Marxist perspective, featuring Native Americans as heroic freedom fighters rather than bloodthirsty nemeses. The Indians, coded as a proud community resisting greedy settlers, corrupt government officials and the relentless capitalist-imperialist powers that these figures represent, stood in "for any number of racial Others" and oppressed people around the globe that the GDR declared solidarity with (Torner 2011: 66).

Indianerfilms soon became the GDR's foremost cinematic exports, as the twelve feature films in the series were enthusiastically received in other ideologically aligned countries. *Indianerfilms* were notably produced in direct response to the successes of the West German *Winnetou* films. The latter were a cycle of adaptations of the nineteenth-century German writer Karl May's Indian-themed novels, which focused on the adventures and the strong bond enjoyed by the Native American Winnetou and the German adventurer Old Shatterhand. These films were banned in East Germany on account of the reactionary values, bourgeois tastes, and markedly ahistorical approaches to American history that the state detected in them (Gemünden 2002). Obviously there is more to these West German-made Westerns than GDR state policy would suggest. For example, Lee Broughton (2016) has provided close readings of the *Winnetou* films that suggest that their content addresses a number of social and political concerns that troubled West Germany during the 1960s.

All of these literary and cinematic works tapped into a wider cultural phenomenon that had a long-standing history in Germany, involving various modes of studying, celebrating, and emulating aspects of the lifestyles and culture of (predominantly) Plains Indians. These activities, termed *Indianthusiasm* by German scholar Hartmut Lutz (2002), have repeatedly been conceptualized through the process of performativity. Christian Feest (2000) has similarly described this phenomenon as "cultural transvestism" while Katrin Sieg's (2002) widely influential theorization of (West) German's impersonations of Native Americans during the post–Second World War period labels it "ethnic drag." Sieg (2002) understands *Indianthusiasm* not only as a way to negotiate the trauma of the Holocaust and questions of culpability and victimhood postwar but also as an ambiguous process by which Otherness is celebrated through an effective effacing of nonwhite bodies by having white people perform as Native Americans.

The most alluring feature of the *Indianerfilms*, beyond their dominant use of scenic vistas from other friendly socialist countries, was unquestionably Gojko Mitić, the socialist sphere's top movie star during this period who became the films' iconic lead protagonist (for a recent study of Mitić's complicated star persona, see Torner 2016). Mitić was a Yugoslav gym instructor turned actor whose chiseled facial features and muscular physique ideally complemented both the socialist message the films were seeking to transmit and the idealized Indian imaginary that had historical roots in German culture. Additionally, his Yugoslav nationality alongside his vaguely nonwhite appearance (augmented in the films by dark makeup and black wigs) communicated refracted and contradictory understandings of ethnic and racial Otherness entwined with the aim of authentically "performing" Native American characters in East German films.

Addressing Reed's appearance in *Blood Brothers* extends the issue of performativity through his performance as an American frontier dweller. As I argue, Reed's role as the film's white American protagonist vacillates between a critical perspective and moments of performativity that uncritically mediate and celebrate his American cowboy star persona, with the latter notably suspending the ideological stakes of the film. Indeed, the exoticized classical Western tropes that Reed's white male frontier identity carries implicitly reinforce the racial and sociocultural hierarchies that an *Indianerfilm* should typically undermine.

An American Cowboy in an *Indianerfilm*

Blood Brothers tells the story of a US soldier Harmonica (Reed), who deserts after witnessing the army massacre a group of Cheyenne villagers. Harmonica subsequently escapes from a military prison with two other inmates. When the trio encounters a young Cheyenne woman, Rehkitz (Gisela Freudenberg), one of Harmonica's accomplices shoots her. Harmonica stays behind to care for Rehkitz and is captured by members of her tribe, including her brother Harter Felzen (Gojko Mitić). They wrongly accuse Harmonica of having assaulted her, but after a series of trials he gains the trust of the Indian village and marries Rehkitz. Their happiness is interrupted when the American army attacks them, killing the young bride, imprisoning Harter Felzen and deporting the rest of the tribe to reservations. After a period of despair, Harmonica has a moment of ideological awakening. He frees Harter Felzen from prison and after their blood bonding ritual, leads an armed rebellion tasked with freeing his Native brothers from the reservations.

Blood Brothers's narrative aptly exemplifies the *Indianerfilm*'s adherence to GDR state ideology. Yet Reed's involvement as a scriptwriter and his presence as the film's unquestionable protagonist markedly shifts its focus away from the Native American cause. Heidi Denzel de Tirado notes how the film foregrounds the ways in which Dean Reed's biography informs the fictional narrative by adding "a dimension of socialist realism" (2018: 127). As she argues, Reed's leftist politics and well-publicized investment in condemning the atrocities committed by American military forces informed the political tone of the film while his Americanness and "famous star image as a 'singing cowboy'" worked to bring a sense of authenticity to the film. As she notes, this gesture also emerged through various interviews in which Reed drew parallels between Harmonica's transformation from "a naïve pacifist" into a "fighter for the communist revolution" and his own life as an "authentic" but now politically enlightened American (2018: 128). At first glance, Reed's presence in the film, which starts with an extra-diegetic insert in which the singer explains the message of brotherhood and solidarity that the film centers on, unquestionably appears to reinforce the ideological dictates of the *Indianderfilm*. Yet as I argue, a closer look at Reed's performance of an American cowboy here confuses this political message.

Blood Brothers dramatically opens with the massacre. Set against a wintry landscape, soldiers riding horses set alight tepees and shoot at women and children. Reed takes an American flag and after witnessing the brutal destruction breaks the flagpole in two. This gesture references Reed's famous protest action during which he washed the American flag in front of the US Embassy in Santiago, Chile, in 1970 to cleanse it of the blood of its victims. Yet soon, Reed undergoes the first crucial transformation of the film, which takes Harmonica away from this overtly ideological characterization. Harmonica sheds his tarnished military identity and is reborn through another symbol of Americanness, that of the vagrant cowboy: after the prison break he appears riding a horse, wearing the quintessential clothing of a frontiersman (a striking yellow shirt with red bandana around his neck), his figure placed in a wide shot against a scenic mountainous vista. In East Germany's *Indianerfilms*, army men are habitually depicted as schemers or weakly compliant, while cowboys are cast as depraved and sadistic men obsessed with material fortunes. In contrast, the Indians are shown to be living in tune with nature. Yet here, Harmonica is insistently framed within the kind of pastoral idylls associated with the protagonists of classical American Westerns, a connection reinforced through his close relationship with horses which symbolically, as John Cawelti notes, serve to connect man and nature in traditional Western narratives (1999: 144).

The character's name, Harmonica, evidently references Charles Bronson's iconic role in Sergio Leone's *Once Upon a Time in the West* (*C'era una volta il West*, 1968) while reinforcing the parallels between Reed's off-screen identity as a singer-performer and his music-loving protagonist. Beyond featuring a nominal wink to the Spaghetti Western, the nickname is incessantly rendered literal through the character's obsessive harmonica playing. Here the instrument, which is "widely perceived as authentically Western" (Kalinak 2012: 5), mediates the diegetic and non-diegetic musical leitmotif of the character throughout the film, providing the soundtrack with a straightforward Western tone, which is unusual for an *Indianerfilm* and undeniably connected to Reed's popularity as a singer/performer.

The central narrative thread of the film concerns the character's growing awareness of the plight of the Indians, channeled through his relationships with Rehkitz and her brother. Harmonica's fate in the Indian village initially hinges on a traditional challenge during which he is forced to flee from the agile Harter Felzen across a mountainous landscape. When the Indian accidentally falls he fails to reach his victim and is thus symbolically (and uncharacteristically for an *Indianerfilm*) relegated to a secondary role throughout the narrative. This narrative contrivance partially reinstates the traditional racial hierarchy of classical American Westerns in which Indian characters are inevitably subordinate to their white counterparts.

After the challenge, Harmonica integrates into the tribe, a process that centers on his education in Native culture. These light-hearted scenes foreground Harmonica's ineptitude in the ways of the Indian, yet at the same time, they feature key performative moments that underline the allure of his (and thus Reed's) American cowboy persona. In one scene, Harter Felzen mocks Harmonica as he fails at bareback horse riding. Harmonica defiantly responds by mounting a saddle on the horse and performing an impressive trick riding stunt, jumping on and off the galloping animal. This action plainly displays Reed's undeniable skills on horseback in a purely performative fashion rather than serving an essential narrative function. This is reinforced by the fact that Reed insisted on executing all of his stunts himself (Allan 2016: 177). Harmonica's action is thus meant to seduce not merely Rehkitz, who is shown gazing captivatedly at his display of riding skills, but also the audience. Yet this scene does not merely reverse "the colonialist and gendered gaze" habitually associated with the white male protagonist (Denzel de Tirado 2018: 131), which would have served the film's revisionist objective. It renders Reed an exotic subject of this gaze specifically through his performance as an American cowboy. Similarly, in a later scene, Harter Felzen taunts Harmonica for failing to hit a target with a bow and arrow. He responds by taking out his gun and performing some flashy trick shooting. While Harter Felzen leaves the scene unimpressed, the audience is nevertheless invited to revel in Reed's on-screen/off-screen image as a convincing cowboy of the West.

Harmonica's playful rivalry with Harter Felzen entwines with his growing romance with Rehkitz, which enacts the well-known classical American Western trope of the doomed interracial romance seen in films such as Delmer Daves's *Broken Arrow* (1950). In one scene, Rehkitz cheerfully praises Harmonica for being well on his way to becoming "a real Indian" and tells him that he will soon learn their "war dance." Enthused by this comment, Reed unleashes a guttural chant, replete with mock ritual dancing and foot stomping, imitating a stereotypical tribal performance. While meant as a moment of comic relief, the humor of this enthusiastic response disengages the overall scene from the film's ideological center, squarely placing Native culture in the realm of playfulness and play-acting. Harmonica's gestures actively trivialize and render laughable indigenous rituals. As such, the American's gestures reinforce what Gerd Gemünden has critically noted about the *Indianerfilm*, which to him "provide us with little more than the well-known clichés of tribal life" while subjecting nonwhite characters to "forms of 'othering' that involve strategies of domination, appropriation and stereotyping" (2002: 245).

Reed energetically follows this performance with a country song in English as he crosses arms with Rehkitz in dance. His brief dual performance ("Indian"/American) thus doubly disavows the Indian theme of the narrative. It portrays Indian culture as purely performative (the white protagonist indulging in playing the Indian for laughs), while subsequently accentuating Reed's own authenticity, channeled through Harmonica, as an American singing cowboy. This gesture is of course especially notable in the context of the East German subgenre that self-consciously celebrated the legitimacy of its cinematic portrayals of Native American culture, all the while casting white Eastern Europeans in heavy makeup to achieve this vision. The extended scene ends with Rehkitz agreeing to marry the white man, as Harmonica's silhouette, framed against the orange-hued sunset, and the by now recognizable musical leitmotif serve to push the tone of the scene into the formal universe of classical American Westerns.

The subsequent wedding ceremony presents Harmonica in a leather outfit suggesting his future assimilation into the tribe. Yet this notion is once again destabilized after he attempts to tame the wild stallion Harter Felzen gifts him. As the Indian village turns into a veritable rodeo, with villagers animatedly standing around the corral, the mise-en-scène directly frames Reed at the center of this performative arena. This frenzied scene produces yet another comedic moment: Harmonica and his horse suddenly burst through the wooden barriers and head straight into a tepee. As he charges through the structure, a length of cloth is caught on his head. He continues his frantic gallop while struggling free from the fabric, which ends up wrapped around his body like a poncho. The scene thus concludes with a visual pun engaging Clint Eastwood's iconic outfit for his Man with No Name character, which reminds the viewer of the ways in which Reed, Eastwood, and other American actors effectively performed their "authentic" national identity in European Westerns.

The last section of the narrative increases the dramatic stakes of the film. Rehkitz's death appears as a punishment for Harmonica's naivety, since he calls on the Natives to trust the US Army men who eventually massacre her along with other villagers. As Harmonica becomes incapacitated with grief, he loses his connection to the Indian tribe and becomes a bum at a frontier town's saloon. He is only shaken into action, and out of his alcoholic stupor, when he catches a glimpse of Harter Felzen and his tribesmen being paraded as prisoners around the town. Freeing Harter Felzen and connecting with him through the blood bonding ritual, Harmonica finally ends up committed to armed struggle.

In the film's final scene, the protagonist is again depicted in cowboy clothes, wearing a somber dark-hued jacket and cowboy hat, with the US Army this time featured as an unquestionable enemy. *Blood Brothers* ends with a momentary freeze frame that shows Harmonica in action alongside Harter Felzen as they jump into the armed confrontation, both men suspended in midair and framed against a barren rock and the blue sky. Once their movement resumes, they fall out of frame and the film's title appears in bold red font on the screen. This still image brings to mind the iconic conclusion of *Butch Cassidy and the Sundance Kid* (George Roy Hill, 1969), in which the freeze frame of the rebellious duo facing their demise turns from color to sepia tones, suggesting the transition of stark historical reality into myth. *Blood Brother*'s evocation of this image does not carry such self-reflexive symbolism. Instead, it appears to construct a myth of cross-racial brotherhood and equality that Reed's performance in the film ultimately disavows.

Sing, Cowboy, Sing, an Explosion of Generic References

Reed had a central role in shaping the production of *Blood Brothers*, but *Sing, Cowboy, Sing* was to be his ambitious solo endeavor. He wrote, directed, and starred in the film that was his final DEFA project. While Reed's role in *Blood Brothers* already drew on his intertextual singing cowboy persona, *Sing, Cowboy, Sing* was explicitly constructed around this motif. As Reed's star began to wane in the early 1980s, it is perhaps unsurprising that his solo project was to center explicitly on the cowboy tropes that crucially shaped his popularity.

The film concerns the adventures of Joe (Reed) and his sidekick Beny (Václav Neckář), two carefree-but-broke, rodeo riders who travel from town to town with their Wild West show. Impressed by their performance, a young girl, Susann (Kerstin Beyer), runs away from home with the aim of convincing Joe to marry her mother, a widow who is engaged to a villainous man who is only after her wealth. As news of Susann's disappearance spreads, Joe and Beny erroneously become wanted as the child's kidnappers, while her future stepfather plans to kill both the vagrants and the little girl. After the trio is embroiled in increasingly absurd hijinks, they eventually wind up in the German migrant settlement of Liebenthal. A series of humorous confrontations with the community's eccentric characters precedes the final showdown. Once the villain is defeated with the help of the townspeople, Joe unites with both Susann and her mother, ready to assume a conventional family life.

Touted as a *Westernkomödie,* the film appeared to spoof the Western's classical tropes and as such also seemed to mock American and—by extension—imperialist frontier mythologies, providing an ideologically satisfactory approach to the genre that aligned it to the East German state's socialist perspective. However, my reading of the film contextualizes some of the transnational generic influences and reference points that serve to show that *Sing, Cowboy, Sing* is more than just a straightforward political critique of American history and culture. I argue that, by drawing upon the tropes of Italian Western comedies as well as the content of the Czechoslovak singing cowboy parody *Lemonade Joe* (*Limonádový Joe,* Oldřich Lipský, 1964), the film stages the frontier as an explosive performative space that generates ambiguity and complexity around Reed's own cowboy persona, notably in opposition to his earlier discussed appearance in *Blood Brothers.* Additionally, my reading explores how the mocking tone of the film more crucially subverts the locally bound *Indianerfilm* and in doing so clearly deviates from the official ideologically revisionist function that Western films were supposed to fulfill in the GDR.

The Singing Cowboy and the Circus: Dean Reed's Frontier Masquerades

Sing, Cowboy, Sing seems to reference different modes of the revisionist European Western comedy and the types of self-reflexivity and performativity they engage in. One is the Italian Western, the other a notable comedic interpretation of the singing cowboy trope.

Reed's film appears to be directly inspired by the excesses of lowbrow Italian Western comedies, which transpose extended slapstick saloon brawls, ridiculous modes of combat, and the unabashed exploitation of scatological humor into their frontier universe. Reed's film also centers on the kind of mismatched comedic duo trope that Terence Hill and Bud Spencer perfected in the Italian context, replaced here with Reed and his ineffectual but endearing sidekick Beny.

The film ultimately imbues the fictional frontier space with absurd elements, such as excessive costumes, gags, and visual references that foreground the artificiality of the fictional West as a playful site of performance. This notably occurs through the literal evocation of the frontier as a circus, as an attraction that fully relegates the narrative to the background. Props from circus performances are used in certain scenes, while Beny appears throughout the film in absurd costumes, performing in one scene as a female flamenco dancer, and in the final showdown as a clown. The circus trope appears to be directly inspired by the Spencer/Hill comedy *Boot Hill* (*La collina degli stivali*, Giuseppe Colizzi, 1969), which placed the Italian duo in the same kind of playfully vaudevillian universe, although its purpose in *Sing, Cowboy, Sing*, as my analysis illustrates, differs from its function within the Spaghetti Western context.

Alongside this generic evocation, *Sing, Cowboy, Sing* systematically foregrounds a focus on a frontier dwelling singer-performer that runs well beyond any narrative purpose. The title directly references a classical singing cowboy vehicle, *Sing, Cowboy, Sing* (Robert N. Bradbury, 1937), which featured the famous Texan country singer and actor Tex Ritter. By partially repurposing an existing Western, Reed appears to place the project in dialogue with this classical subgenre and by extension align himself with the great musical cowboys of the

American West. Yet the film's appropriation of this motif ultimately destabilizes the singing cowboy image at its basis.

Peter Stanfield's (2002) historical study of the singing cowboy locates its origins at the intersection of a number of popular performance contexts and cultural traditions within late-nineteenth- and early-twentieth-century America that developed separately from the cinematic Western. His historical outline notably highlights that the celebrity of the main characters as country singers, rather than actors, unquestionably contributed to their popularity, a trajectory that mirrors Reed's own career. Yet instead of merely referencing the traditional cross-media career paths of the original singing cowboys, Reed's comic evocation of the West as a site of performance draws on vaudevillian excesses too. In doing this, it calls to mind the well-known Czechoslovak Western comedy *Lemonade Joe*, which depicts the absurd adventures of a teetotal singing cowboy. Joe (Karel Fiala), impeccably dressed and inexplicably prone to bursting into song, mocks the excessive sartorial perfection, overwrought vocal presence, and impeccable moral decency that defined heroes in the classical singing cowboys films.

The eponymous Lemonade Joe initially appears as the heroic savior of the fictional town of Stetson City, yet ultimately reveals himself to be nothing but a peddler for the fictional beverage Kolaloka—an unmistakable reference to America's most successful corporate product. The film has been variably read as an indictment of American imperialism (Miller 2013) and a critique of the Manichean worldview propagated by Soviet ideology (Imre 2011). But these nuanced political aspects of the Czechoslovak film seem to be entirely beyond Reed's interest. *Sing, Cowboy, Sing*'s fictional frontier universe of mistaken identities, vaudeville performance, and playful masquerade serves instead to underpin Reed's own malleability as a Western hero.

Reed's Joe first emerges in the film mounted on a horse and sporting an embellished white shirt and cowboy hat, mimicking the spotless white look and impeccable sartorial style of the classical singing cowboys and *Lemonade Joe*'s humorous evocation of this look too. The color, as the indisputable symbol not only of implausible physical cleanliness but also of moral purity on the frontier, is evoked here ironically. Throughout his early adventures, Joe reveals himself to be shamelessly pursuing financial gains and the moral dirtiness of his endeavors is rendered literal at times. For instance, in one scene he enthusiastically engages in a pig-wrestling contest and emerges from the fight covered in muck.

Rather than implicitly negotiating the constructedness of Reed's good cowboy persona in the film's narrative, these early scenes present it in the distinctively artificial framework of the Wild West show. The mise en abyme of Joe's performance as a pretend frontiersman within the diegesis is referenced throughout the film, and as such self-reflexively suggests that Reed's own real-life cowboy persona was merely artifice as well. Early on, Susann expresses bewilderment at Joe's daytime job as a performer, asking him why he "plays a cowboy" when he's "old enough to be a real cowboy." Although the parameters of what constitutes an authentic or pretend version of a frontier dweller are never made explicit in the film, Reed's performance effectively draws on the perceived truthfulness of his popular off-screen cowboy persona, while at the same time foregrounding this crucial aspect of his celebrity and rendering it a playful charade. The significance of this conversation is heightened in a later scene. Right before the final shoot-out, Susann and Joe have an emotional confrontation, as the man tearfully confesses to Susann that he is incapable of fighting her evil stepfather as he has always been "just playing a cowboy," adding that he is "a clown," "a nobody." In an inevitable move toward a happy ending, Susann comforts Joe who regains faith in himself. Yet the dramatic confrontation with the villain never confirms the protagonist's skills as a gunman, as the expected shoot-out mobilizes the entire town and ends with a series of chaotic slapstick moments. In Reed's frontier universe cowboys and clowns thus become virtually exchangeable modes of masquerade. Joe and Beny's musical performance in Liebenthal preceding the final shoot-out also emphasizes this iconographic fusion. Before getting on stage, Joe interrupts Beny as he is putting on his clown makeup for the show to generously offer him the role of the lead singer. Beny thus stages a song in English (with Reed cast in the supporting role) that recounts his "dream to be a real cowboy." While doing this, Beny is dressed in the clothes that Joe wore during the introductory Wild West show, suggesting the full transferability of the superficial cowboy identity.

An Ironic East German Frontier Imaginary

Allan notes that *Sing, Cowboy, Sings*'s depiction of the German migrant settlement of Liebenthal evokes the socialism found in East Germany (2016: 184). In this way, its town hall gatherings call to mind party meetings, and a series of signs display absurd rules and regulations designed to tightly control the behavior of its citizens. Beyond these references to GDR reality, there are also intertextual allusions to the *Indianerfilm* specifically, that often carry a similarly derisive tone. The film's opening montage shows in extreme close-up a male figure as he dons the key attributes of an Indian warrior's attire: war paint, leather moccasins, and a beaded necklace. Finally a hatchet and a tomahawk are placed in his colorfully decorated belt. The sequence then jump-cuts to a close-up of the figure's face, framed by a war bonnet, as he gallops, terrified, at full speed toward his presumed enemy, letting out a decidedly unmanly and un-Indian-like shriek. This gesture, as it is immediately revealed in the next shot, is performed as part of the aforementioned Wild West show, with the Indian character appearing opposite Dean Reed's cowboy persona.

This staged Wild West show self-reflexively defines the frontier narrative as Reed's performative place of play. But this sequence also unambiguously places the (faux) Indian of the film, played by Beny as it turns out, into a space of derision. It becomes a spoof of a crucial Western frontier encounter in which—according to GDR filmmaking tradition—masculine heroism is always attributed to the Indian character. By flipping the expectations with regards to how the *Indianerfilm* would treat this Western trope, and by establishing the character as a ridiculous clown, especially through Beny's recurrent appearances in this guise, the sequence unquestionably subverts DEFA's take on the Western's narrative and visual structure. Having the Czechoslovak actor and singer Václav Neckář play Beny reinforces this idea. Neckář was best known internationally for his starring role in *Closely Watched Trains* (*Ostře sledované vlaky*, Jirí Menzel, 1966), and as such, embodied one of the most iconic and quintessentially unmanly characters in the region's socialist film culture. In having this minor Slavic figure perform as an Indian, the film arguably renders absurd the heroism of these characters in *Indianerfilms* and more specifically destabilizes the truthfulness of Gojko Mitić's stoic Slav-turned-Indian persona.

Sing, Cowboy, Sing as a whole manifestly avoids focusing on Native themes and subjects. A brief encounter with an "authentic" Indian early on in the narrative reinforces this explicit lack. Walking around in a frontier town, Joe and Susann spot an Indian confined in a wooden shackle. The man appears dazed, as he is displayed as a target for relentless egg throwing by the amused locals. Susann, outraged by the humiliating scene, asks Joe to do something to which he laconically replies that it is none of his business. The scene is primarily meant to underline the narrative transformation of the protagonist from a selfish, unethical loner to a caring patriarchal figure. Yet when considered within the broader framework of Reed's well-publicized politics, it emerges as a shocking disavowal of human solidarity and brotherhood. But rather than seeing this disavowal as merely a personal political statement, it also appears as a crude rejection of the solidarity and internationalism that marked GDR politics and culture as channeled through *Indianerfilms*. Indeed, Reed's cinematic frontier universe is more generally devoid of nonwhite characters. The film's sole Asian character is a Chinese cook whose depiction as a cartoonish oddball conveys offensively racist stereotypes, starkly opposing any meaningful engagement with the historical or sociopolitical plight of such subjects. Lee Broughton's (2016) study on the Euro-Western and race highlights the ways in which the aforementioned Italian Western *Boot Hill* negotiates the representation of its black character Thomas (Woody Strode) through the circus motif. As he explains, the film stages the circus as a carnivalesque setting that destabilizes the rigid racial hierarchies of Hollywood Westerns and more broadly rejects the racial injustices of American society. While Reed's absurd frontier was probably inspired by this Italian film's evocation of the circus theme, his production markedly disengages from *Boot Hill*'s critical message. In slyly subverting the clichés of the *Indianerfilm*, Reed's comedy actually reinstates the racist tropes that underpin Hollywood's classical vision of the American West and as such, significantly contradicts the sense of revisionism habitually associated with Western comedies like Mel Brooks's iconic *Blazing Saddles* (1974).

The references to the *Indianerfilm* extend to the final image of *Sing, Cowboy, Sing*. As Susann excitedly lets off some firecrackers near Beny and Joe to celebrate their victory, they instinctively jump into a trunk situated behind them, which visibly displays the word "circus." The chest features earlier in the film, as it contains props, including some live snakes that are the source of an extended slapstick scene in which Joe and Beny attempt to corral the dangerous reptiles. Their reappearance serves as a final reminder of the light-hearted circus trope that prominently permeates the film's iconographic frontier universe. Yet the freeze frame that concludes the scene, which shows Joe and Beny suspended as they jump away from the animals, unmistakably ridicules the already discussed final still image of *Blood Brothers*, irrevocably spoofing its message of solidarity and heroics.

Sing, Cowboy, Sing was to be Reed's final film for DEFA. Increasingly (and vocally) unhappy about his life in the GDR, Reed was found dead in 1986 under mysterious circumstances that some interpreted as a suicide and others as the ultimate proof of his dramatic fallout with the socialist regime. His leftist American cowboy persona, so usefully absorbed within the fabric of state-dictated East German popular culture during the 1970s, had become increasingly irrelevant within the shifting cultural and political landscape of the country's final decade of existence.

Conclusion

Reed's widely publicized socialist frontier identity unquestionably fit the ideological dictates of the Soviet Bloc. Yet a closer analysis of the two films that centrally evoked this persona in an East German context reveals a more complicated picture. In *Blood Brothers*, the celebratory foregrounding of his alluring American cowboy identity, staged through classical Western tropes, ultimately dilutes the ideological aims of the revisionist *Indianerfilm*. By turn, in *Sing, Cowboy, Sing* Reed's image as a cowboy becomes embedded in a self-reflexively artificial frontier space that draws upon the circus motif to reinforce this gesture. His absurd treatment of the singing cowboy trope at first glance appears to spoof the classical iterations of this genre. Yet the film's distinctly mocking visual and narrative references to the *Indianerfilm* confirm that Reed's crude comedy actually highlights the ways in which the Western genre was appropriated and reconfigured within the ideological context of East Germany. As such, these films illustrate the limits of Reed's American cowboy persona at the service of state socialist ideology.

Bibliography

Allan, Seán. "Transnational Stardom: DEFA's Management of Dean Reed." In *Re-Imagining DEFA, East German Cinema in Its National and Transnational Contexts*, edited by Seán Allan and Sebastian Heiduschke, 168–88. New York: Berghahn Books, 2016.

Broughton, Lee. *The Euro-Western: Reframing Gender, Race and the "Other" in Film.* London: I.B. Tauris, 2016.

Cawelti, John. *The Six-Gun Mystique Sequel.* Bowling Green: Bowling Green State University Popular Press, 1999.

Denzel de Tirado, Heidi. "Interracial Romance, Taboo, and Desire in the Eastern Counter-Western *Blutsbrüder*." In *Gender and Sexuality in East German Film: Intimacy and Alienation*, edited by Kyle Frackman and Faye Stewart, 126–45. Woodbridge: Boydell and Brewer, 2018.

Dika, Vera. "An East German *Indianerfilm*: The Bear in Sheep's Clothing." *Jump Cut*, 50, Spring (2008). Available online at: https://www.ejumpcut.org/archive/jc50.2008/Dika-indianer/ (accessed February 12, 2019).

Dyer, Richard. *Pastiche*. New York and London: Routledge, 2007.

Feest, Cristian, F. "Germany's Indians in a European Perspective." In *Germans and Indians: Fantasies, Encounters, Projections*, edited by Colin G. Calloway, Gerd Gemünden, and Suzanne Zantop, 25–46. Lincoln and London: University of Nebraska Press, 2002.

Gemünden, Gerd. "Between Karl May and Karl Marx." In *Germans and Indians: Fantasies, Encounters, Projections*, edited by Colin G. Calloway, Gerd Gemünden, and Suzanne Zantop, 243–58. Lincoln and London: University of Nebraska Press, 2002.

Imre, Anikó. "Eastern Westerns: Enlightened Edutainment and National Transvestism." *New Review of Film and Television Studies*, 9, no. 2, June (2011): 152–69.

Kalinak, Kathryn. *Music in the Western: Notes from the Frontier*. New York and London: Routledge, 2012.

Kasson, Joy S. *Buffalo Bill's Wild West: Celebrity, Memory, and Popular History*. New York: Hill and Wang, 2000.

Lutz, Hartmut. "German Indianthusiasm: A Socially Constructed German National(ist) Myth." In *Germans and Indians: Fantasies, Encounters, Projections*, edited by Colin G. Calloway, Gerd Gemünden, and Suzanne Zantop, 167–85. Lincoln and London: University of Nebraska Press, 2002.

Miller, Cynthia J. "Comedy, Capitalism and Kolaloka: Adapting the American West in Lemonade Joe (1964)." In *International Westerns: Re-Locating the Frontier*, edited by Cynthia J. Miller and A. Bowdoin Van Riper, 104–20. Lanham: Scarecrow Press, 2013.

Mularski, Jedrek. "Mr. Simpático: Dean Reed, Pop Culture, and the Cold War in Chile." *Music & Politics*, 8, no. 1, Winter (2014). Available online at: http://dx.doi.org/10.3998/mp.9460447.0008.102 (accessed February 12, 2019).

Nadelson, Reggie. *Comrade Rockstar: The Life and Mystery of Dean Reed*. New York: Walker Company, 2006.

Rebhorn, Matthew. *Pioneer Performances: Staging the Frontier*. Oxford: Oxford University Press, 2012.

Ribke, Nahuel. *A Genre Approach to Celebrity Politics*. London: Palgrave Macmillan, 2015.

Sieg, Katrin. *Ethnic Drag: Performing Race, Nation, Sexuality in West Germany*. Ann Arbor: University of Michigan Press, 2002.

Stanfield, Peter. *Horse Opera: The Strange History of the 1930s Singing Cowboy*. Champaign: University of Illinois Press, 2002.

Torner, Evan. "The DEFA *Indianerfilm*: Narrating the Postcolonial through Gojko Mitic." In *Re-Imagining DEFA, East German Cinema in its National and Transnational Contexts*, edited by Seán Allan and Sebastian Heiduschke, 227–47. New York: Berghahn Books, 2016.

Torner, Evan. "The Red and the Black: Race in the DEFA Film Osceola." *New German Review*, 25, no. 1, (2011): 61–81.

8

An(Other) West:
The Limits of National Identity in
The Proposition

Chelsea Wessels

The landscape, the history, the communities of outcasts that surround the bushrangers are variant displays of the bushranger, different ways of figuring the same thing. Together with the figures of the bushrangers themselves, they suggest a single image refracted in different ways, a phantom beast that can be known only by a discrete trunk and ear, leg, skin and tail.

(William Routt 2001)

Introduction

This chapter will examine how *The Proposition* (John Hillcoat, 2005) deals with the fragmentation of Australian national identity by utilizing the western[1]—in dialogue with the bushranger genre—to address Australia's colonial history. By tracing the influence of the bushranger genre as it is reworked in a later example, I argue that the western reveals its openness to specific concerns of national identity: in this case, the contested national identity of Australia. In *The Proposition*, the codes of the western are employed to foreground questions of nation, space, and the myth of the past. By mapping these codes onto an Australian context, however, the limits of the western as a vehicle of the "dominant fiction" are exposed, and instead of creating a binding, cohesive national mythology, the contemporary Australian western articulates an understanding of the conflicting forces that shape Australia's national identity.

---

[1] I use the term 'western' to refer to the western as a global genre, whereas 'Western' is used in relation to the American West.

The western genre, particularly in its American form, appears to set forth what Jacques Rancière terms a "dominant fiction"—the "privileged mode of representation by which an image of social consensus is offered to members of a social formation and within which they are asked to identify themselves" (as cited in Silverman 1992: 30). Rancière describes this fiction in terms of the birth of the American nation, which hinges on binary oppositions: "whites versus Indians; North versus South; Law versus outlaw, etc" (as cited in Burgoyne 2010: 2). However, unlike the neat distinctions laid out by Rancière and supported by the mythology of the Hollywood Western, in Australia, the western functions differently: as a picture of the struggle to define national identity in an Australian context. The western genre's connection to a nation-building mythology, deeply ingrained in the majority of writings on the western as an American form, makes its use in Australia particularly complex. Here, the western functions in dialogue with the bushranger genre to expose the limits of using the western to establish a national mythology. *The Proposition*, I argue, uses genre to work against the notion of a dominant fiction and contests attempts to write a unified history from the colonial past.

While the early bushranger films might have served as dominant fictions, with their clear binaries between good and evil and civilization and the wild, later Australian westerns begin to revise the neat distinctions of the bushranger genre to articulate a more complex notion of national identity. *The Proposition* foregrounds questions of nation, space, and the myth of the past, not to bind together the disparate histories of colonization into one overarching mythic construct but rather to challenge mythic constructs of national identity. Revising the bushranger genre, then, allows for a consideration of national identity that does not rely on a dominant fiction, or a narrative of belonging, but rather uses the codes of the western to represent, and articulate, a response to colonial history. While the term "Aboriginal" has complex connotations throughout history, I will employ it here as it is commonly used to refer to indigenous Australians.

Antipodal Cinema and the Bushranger Genre

Australia and Great Britain occupy antipodal positions, which is to say that they are positioned in exact opposition on the globe. To be antipodal refers to both the geographic location and the issues raised in occupying this position: Australia is caught in the tension between a removed geographic position and a close connection through culture and language to its colonial British influences. This can be extrapolated further to consider the relationship between Australia and other dominant English-speaking nations, such as the United States. This is especially pertinent when discussing film, as the cinematic development of Australia is always linked to that of Britain and the United States—the major English-speaking cinemas that compete for dominance within the Australian market.

Antipodal suggests a position of both isolation and relation, and, while in many constructions this is seen negatively, these unequal relations have been interpreted positively in the work of William Routt (2001), McKenzie Wark (1995), and Tom O'Regan (1996), among others. For O'Regan, in particular, Australia's antipodal position, especially in regard to Hollywood, leads to a productive tension in Australian cinema:

> Trying to be the same leads to a confrontation with difference, to questions of accent, domestic social texts, scale, budgets—questions of what can or cannot be staged, in other words, the need to differentiate, to occupy the spaces that Hollywood does not. (1996: 107)

Rather than focusing on sameness or difference, then, the antipodal cinema becomes distinct in its clear tension between fitting in with other major cinemas and celebrating a uniquely national cinema. It is this in-between state, the antipodal condition, that is "central to the Australian negotiation of its possibilities" (O'Regan 1996: 110).

By focusing on the antipodal position, I argue that these Australian films, regardless of Hollywood's influence, are primarily an engagement with the tension between sameness (modeling films after Hollywood productions) and difference (the influence of local cultural and industrial circumstances) outlined earlier by O'Regan (1996). While they have undeniably been influenced in later years by Hollywood's dominance, the films are also very much a product of the Australian context. Before turning to *The Proposition*, I would like to examine how the development of the bushranger genre figures prominently in both establishing the Australian film industry and thinking about representing "Australia" on-screen, as well as its connection to the western genre.

The Story of the Kelly Gang, made by Charles Tait in 1906, is the earliest known feature-length narrative film, once clocking in at nearly seventy minutes. However, less than twenty minutes of this footage has survived, and much of the nitrate is so badly decomposed that parts are nearly unwatchable. This film, then, demonstrates the very real issues of fragmentation that arise in working with early cinema, in that there is no "whole" available for study and the surviving fragments are only bits and pieces of a narrative and generic body. The fragmentation on a physical, narrative, and generic level here typifies the mobility of generic conventions associated with the American Western and their potential for movement not only outside of the West but as part of a separate generic tradition, the bushranger genre, which specifically reflects Australian history and identity. In examining *The Story of the Kelly Gang* as an early western, I would like to focus on how its position as an early bushranger film demonstrates the applicability of three early types of generic conventions: rescues, holdups, and visual tourism/spectacle.

First, it is important to briefly understand what a bushranger film is and how this particular genre clearly paralleled and influenced stories of the early West. A bushranger is an outlaw, known for robbing banks or coaches, and later, symbolizing a figure who is antiestablishment. The term originated in Australia to describe early convicts who would escape and hide out in the bush, using robbery and violence to support life on the run. Early fictional representations popularized the term, such as the Rolf Boldrewood serial *Robbery Under Arms*, published from 1882 to 1883 and often read as an influence on Owen Wister's *The Virginian* (1902). Edward "Ned" Kelly and his gang captured the interest of writers and filmmakers with their riveting actions and bifurcated status as killers and heroic rebels against the repressive British government, making Ned Kelly one of the most popular real-life bushrangers. The violence and lack of morality associated with these characters, and their subsequent filmic representations, led to the banning of the genre across Australia by 1912. There are two key connections here to the western: first, the important role that the Australian landscape plays—as a wild space that exists beyond the boundaries of civilization—in creating and othering these characters, and second, the intensely violent nature of their stories.

The dichotomy between civilization and wilderness has long been at the center of discussions of the western genre. Notably, Jim Kitses, in his 1969 piece "Authorship and Genre: Notes on the Western," outlines a series of antimonies between civilization and wilderness that represent a constant ideological tension in the genre. This can play out in the landscape itself, which is both "inspiring" and "barren and savage, surroundings so demanding that men are rendered morally ambiguous, or wholly brutalized" (Kitses, 1969: 59). In Australia, the contrast between the colonized spaces occupied by the English and the vast expanse of the outback sets up this dichotomy, and the bushrangers' ability to move between these two spaces renders them "morally ambiguous," as opposed to the Aboriginal people, who are wholly aligned with the savagery of the landscape. While Kitses argues that this ideological tension specifically applies to America, it is possible to see the connections to Australia when he writes about the impact of "the isolation of a vast unexplored continent" and "the clash of allegiances between Mother Country and New World" (1969: 60). I will return to this struggle over national identity later in the chapter with regard to *The Proposition*, but it is worth raising here in terms of how it reveals the way the bushranger genre, even in its earliest form, resonates with later discussions of the western genre.

In terms of the specific generic conventions outlined earlier (rescues, holdups, and visual tourism/spectacle), the surviving footage of *The Story of the Kelly Gang* provides several complex examples. First, one of the early surviving scenes from the film illustrates the way in which the rescue is used to establish Kelly as more than a cold-blooded outlaw. This scene fictionalizes what has become known as the Fitzpatrick incident. In contemporary reports of the incident, Constable Fitzpatrick arrives at the Kelly home to arrest Dan Kelly for horse stealing in 1878, lacking a warrant and appearing drunk. In Fitzpatrick's official police report, he claims Ellen Kelly hit him with a shovel and Ned Kelly shot him in the wrist—leading to the arrest of Ellen and forcing Ned to flee (*Culture Victoria* 2016). By contrast, the film shows Constable Fitzpatrick arriving at the Kelly home and subsequently making an inappropriate overture to Kate, Ned's sister. The constable is shown waiting impatiently outside the house, eventually gesturing for Kate to come out and join him. Kate fidgets uncomfortably as he moves closer and struggles wildly as he tries to embrace her. As she escapes back into the house, Fitzpatrick follows, raising his arm to strike her before Ned emerges and knocks him to the ground. Fitzpatrick clearly reaches for his gun before Ned brings out his own weapon, and the Kelly brothers rush outside to help. They subdue Fitzpatrick, and then quickly mount their horses and ride away, presumably in order to avoid arrest. While this is not the first scene of the film, by including this moment early on, Ned is established in a sympathetic light, only using violence to protect his sister, and drawing his gun in order to keep Fitzpatrick from shooting him. The rescue scene, then, is a generic fragment that can be used to establish sympathy for a character. In this case, we see the outlaw figure rescuing his sister from the corrupt lawmen, but there are a number of binary positions created in the rescue. In fact, the binary opposition created by the need for a rescue returns us to the consideration of how "othering" works to create identities. Here, the rescue cements three key figures: the person in need of rescue (Kate Kelly), the pernicious force posing a threat (Constable Fitzpatrick), and the sympathetic source of deliverance (Ned Kelly). In *The Story of the Kelly Gang*, the inclusion of a rescue in a film centered around a controversial outlaw (who does spend much of the film enacting violence) complicates the clear binary between "good" and "bad" characters and situates them in a more liminal space that typifies the complex nature of the frontier as a space between civilization and wilderness.

The liminal nature of the characters is also emphasized in the holdup scenes, of which there are several among the surviving footage. In one of the earlier ones, Ned and his gang hold up the campsite of some of their pursuers. Here, the wilderness of the landscape again establishes the characters as existing outside of society, as the gang creep up on the tent out of the brush while the soon-to-be captive campers fire their guns into the trees and generally make a spectacle that contrasts sharply with the serene nature of the deserted forest. As supporting forces appear in the distance, the gang quickly abandons the comfort of drinking around the captured camp fire and melts back into the trees. A captive attempts to direct his friends to where the gang are hiding, but while the police constables fuss with their guns and horses, Kelly and his gang are able to quickly shoot down their attackers as they emerge from behind the camp's tent. The setup of the scene does not imply that the bushrangers are wholly uncivilized, but their ability to use the landscape to their advantage puts them at odds with the clearly out of place police constables who are the agents and representatives of civilized society. Later, we will see them hold up small coaches, lone men on horseback, and even an entire building full of people. It is clear through the holdups that the Kelly gang is on the wrong side of the law, as represented by the constables, but it is not clear whether the lawmen are on the right side given the way that Constable Fitzpatrick behaved toward Kate in the sequence described earlier. By positioning the bushrangers as both sympathetic and violent characters, through rescue and holdup scenes, the film establishes these outlaws as existing between civilization and the wilderness.

Finally, we can turn to the third type of generic convention, which offers a sense of visual tourism via the on-screen representation of a heightened or spectacular reality. In the surviving footage of *The Story of the Kelly Gang*, we do not see any train rides or prolonged shots of the landscape as in the "phantom ride" train films that were popular in early cinema. What we do get, however, is a sense of spectacle, through both the dramatized versions of true events and the violent action of the narrative. While violence might not be exotic to viewers, the scene where the Kelly gang is literally burned out of hiding takes the viewer inside of the burning building and makes them privy to the dramatic events unfolding. Here several members of Kelly's gang are holed up in a hotel bar when a shoot-out with the police ensues, leading to them setting the building on fire in an effort to smoke out the bushrangers. The prospect of burning to death leads Steve and Dan, two of the outlaws, to shoot each other in a suicide pact. Historically, the details of Steve's and Dan's deaths are unclear, so with this probable fictionalization, the film offers viewers an overly dramatic coding of real events. The final shot of this scene is a fixed medium shot of the doorway, as smoke and flames envelop the building. One of the crucial elements of a phantom ride is the spectacle arising from observing the unfamiliar or the familiar presented in a dramatic way; the view of a landscape passing by might not be an unfamiliar sight to a train passenger who was used to looking out of a train's window while traveling. But seeing the same journey shot by a camera mounted on the front of the train would create a new visual spectacle for the same passenger. Here, while both the true story of Ned Kelly and the events popularized through fiction might not be unfamiliar, the dramatic staging of the fire and the double suicide elevates the events above a simply realistic depiction. In early screenings of the bushranger films, there would have been not only a narrator to provide certain explanations but also quite often an orchestra of sound effects created to accompany certain scenes, with audio accompaniment such as gunshots or galloping hooves. These cues would work with the on-screen visuals to offer the viewer a chance to engage with violent events from the safety and comfort of their cinema chairs. We are used to these principles applying to elements that typically lie beyond the narrative, such as spectacular representations of landscape or exotic representations of the "other," but in this case, the spectacle of the clash between the law and the bushrangers provides a template for the ways in which violence became a core component of the western.

What these fragments and their generic codings imply, then, is that elements that have often been co-opted as part of the American Western began to develop and exist in distinctly separate ways throughout early global film. While later remakes of the Ned Kelly story adopt more of the coded elements of a western by placing more emphasis on Kelly as a lone hero or featuring more dramatic shoot outs instead of burning buildings, this early film emphasizes the core types of generic conventions (rescues, holdups, and visual tourism/spectacle) that can be identified across a body of early generic iterations. This is key in two ways: First, this early Australian film illustrates the distinct development of the bushranger genre and the genre's use of codings that are similar to those found in early westerns. Second, early examples of bushranger films demonstrate the clear connection between a place, Australia in this case, and the types of generic conventions that are likely to develop as a consequence.

The bushranger genre was developed further as a marketing strategy, similar to the Americanization of early westerns in the United States. In *The Red Rooster Scare: Making Cinema American 1900–1910*, Richard Abel (1999) analyzes the history of Pathé in America in order to demonstrate how a particular approach by the press effectively degraded this French powerhouse production company from its position as one of the key cinema studios in America to a specialized and foreign position. Abel argues that by promoting the western genre as representative of a cohesive national identity, seen in the figure of the cowboy, and critiquing Pathé's western films for their lack of American authenticity, the press contributed to building what became seen as an inherent connection between American ideology and identity and the western. In the same way that the American film industry developed westerns as a national product, the bushranger films were critical to early Australian film production. As Routt argues:

> [It] is not unreasonable to claim that bushranger films were, in fact, the single most significant component of the first five years of Australian feature production. . . . Moreover, the circumstances of early Australian production and of Australian culture in the first decades of this century strongly suggest that, despite their parallels with certain early Westerns, this type of film is likely to have played a key role in Australian film history even in the (unimaginable) absence of the American cinema. (2001)

Routt here affirms the isolated, and nation-centric, development of the bushranger genre. What is also important about his argument is the suggestion that these bushranger films were, in fact, an early definition of an "Australian" film genre. By positioning these films as Australian, developed largely in isolation from American cinematic influences, they represent the beginnings of a reflection of "the national" in film. Indeed, these early bushranger stories function as localized myths unique to the Australian context.

At the same time, the content and features of the bushranger film reveal the complexities in attempting to represent an Australian national identity, particularly when the country's colonial history is taken into account. In *The Story of the Kelly Gang*, for example, the surviving fragments of the film focus largely on the conflict between Kelly and the Victorian police. This situates the outlaws (in this case, Kelly and his gang) as "Australian," defined in their opposition to the English colonial presence. However, this configuration of Australian identity completely ignores the Aboriginal presence, instead formulating identity through the antipodal positioning of white Australians versus white Britons. The absence of the Aboriginal in this early construction of the national alters the focus of defining Australia from racial opposition to spatial difference. The logical racial opposition would be white Britons and Australians versus black Aborigines. However, we are instead presented with two distinctive spatial oppositions. The antipodal space of Australia versus Britain and also the "civilized" colonized spaces *within* Australia that are occupied by British forces versus the "outside" wilderness spaces that are claimed by Kelly and the outlaws.

In tracing the story of the Kelly gang from its early cinematic formulations to contemporary productions, the influences of other film industries and the global market come into play. The "Australian" film genre Routt describes comes into contact with, and is in competition with both the Hollywood and the British films that were also being made available to audiences in Australia and worldwide. The Kelly story has in turn found audiences outside of Australia, necessitating a negotiation between its Australian roots in the bushranger genre and the generic content of films made outside of Australia in order to appeal to audiences throughout the wider world. In this way, the contemporary reimaginings of the figure of Ned Kelly and the bushranger genre present a case study in how the tensions of an antipodal position play out in the retelling of a local story on a global scale. In addressing national identity here, the clear oppositional coding of the original *The Story of the Kelly Gang* film is complicated through the multiple "otherings" that occur when both the English and the Aboriginals are included in the construction of the national imaginary.

National identity is the primary thrust of the common linkage between the western and America. However, constructions of national identity through binary relationships, liminal spaces, and the "other" are hardly unique to American history. As Richard Abel (1999), Robert Burgoyne (2010), and others have shown, the "other" of the Native American, and their position as part of a binary opposition to white civilization works to construct a particular idea of a national narrative and cohesive identity. In Australia, this is complicated through the colonial past, which situates multiple "others": Australian as "not" Aboriginal, Australian as "not" English, and Australian as "outlaw."

The Proposition: The Dirty Business of Creating a Nation

To further complicate reading contemporary Australian westerns in terms of national identity, it is important to consider the context in which these films are produced and shown. Australia has a similar cinema market to other English-speaking countries, in that the dominance of Hollywood must be acknowledged not only in the attempts by Australian filmmakers to subvert this pressure through the creation of "homegrown" productions but also in negotiating the content of these productions in ways that allow them to engage audiences in competition with Hollywood films. In thinking about Australia as an English-language cinema, and what this means for its westerns, its antipodal position again becomes a key consideration. As O'Regan argues:

> Acutely posed are the problems of both its own distinctiveness and its own capacity to pass for being American and British. These structural characteristics see Australian cinema operating in conditions of permanent and unequal cultural exchange with respect to the international cinema(s). (1996: 110)

Australia, thus, is always intimately connected, through both its spatial position and colonial history, to both Britain and the United States. Furthermore, these connections carry over into each country's film markets, which creates a triangulation of influences on both form and content in Australian films that can be seen to play out in the western.

Specifically, we see this in returning to the bushranger genre. While the tensions between the outlaws (and the ordinary settlers that they represented) and the "sqauttocracy" of the rich landholders were the focus of the early bushranger films, this conflict was usually presented with a clear moral dualism: good (bushrangers and ordinary settlers) versus evil (rich landowners and their representatives). However, in order to present such a view, these films ignored dealing with any kind of native presence, and often continue to do so, as retellings such as *Ned Kelly* (Gregor Jordan, 2003) clearly illustrate when the complexities of colonial history are avoided by simply not including representations of the colonized. In many ways, this approach connects to reading Australian films as English-language cinema, in that films like *Ned Kelly* are easier to translate across similar markets with a broad appeal, for example, through their use of Hollywood-friendly stars.

In tracing the bushranger genre to the contemporary Australian western, however, films like *The Proposition* do increasingly grapple with the complicated questions arising from Australia's colonial history and the position of the Aboriginals. On the flip side of a modern day bushranging story like Jordan's *Ned Kelly*, which leans more toward "passing" as American or British, *The Proposition* focuses more on the distinctiveness of Australia and its layered history. Written by Nick Cave and directed by John Hillcoat, both Australians, the film explores the murkier morality of Australia's colonial history and refuses to offer a clear distinction between notions of good and evil. The film draws on the bushranger genre with the central conflict between the Burns brothers (Guy Pearce, Danny Huston and Richard Wilson), an outlaw gang, and the law, led by Captain Stanley (Ray Winstone) who is out to civilize the outback with his brand of British law and order. However, neither party is presented in a wholly sympathetic manner, and the internal tensions between the brothers contribute further to the ambiguity.

But what is perhaps most interesting about the development of the bushranger genre into a contemporary western here is the way *The Proposition* not only engages more fully with the outlaw/settler/colonial landlord conflicts but also presents the treatment of the Aboriginals without either promoting an assimilationist fantasy or incorporating them as a brief aside. *The Proposition* instead uses the Aboriginals to engage with issues relating to Australia's settlement in the late nineteenth century. These issues, when revisited from a contemporary standpoint, might offer insight into considering how Australia, through the western, conceives of its own history and identity.

The film opens with a warning:

> *Members of the Aboriginal and Torres Strait Islander communities are advised that this film contains images which may be offensive to indigenous people. It includes historical photographs of people now deceased.*

These photographs, depicting both Aboriginal people and white settlers, are shown against a black backdrop while the opening credits play. This serves to immediately enforce the historical context of the coming narrative, both through the warning, which emphasizes the authenticity of the photos, and through the subject matter, which largely focuses on the Aboriginal relationship with the white settlers, through photos of Aboriginal men dressed as soldiers or Aboriginal women working as domestics. These images, providing historical context for colonial life in Australia, will later be echoed in the narrative of the film. Interestingly, these photographs also feature the faces of actors from the film transposed onto the images, signaling the link between historical "accuracy" and the fictional world of the film from the very start. In this way, *The Proposition* immediately seeks to demonstrate a concern for historical accuracy in terms of the "look" of the film and its treatment of Aboriginals. (It is worth noting here that the extra features on the DVD spend a considerable amount of time on the historical accuracy the film was aiming for, including interviews with its Aboriginal actors.)

The almost haunting solemnity of the opening credits is immediately shattered as the film proper begins in the middle of a shoot-out, which finds two of the Burns brothers besieged in a shack by soldiers. The viewer quickly learns that the "proposition" referred to in the film's title is one offered to Charlie Burns (Pearce) after he and his younger brother Mikey (Wilson) are subsequently captured by Captain Stanley: Charlie must track down and kill his older brother Arthur (Huston) by Christmas Day, or Mikey will be hanged. After making his offer to Charlie, Captain Stanley emphasizes the deadly seriousness of it by striking Mikey across the face with his pistol. He then moves to look out of the window, and the next cut finally takes the camera out of the bullet-ridden shack that the first five minutes of the film takes place in—revealing "Australia" to the viewer. As the camera slowly pans across several soldiers and an Aboriginal digging graves for casualties of the shoot-out, the landscape is hazy from the oppressive heat. "Australia, what fresh hell is this?" Stanley murmurs, as he wipes sweat and grime from his face.

Within less than ten minutes, then, the film reveals the brutality of life in the Australian outback, from the overbearing heat and the noticeable filth that coats everyone, regardless of their station, to the violence exhibited by those on both sides of the law. There are no exceptions to violence in this film. Whites of all stripes mete it out and suffer it and the same goes for Aboriginals: a group of Aboriginals attack Charlie while he is looking for his brother while another scene features the grotesque rounding up and interrogation of Aboriginals by Stanley's men. The violence perpetuates further violence on all sides, and *The Proposition* uses this as a way of examining colonial expansion and oppression.

Australia's expansion can be thought of as circular, which distinguishes it from the expansion of the United States—which was a linear, western march across the continent. In Australia, the vastness of the outback meant that expansion moved outward from settlements, slowly and haphazardly. Aboriginals were still "emerging" from the outback in the 1960s, often completely unaware of the colonization that had been taking place over the last two hundred years or so. *The Proposition* deals explicitly with these spaces that colonialism cannot reach, without glorifying the outback as an idealized frontier. Captain Stanley cannot fulfill his orders from England to "civilize" the area, while Charlie, as an outlaw, is caught between the law of Captain Stanley, his criminal family connections, and the threat of trying to live outside civilization, where if the Aboriginals do not kill him, the harshness of the land just might. Meanwhile, the Aboriginals are being hunted down and killed, while they fight to keep their own land and way of life from the encroaching white settlements. There are no civilized spaces in *The Proposition*, and in this way, the landscape of the film resists simple divisions between civilization and the wild in the same way the characters resist simple moral classifications.

The blurred distinctions that *The Proposition* presents between the clear binary divisions that were found in the early bushranger films—law and outlaw, civilization and wilderness, and so on—confirm that a straightforward mapping of the codes of the Hollywood Western onto an Australian context challenges the expectation that it will elicit a similar mythology about nation-building. However, by approaching the western from a global perspective, where its codes are disengaged from a US origin, we can make connections between the way the western has been used to create a variety of dominant fictions in the United States and how it fails to construct such fictions in other countries. For example, Lee Broughton's (2016) work on European westerns highlights the ways in which the producers of westerns in Great Britain, Italy, and West Germany were able to restructure the codes of the Hollywood Western in order to include progressive representations of strong women, African Americans, and Native Americans, respectively, that reflected local cultural and political discourses concerning race and gender. In the case of Australia and *The Proposition*, the key component is the way that violence is deployed in conjunction with revised elements of the bushranger story in order to confront issues of national identity.

For Routt, *The Proposition* is not a bushranger western but rather an art film about violence—"a movie about faces and souls" (2005). He argues that the close-ups used throughout the film emphasize the characters and their more individual narratives as snapshots. While there is a focus on the "snapshots" of life in the outback throughout the film, and the themes of family and home are constantly being questioned, to disconnect the film from what I would argue are its bushranger roots is also to disconnect it from what makes the film Australian. To focus on these smaller narratives, and the fragmented narrative structure, suggests that the film could take place anywhere and that Australia is simply a backdrop for the depiction of "faces and souls." However, the explicit use of Australian history and national issues, clearly foregrounded in the opening photographic montage, immediately emphasizes that this is a story grounded in *terra nullius*, and that Australia is as much one of the film's characters as Captain Stanley or Charlie. The most intense moments of brotherly bonding between Charlie and Arthur take place as the brothers watch the sun set over the outback, where the landscape not only provides a backdrop to the action, but also serves as a reminder of *place*. In this way, the landscape constantly refers the viewer back to the fact that the film is Australian, be it through shots of sunsets over the emptiness of the outback or scenes featuring the rocky caves where Arthur takes refuge (specifically because neither the police or the Aboriginals will dare to enter the area). The landscape of Australia, then, is more than a backdrop to *The Proposition*—it is a highly visible site that defines the film as Australian and makes the conflicts and issues, familiar to the bushranger genre, distinctly national.

Felicity Collins also reads the film in terms of Australian history, focusing on the ways in which it works as an allegory of issues of colonial violence in Australia. For Collins, the intimacy of the close-ups Routt uses as the basis for his classification serve to deconstruct "a longstanding myth of Australia as a place where the transcendent image of the landscape redeems a melancholy settler history of incompetence and failure in a harsh new world" (2008: 65). This reading invites clear evidence of the failure of the Hollywood Western's dominant fiction to work in an Australian context, in that the violence plays out not as a nation-building force but rather as representative of the struggle to define a cohesive national identity among the fragmented occupants of the landscape. As a western, *The Proposition* foregrounds the connections between nation and space in its depiction of the land, and between nation (or lack of nation) and violence in the constant clashes between the various characters who fill the space.

Where Routt (2005), Collins (2008), and nearly all other critics agree is that the film can be compared to the revisionist westerns of, for example, Sergio Leone and Sam Peckinpah. Superficially, this is easy to see in the violence and the lack of a clear moral center or any kind of redemption. However, Will Self, in his review for *The Independent*, reads the film as more original than revisionist, in terms of the western genre. Self argues that Australia lacks the same history of westerns as America, in that there is no "classical" model of an Australian western for comparison (2006). In order for the film to be revisionist, then, it would have to be read comparatively with Hollywood Westerns, rather than in terms of its Australian influences. For Self, the revision comes not from revising Hollywood Westerns but rather from the way the film engages with the bushranger stories of early cinema, a point with which I would readily agree.

These bushranger stories, which are revised from a contemporary perspective here, provide the basis for reading violence in terms of national identity. If the early bushranger stories deployed violence in support of clear binaries between law and outlaw, English enforcers and "Australian" (typically Irish) settlers, *The Proposition* returns to this mythology from a far more complicated contemporary position. Collins proposes that the film, rather than "redeeming the past for new national myths," might instead serve as a model for realizing "a different history, one that might recognize the potential of a 'Secondworldish' subjectivity—at home with defeat—to transform national identity into something other than a 'sacred parable' built on the hellish repetition of violence and catastrophe" (2008: 69). In this way, *The Proposition* can be read as revisionist not only in terms of its generic labels but also in terms of rethinking the national history the film seeks to depict. Here, at last, we see glimpses of cinematic rewritings of a national history, as *The Proposition* returns to the "violence and catastrophe" of the bushranger era but reworks the conventions of the bushranger genre to avoid the simple binary divisions of the early bushranger films.

Conclusion

As the epigraph of this chapter suggests, the bushranger genre hinges on the interaction between landscape, history, and the bushranger figure in relation to communities. As one of the earliest forms of distinctly Australian film, the genre offers a clear connection between nation and film. However, early bushranger films work from basic binary divisions, for example between law and outlaw, and often operate from a place of moral dualism where it is easy to define the moral natures of the sides in a conflict. From *The Story of the Kelly Gang* and the bushranger genre more generally to contemporary films, westerns in Australia have changed and developed in a global context, where funding, stars, and even generic elements are all affected by relationships between Australia and other markets. In particular, these contemporary films seek to create a local dominant fiction by engaging with Australia's colonial past by drawing on both the bushranger and the western genres.

While *The Proposition* is grounded in Australian history and context, it also fails to capture a dominant Australian identity that might function as a unifying national mythology as the dualism of the early bushranger films ultimately begins to break down. As *The Proposition* delves more deeply into the murky colonial past, it moves further away from a dominant fiction by breaking down the oppositional binaries fundamental to Rancière's definition. The settlers are no longer a single, definable group, and even the distinction between law and outlaw—a key element at the center of the bushranger genre—no longer holds firm. Finally, *The Proposition* fully revises the bushranger genre in returning to the violence of the era but from a modern perspective. By attempting to give equal consideration to Aboriginals, the English colonial forces, and the Kelly-esque outlaws, the film offers not a mythology of a unified nation but rather something darker, and perhaps more realistic. Here, the colonial past of Australia, and the way it shaped any conception of the nation, is not the "sacred parable" put forth in the bushranger films, but rather a violent allegory of the traumatic colonial past.

Bibliography

Abel, Richard. *The Red Rooster Scare: Making Cinema American, 1900–1910*. Berkeley: University of California, 1999.

Boldrewood, Rolf. *Robbery under Arms: A Story of Life and Adventure in the Bush and in the Goldfields of Australia*. Vol. 510. London: Oxford University Press, 1949.

Broughton, Lee. *The Euro-Western: Reframing Gender, Race and the "Other" in Film*. London: I.B. Tauris, 2016.

Burgoyne, Robert. *Film Nation: Hollywood Looks at U.S. History*. Revised ed. Minneapolis: University of Minnesota, 2010.

Collins, Felicity. "Historical Fiction and the Allegorical Truth of Colonial Violence in *The Proposition*." *Cultural Studies Review*, 14, no. 1 (2008): 55–71.

The Fitzpatrick Incident, *Culture Victoria*, 2016. Available online at: https://cv.vic.gov.au/stories/a-diverse-state/ambush-ned-kelly-and-the-stringybark-creek-murders/the-fitzpatrick-incident/ (accessed January 22, 2019).

Kitses, Jim. "Authorship and Genre: Notes on the Western." In *The Film Studies Reader*, edited by Joanne Hollows, Peter Hutchings, and Mark Jancovich, 57–68. London: Hodder Arnold, 2000 [1969].

O'Regan, Tom. *Australian National Cinema*. London: Routledge, 1996.

Rancière, Jacques. "Interview: The Image of Brotherhood." *Edinburgh 77 Magazine*, 2 (1977): 26–31.

Routt, William D. "The Evening Redness of the West." *The Age*, October 1, (2005). Available online at: http://www.theage.com.au/news/film/the-evening-redness-in-the-west/2005/09/29/1127804605041.html (accessed March 12, 2012).

Routt, William D. "More Australian than Aristotelian: The Australian Bushranger Film, 1904–1914." *Senses of Cinema*, 18 (2001). Available online at: http://sensesofcinema. com/2001/feature-articles/oz_western/ (accessed March 12, 2012).

Self, Will. "The Proposition: Bringing the Revisionist Western to the Australian Outback." *The Independent*, March 3, (2006). Available online at: http://www.independent.co.uk/ arts-entertainment/films/features/the-proposition-bringing-the-revisionist-western-to-the-australian-outback-468212.html (accessed April 15, 2012).

Silverman, Kaja. *Male Subjectivity at the Margins*. New York: Routledge, 1992.

Wark, McKenzie. "Cinema II: The Next Hundred Years." In *A Century of Australian Cinema*, edited by James Sabine, 198–212. Port Melbourne: William Heinemann.

Wister, Owen. *The Virginian: A Horseman of the Plains*. New York: The MacMillan Company, 1902.

Part Three

Contemporary Cult Westerns and Contemporary Concerns

9

The Return of the Repressed:
Locating the Supernatural in US Civil War
Westerns

Lee Broughton

Introduction

The American Civil War (1861–65) is a historical conflict of such enormity that
a public memory of the event persists worldwide. However, public memory
concerning the war within the United States itself remains highly contested, with
outlooks being dictated by factors such as geographical location, family history,
and personal politics. In seeking to determine how Americans made sense—
and, indeed, continue to make sense—of the war, Gary W. Gallagher (2008)
has identified a number of major interpretive traditions. Up until the 1960s,
much of Hollywood's Civil War–related output drew upon just two of these
traditions. "The Lost Cause tradition" sought to "cast the South's experiment
in nation-building as an admirable struggle against hopeless odds, played
down the importance of slavery in bringing secession and war, and ascribed to
Confederates constitutional high-mindedness and gallantry on the battlefield"
while the "Reconciliation Cause tradition" "represented an attempt by white
people North and South to extol the *American* [Gallagher's emphasis] virtues
both sides manifested during the war, to exalt the restored nation that emerged
from the conflict, and to mute the role of African Americans" (2008: 2).

Another major interpretive tradition identified by Gallagher is the
"Emancipation Cause tradition" (2008: 2). This tradition "interpreted the war
as a struggle to liberate 4 million slaves and remove a cancerous influence on
American society and politics" (2008: 2). While mild references to this tradition
were found in some Hollywood Civil War–related films during the 1960s, its
presence became more prominent in Westerns produced during the early 1970s.

This chapter will critically consider how all three of these traditions are employed in a range of US Civil War–related films that also incorporate supernatural elements. In horror studies, Sigmund Freud's (2001 [1957]) work on repression has been adapted in order to argue that supernatural activity represents the "return" of the repressed (the repressed usually being a painful or disturbing memory or action). Ultimately, by determining which of Gallagher's interpretive traditions they foreground and considering what painful or disturbing public memories or actions might be represented by the films' supernatural elements, I will seek to establish whether the films under review—three American productions and one Italian production—offer an unorthodox representation of the US Civil War that might in turn provide interesting insights into national unity, race relations, and the state of their respective nations more generally at the time of their production.

The American Civil War on Film

In the course of discussing Hollywood's frequent use of the Reconciliation Cause tradition, Brian Steel Wills suggests that "the Civil War often found itself mistaken for the West in films, as producers sought to exploit both worlds in a fashion that would not offend supporters (and ticket-paying moviegoers) of either North or South" (2007: 97). While Hollywood's need to turn a profit must of course be taken into consideration as a contextual factor, it would seem that the content of Hollywood's Civil War-themed Westerns from the 1960s was also informed by more forthrightly ideological and political concerns too. Robert J. Cook indicates that preparations for the Civil War's centennial commemorations at the start of the decade revealed tangible differences in the way that significant numbers of Southerners and Northerners wished to remember and memorialize different aspects of the war (2007: 52).

This apparent lack of a national consensus with regard to how the Civil War should be commemorated was further complicated by the fact that America was making preparations for an ever-deeper physical involvement in the war in Vietnam while also fighting the ideological Cold War on several fronts. As a consequence, Hollywood seemingly felt duty-bound to produce Civil War films that showed a united American nation fighting a common enemy. Sam Peckinpah's *Major Dundee* (1965) is perhaps the classic example of this ideological approach in practice. In this film Northern Union troops, Southern

Confederate prisoners and a motley group of frontiersmen become reconciled before banding together and becoming a fearless volunteer fighting force that travels to Mexico in order to engage an army of renegade Indians.

Possibly reflecting the advances being made by the civil rights movement in America during the early 1960s, there are hints of the Emancipation Cause tradition to be found in *Major Dundee*. Brave black Union troopers are briefly featured and a Confederate soldier causes outrage when he expects one of them to act deferentially. However, perhaps reflecting the more militant attitudes of the contemporaneous Black Power movement and the concomitant popularity of Blaxploitation films, the tradition would feature more prominently in Hollywood's Civil War Westerns during the early 1970s. For example, in Larry G. Spangler's *The Soul of Nigger Charley* (1973) the renegade former slave Charley (Fred Williamson) and his band of ethnic brothers fight against rogue Confederates who have refused to accept that the Civil War has ended. In their efforts to establish a colony in Mexico, the Confederates are press-ganging free African Americans into becoming their slaves until Charley intervenes and frees them. Clearly the presence of the Emancipation Cause tradition in Civil War Westerns is a useful tool for examining race relations in America more generally at the time of a film's production.

American Films, the Civil War, and Horror

Cynthia J. Miller and A. Bowdoin Van Riper note that the "supernatural first began to menace the West on-screen in the late 1950s" when Edward Dein's *Curse of the Undead* (1959) was released (2016: 32). *Curse of the Undead* is an innovative horror Western that deftly transposes tropes more commonly associated with vampire films to its old West setting. But while *Curse of the Undead*'s singular content offered a bold new direction for both the horror film and the Western, Hollywood was slow to respond and horror Westerns remained relatively scant in number until the turn of the new millennium when their numbers began to increase substantially.

One Civil War-oriented film of interest to this chapter is Herschel Gordon Lewis's *Two Thousand Maniacs!* (1964) which was released toward the end of the Civil War's centennial commemoration period. Although Lewis's film is not strictly a Western, it does likely mark the first time that an American Civil War–related film had been infused with extreme horror elements. Karl Betts of the Civil War Centennial Commission had called for popular entertainments that would involve the whole community to be incorporated into the Commission's program of celebrations (Cook 2007: 46–47) and Lewis appears to have taken this appeal to heart when writing *Two Thousand Maniacs!* Similarly, the Commission's chairman Ulysses S. Grant III had recommended that the themes of local centennial commemorations should "not be directed from Washington: they should spring into being in response to the wish of the people in each political subdivision" (quoted in Cook 2007: 35) and the Southerners in Lewis's film follow this recommendation to the letter, cooking up celebrations that reflect their own murderous desire for revenge against the Yankees. The Southern historian Bell Wiley had told the Commission that he hoped any celebrations would "avoid any sort of activity that will tend to revive the bitterness and hatred engendered by the conflict of a century ago" (quoted in Cook 2007: 34) and the centennial celebrations found in *Two Thousand Maniacs!* play as if Lewis was pointedly going out of his way to mock Wiley's words.

Here six hapless Yankees are lured to the rural Southern town of Pleasant Valley on the pretext that they will play the part of honored guests in the locals' Civil War centennial commemorations. However, it transpires that the town is actually populated by the ghosts of Confederates who were slaughtered there one hundred years earlier by renegade Union soldiers. These Southern phantoms now have a limited amount of time in which to exact their revenge against the modern day Yankees. As part of Pleasant Valley's celebrations Bea Miller (Shelby Livingston) is hacked to death before being served up as the centerpiece for the centennial's communal barbecue, while John Miller (Jerome Eden) is torn limb from limb when his arms and legs are tied to four horses. Later on, David Wells (Michael Korb) is forced into a barrel that is lined with metal spikes before being rolled down a bumpy hill and spiked to death while Beverly Wells (Yvonne Gilbert) is the centerpiece in a funfair like game: she is placed below a high steel tower that has a large boulder balanced at its top. The boulder falls and crushes her as a prize for the lucky local who manages to hit a mechanically connected target with a softball.

As noted earlier, the Civil War–related Westerns that were produced by Hollywood at this time sought to promote narratives that managed to show a united America on screen via the employment of the Reconciliation Cause tradition. By contrast, *Two Thousand Maniacs!* comprehensively flies in the face of Hollywood's harmonious approach and instead delights in telling a story that reveals that old regional animosities still run deep. Similarly, there is little evidence of the Lost Cause tradition and its attendant notion of Southern gallantry on the battlefield to be found here. If we were to conduct a surface reading of *Two Thousand Maniacs!*

today we might conclude that the film was an early take on the backwoods horror genre that also cleverly incorporated timely satirical comment regarding America's Civil War centennial commemorations. However, deeper considerations of the political symbolism (not least, the plethora of enthusiastically waved Confederate battle flags on display) and the anti-Northern sentiments (the town's children amuse themselves by lynching a cat that has a label that sports the words "damn Yankee" attached to it) that are found in *Two Thousand Maniacs!* might—when viewed with the defiant mood of the contemporary South in mind—result in a more radically subversive reading of the film. Lewis and his producer David F. Friedman produced their films primarily for sale to Southern exhibitors, and they actually shot *Two Thousand Maniacs!* in St Augustine, Florida using enthusiastic locals as extras. As such, it could be argued that the film did perhaps capture the more extreme aspects of the local zeitgeist.

Indeed, this is one conflict that the South wins. The film's nominal Northern hero Tom (William Kerwin) is actually an ineffectual and emasculated academic who never gets physical with the Southerners. He only manages to initiate his and Terry's (Connie Mason) escape by duping a child into revealing the whereabouts of his car keys. During the escape, one of the Southerners, Harper (Mark Douglas), appears to have been killed, but his apparent death is accidental—he runs into a pool of quicksand while chasing Tom and Terry. Even this strike against the South counts for nothing as Harper rises from the quicksand to return to his proper resting place with the rest of the town's revenants at the film's end. So the final kill count remains "4" to the Southerners and "0" to the Northerners. The Confederate phantoms depicted in *Two Thousand Maniacs!*— and the anti-Northern sentiments that they express—would seem to represent the return of the repressed in the form of sectional attitudes that challenge Hollywood's tales of North-South reconciliation. Furthermore, the film's ending suggests that the phantoms' hate—and, by extension, the ill will harbored by some contemporary Southerners—will endure forever, with the inhabitants of Pleasant Valley returning again and again, every hundred years, to wreak violent vengeance on future generations of Yankees.

The US Civil War on Film: The Italian Context

It should of course be acknowledged that American filmmakers are not the only filmmakers who have made US Civil War–related Westerns and, by extension,

Civil War–related horror Westerns. As I have argued elsewhere (Broughton 2016a), when Italian-made Spaghetti Westerns that feature American Civil War–related scenarios are viewed with Italy's own historical North-South conflicts in mind, it is often possible to detect instances where the films' employment of symbols from American history appear to be being used in order to allegorically pass comment on specific episodes from Italy's own history.

Such episodes include the North-South civil war (which ran from 1861 to 1865, the same years as its American counterpart) that ensued when Southern rebels became insurgent agitators and bandits following Italy's unification, which had been secured via the Northern Kingdom of Piedmont's annexation of the Southern Kingdom of the Two Sicilies (Davis 1988). Similarly, during the final years of the Second World War (1943–45) Italy was split into two states that were caught up in another North-South conflict. The newly formed Royalist Kingdom of the South had become both occupied by and militarily aligned with the Allies while the fascist Italian Social Republic that had been established in the north of Italy was both occupied by and militarily aligned with Nazi Germany. Small armies that fought alongside their respective allies were raised by both of these Italian states and there were occasions when these Italian armies met face-to-face on the battlefield (Lamb 1993: 190), effectively finding themselves at the center of the Allies and the Germans' larger North-South conflict.

John A. Davis notes that, during the Italian Civil War of 1861–65, the Northern Piedmontese authorities dealt with the insurgent activities of Southern rebels by simply ordering "more cavalry patrols and more troops" to carry out more "mass executions" (1988: 173). Similarly, massacres carried out by the Nazis and the Fascists in Northern Italy toward the end of the Second World War are well documented (Lamb 1993). Significantly, the Italian Westerns that feature US Civil War scenarios often tend to code their Northern Union officers as invading fascist-like authoritarians who act in cruel and merciless ways that ultimately bring them into conflict with Southern Confederate foot soldiers who are coded as brave and noble individuals (Broughton 2016a). Clear examples of this approach can be found in films such as Alfonso Brescia's *Days of Violence* (*I giorni della violenza*, 1967) and Leon Klimovsky's *Raise Your Hands, Dead Man, You're Under Arrest* (*Su le mani, cadavere! Sei in arresto*, 1971).

During the 1960s and early 1970s a number of Italian films from a variety of genres—examples include Luchino Visconti's *Rocco and his Brothers* (*Rocco e i suoi fratelli*, 1960) and the same director's *The Leopard* (*Il gattopardo*, 1963)— employed Northern and Southern symbolism that appeared to pass comment on the state of the nation, both past and present, and the Spaghetti Westerns cited earlier can be understood to be part of this wider trend. These films were topical and captured the local zeitgeist since an acute North-South economic and cultural divide had caused much disunity in Italy during the 1950s and 1960s. Since a sense of unity between the North and South of Italy was not an obvious feature of their understanding of Italian history or of their lived experience, the producers of US Civil War–related Spaghetti Westerns were thus inclined to pointedly reject the themes of reconciliation that were promoted in Hollywood's contemporaneous Civil War Westerns. Furthermore, Charlotte Heath-Kelly notes the sense of continuity that has been assumed to link Italy's internal political struggles during the Second World War and the fratricidal terrorist violence (a civil war of sorts fought between the extreme political left and the extreme political right) that divided the nation during the "years of lead" that ran from the late 1960s to the early 1980s (2013: 35).

Sergio Garrone's Spaghetti Western *Django the Bastard* (*Django il bastardo*, 1969) is distinguished in two interesting ways: it is a supernatural Civil War Western and its storyline appears to allegorically reference the key moment in the Second World War that divided Italy both politically and geographically while also sowing the seeds for the country's future internal conflicts. Italy surrendered to the Allies on September 3, 1943, and a public announcement to this effect was made on September 8, 1943. Pietro Badoglio's government and the country's monarch, King Victor Emmanuel III, hurriedly left Rome and set up new headquarters in Brindisi on the South East coast of Italy under the protection of the Allies in the new Kingdom of the South. A lack of clear instructions from the Italian High Command on September 8, 1943—and a subsequent breakdown in communications—resulted in military chaos. On the ground, "many officers . . . decided not to face up to their responsibilities to their men, slipping away themselves without telling them or leaving them with any orders or guidance" (Morgan 2007: 100). Some Italian regiments, who assumed that the Germans were now their enemy, attempted to hold their positions and were duly executed by the Nazis when they subsequently tried to surrender (Lamb 1993: 2). Emilio Gentile describes the actions of Badoglio, his government and the King as "a ruling class abandoning its responsibilities of command to take flight" (2009: 211) while Philip Morgan observes that "the sense that they had been abandoned and let down by their officers featured strongly in the memories of the aftermath of 8 September" (2007: 100). Claudio Pavone quotes the testimony of an Italian soldier who opined that "it was our leaders . . . who sold us out" (2013: 57).

Django the Bastard tells the story of a vengeful Confederate revenant, Django (Anthony Steffen), who suddenly appears years after he and the rest of his regiment were massacred by Union troops. Cadaverous-looking, impassive, and dressed all in black, Django sports a threadbare black poncho with severely frayed and ragged seams that serve to make his spectral profile even more ghost-like. Although he is physically present—and thus seemingly susceptible to physical injuries and impediments (much like Clint Eastwood's characters in *High Plains Drifter* [Eastwood, 1973] and *Pale Rider* [Eastwood, 1985])— Django does appear and disappear with supernatural ease and, at a formal level, the film knowingly draws upon many of the tropes of the supernatural horror film. Django alerts his victims to his intentions by dramatically presenting them with grave marker-like wooden crosses that have their name and date of death (that very day's date) inscribed on them. It transpires that his three targets—Sam Hawkens (Victoriano Gazzarra), Howard Ross (Jean Louis), and Rod Murdock (Paolo Gozlino)—were his regiment's traitorous commanding officers.

In the film's explanatory flashback a Confederate trooper called Evans returns to the regiment's camp with a bottle of whiskey that he found while on patrol. Django wants a glass of it but Evans explains that "some of the boys think that we should give it to the officers." However, when the pair enter the officers' tent they are nowhere to be seen. Evans observes that it "looks like they've all gone, deserted, left us! I don't understand, why would they do that?" When Evans and Django search for their colleague Collins, who is supposed to be on watch, they find him dead with Major Murdock's knife in his back. Evans is suddenly shot and Django raises the alarm as Union troops mount a surprise attack. Despite their attempts to rally an impromptu defense, the whole regiment is soon massacred by the Union troops while Murdock, Howard, and Hawkens look on from a safe distance. Thus, in common with a significant number of other Spaghetti Westerns, *Django the Bastard* presents its Southern Confederate foot soldiers as brave and noble individuals and its Northern Union troops as merciless aggressors.

The basic narrative structure of the flashback (the regiment's officers deserting and leaving their men at the mercy of the enemy), the symbolism employed (the stab in the back), and the tone of the scene's dialogue can be fruitfully compared to events in Italy on September 8, 1943, at a micro level (officers deserting individual regiments) and the macro level (Badoglio, his High Command, and the King deserting the center and north of Italy) and the fatalities that ensued in both cases. Furthermore, the words that Django uses when he finally confronts Major Murdock—"they were all brave soldiers in our regiment . . . [but they were] deserted, sold out . . . their own officers betrayed them"—sound like they could just as easily have been said by an Italian soldier providing testimony about their September 8, 1943, experiences. Claudio Pavone indicates that the trauma of the events that unfolded inside Italy during the final years of the Second World War prompted a tendency for Italians to "forget a past charged with sufferings that could not easily be re-processed in memory" (2013: 6). As such, if it is accepted that the spectral Django represents the return of the repressed (suppressed memories of Italy's the Second World War experiences on and following September 8, 1943), the content of *Django the Bastard*'s flashback can be read as a necessarily coded way of addressing national memories that were still raw, painful, and rarely openly discussed even though they were continuing to have a direct effect on Italian politics and society at the time of the film's release.

American-Made US Civil War–Related Horror Films

As noted earlier, the presence of the Emancipation Cause tradition in Civil War Westerns is a useful tool for examining race relations in America more generally at the time of a film's production. And race relations in America during the early 1990s suffered a highly testing time, sparked primarily by the beating of Rodney King. As Ronald N. Jacobs reports:

> [In Los Angeles] on March 3, 1991, an African American motorist, Rodney King, was pulled over for speeding. After a brief chase, King was met by twenty-one police officers. . . . In full view of all who were present, King was severely beaten by three white LAPD officers. . . . The event was videotaped by an amateur cameraman, George Holliday, . . . and subsequently broadcast on television thousands of times. (2000: 81)

The outrage that the footage provoked would subsequently be eclipsed by the outrage that followed King's assaulters' court case. As Lynn Mie Itagaki notes, "In April 1992, the acquittal and mistrial verdicts of the four police officers involved . . . sparked one of the most deadly and destructive civil disturbances in U.S. history" (2016: xvi). In the same year the legal scholar and civil rights activist Derrick Bell opined that "racism is an integral, permanent, and indestructible component of this society" (1992: ix) while the political scientist Andrew

Hacker argued that "a huge racial chasm remains, and there are few signs that the coming century will see it closed" (2003 [1992]: 219).

George Hickenlooper's *Grey Knight* (1993) is a Civil War–related horror film that appears to reflect the debates on race relations that were taking place in America at the time of its production. In the commentary track on the 2004 Vanguard Cinema DVD release of *Grey Knight*, director Hickenlooper and the film's writer Matt Greenberg briefly allude to the fact that the film's content does tangentially resonate with contemporaneous events without actually indicating whether they purposefully intended the film to be a comment on race relations in America at that time. For example, Hickenlooper recalls at one point that

> it was real interesting because here we are dealing with these issues of racism during the Civil War and every day when we drive to the set we pass by the Simi Valley Courthouse, where just two months before they had basically acquitted the four policemen accused of beating Rodney King. (2004)

And when discussing the film's flashbacks, which depict slave traders massacring natives in Africa, Hickenlooper recounts that

> we needed to get fifteen African American guys basically to play these Africans who are hunted down by the slave traders . . . keep in mind that we shot this film three months after the 1992 Los Angeles riots so tensions were still really high. . . . So we get up to the set that morning, these fifteen guys get off the bus, they say to me "So, what are we doing today?" I said, "Well, you're going to take off all of your clothes and we're going to put [tribal] paint on you and we're going to have you chased around by a bunch of fat white guys with guns." And you can imagine that didn't go over too well. (2004)

In any event, it can be argued that *Grey Knight* captures the zeitgeist of early 1990s America.

Set in Tennessee in 1863, the film at first appears to put the Reconciliation Cause tradition at the center of its narrative. Here the Union's General Howarth (Martin Sheen) sends two of his officers, Captain John Harling (Adrian Pasdar) and Colonel George Thalman (Ray Wise), and a small unit of men to investigate reports that members of the Confederacy's 51st Alabama regiment have risen from the grave and are now attacking both Northern and Southern troops alike under the command of Major Josiah Elkins (Roger Wilson). Also traveling with Harling and Thalman is Colonel Nehemiah Strayn (Corbin Bernsen), a Confederate prisoner of war and the erstwhile commander of the 51st Alabama regiment who saw Elkins and the rest of his men die when Union soldiers, who refused to accept their surrender, massacred them (an element of the Lost Cause tradition is thus present here too).

Passing comment on reports that Elkins's new regiment is recruiting men from the ranks of both the Union and the Confederate regiments that they defeat, Howarth observes, "Sometimes in this war, things get very confused. Particularly in our border states of Missouri and Kentucky where there are so many young men fighting each other from the same extended family. Blue and Grey is not always black and white for any of us here in Kentucky." His words suggest that the two sides have more in common than the war would indicate, and, further to Elkins's recruitment policy signaling an act of North-South reconciliation of sorts, Harling also finds himself at the center of a number of North-South reconciliations. At a personal and a professional level he reconciles with the Confederate Strayn, his former mentor who he had subsequently fallen out with following their duel over the love of a woman. And, at the film's end, Harling's Yankee unit teams up with the remnants of the Confederacy's 31st Tennessee regiment in order to fight Elkins's supernatural soldiers together. Throughout the film, period photographs of real casualties and diegetic images of maimed men, mass burials, and field hospital procedures hammer home the horrors of war. Given the nature of Howarth's comments noted earlier, on one level it might be that the return of the repressed signaled by the supernatural in *Grey Knight* is the tragedy of fratricidal fighting, as actually experienced in the Civil War and as depicted throughout the film. A more pointed comment on this is made toward the film's end when the Confederate Strayn begins to defiantly whistle the Union army's rallying song "Yankee Doodle" as he walks away from a final meeting with Elkins, who subsequently screams "we're brothers Nehemiah."

However, there is a further level of reconciliation that, in the course of being enacted, offers a further example of the film's supernatural elements signaling the return of another repressed, namely the horrors of the slave trade, Southern slavery, and racism. This story strand ultimately sees *Grey Knight* robustly employing the Emancipation Cause tradition. When Strayn is first introduced he is an openly racist individual. When he has his boots cleaned and his face shaved by African Americans after being released from his prison cell, he tries to rile them by saying, "Great service boys, just like home." Furthermore Rebecca (Cynda Williams), a mute runaway slave who survived an attack by Elkins's men, is traveling with Harling's unit and when Strayn first sees her he asks, "She gonna be shining our boots?" When he is subsequently shackled to her, Strayn protests "You can't chain me to a nigger. You can't humiliate me this way."

In a later conversation with Harling, Strayn observes that "God is a Southerner," to which Harling replies, "You think he keeps slaves too?" Strayn comes back with "Since when has this war been about slavery? I don't own a slave, most of my army don't. That's how the South works. Until we come up with something better on our own terms, that's the way it'll stay." When Harling protests, "I don't think that's a popular opinion, Colonel," Strayn suggests, "Why don't we put it to a vote?" This leads a showboating Strayn to put a series of votes to the Union troops around him: "Hey boys! How many of y'all think the South should listen to Mr. Lincoln?" The response is a resounding "yes." But when he asks, "Think niggers should vote?" the response is a resounding "no." The idea that both Northerners and Southerners would deny African Americans the vote—and thus deny them a political voice—can be symbolically linked to the fact that the mute Rebecca also lacks a voice. Furthermore, given the outcome of the trial of Rodney King's beaters, it could also be argued that Rebecca's muteness represents the African American community's own lack of a significant voice in early 1990s America.

However, Rebecca possesses the knowledge needed to defeat Elkins's supernatural soldiers, and she chooses to communicate this knowledge by establishing a telepathic link with Strayn. Telepathically projected flashbacks reveal that slavers operating in Africa slaughtered a local tribe who had been tasked with ensuring that a supremely evil force never be permitted to escape from a hole in the ground that it had been cast into. When the head slaver enters the hole, he emerges possessed and the force is subsequently transported to America. Rebecca's ancestors had managed to reinter the force in a cave beneath a river in Tennessee, but when Strayn encounters his reanimated dead nephew Thomas (A. J. Langer) in the cave, the 51st Alabama regiment's drummer boy explains that Union cannon fire during the massacre of Strayn's regiment facilitated its escape and allowed it to bring Elkins and his men back to life as evil revenants.

When discussing this scene, Hickenlooper observes, "Basically . . . the origin of all this conflict that they're dealing with stems from this cave, which was imported again from Africa by the slave traders" (2004). While this observation would seem to clearly suggest that the slave trade itself is being metaphorically blamed for the conflict in the film and, by extension, conflict in American society during the early 1990s, Matt Greenberg is keen to ensure that no viewer gets the impression that the film's narrative is demonizing Africa or African Americans when he adds:

> It's not so much a black or white issue. . . . Africa is the origins of man. . . . Africa is where originated man, his angels *and* his demons essentially . . . the whole metaphor of course of having a slave trader bring back that evil obviously in

his line of work, which in and of itself was borne of greed and thoughtlessness
. . . it's kind of, in one sense, metaphorical of our attitudes towards third world
countries today. (2004)

This insight from the film's writer appears to indicate that, from his point of view,
Grey Knight was not a conscious comment on contemporaneous race relations
in America during the early 1990s.

When Thomas bites Strayn, he becomes infected by the evil and needs to
consume blood, but Rebecca nurses him and lets him feed on her blood, which
effects a cure. This transfer of bodily fluids—and the intimate but platonic nature
of Rebecca's nursing—effects other changes in Strayn: his racism is eradicated
and he comes to care for Rebecca, as is evidenced when he gently holds and
assists her when she struggles to walk over rough country. Furthermore, with
his formerly closed mind now symbolically opened, Strayn is able to hold
conversations with Rebecca (who speaks to him telepathically) and enjoy a sense
of physical closeness with her. So much so that Harling makes the following
entry about Strayn and Rebecca in his diary:

> My only question [is] his newly found friendship with the Negress. It concerns
> me to the degree that he could lose his credibility with any surviving members
> of the [Confederacy's] 51st should we encounter them. I also fear it disturbs
> Thalman's [Union] men, whose own disposition to the darker race is really no
> different than our brethren to the South.

This diary entry serves as a reminder that racism in America—both historically
and in the early 1990s if Rodney King's beating is accepted to have had a racial
dimension—cannot be classed as a purely Southern phenomenon. But, equally,
Strayn and Rebecca's developing relationship also serves as a reminder that not
all Southerners were or are racist. When Harling subsequently barks, "Don't
you talk to her," Strayn defends Rebecca's right to be acknowledged as a person
and an individual by spitting back, "'she' has a name." Strayn eventually gifts his
prized silver pocket watch to Rebecca with the words, "I want you to have this.
My daddy'd kill me if he knew I'd given his watch to a Negr . . . nice girl like you."
The positive way in which Strayn and Rebecca's relationship develops serves to
show that an individual's racist outlooks are not necessarily fixed in perpetuity.

In the film's tumultuous final battle, Rebecca joins in the fighting and uses a
pistol loaded with silver bullets to kill one of the supernatural soldiers. She also
wounds Elkins and intervenes physically when he attacks Strayn. Her actions
result in Elkins infecting her, and she elects to sacrifice herself by shooting

a silver bullet into her own chest (which results in her letting out a piercing scream), knowing that it will pass through her and also penetrate Elkins, who has grabbed her from behind. As she lies gravely wounded, the formerly mute Rebecca begins to quietly sing to herself. There appears to be much of symbolic interest occurring in Rebecca's final scene. As I have discussed in detail elsewhere (Broughton, 2016b), the American Western's prescriptive representational "rules" regarding African American characters handling guns and shooting at white characters in Hollywood Westerns began to be relaxed in the early 1970s during the Blaxploitation film boom. It is therefore interesting to note that in *Grey Knight*, a film produced during a peak in racial tensions in America, a black woman who takes up arms and kills white men (even if they are monstrous enemies of the protagonists) must subsequently suffer the gravest of narrative punishments. As a further point of comparison that confirms a reversal in the fortunes of assertive black characters in American-made Westerns at this time, Ned Logan (Morgan Freeman) suffers a similarly grave narrative punishment in Clint Eastwood's *Unforgiven* (1992).

Furthermore, Rebecca finds her voice after she has enacted violence against white characters and has subsequently begun to take on a monstrous form, which necessitates her destruction and Harling finishes her off in spite of Strayn's emotional protests. Of this narrative turn, Hickenlooper observes, "By itself, in the context, when she begins to speak—this black slave woman—she's silenced— mercifully, of course, by Harling—but nevertheless silenced, which to me says a lot about race relations" (2004). Here Hickenlooper appears to point toward a meaningful metaphor, perhaps the idea that any genuine appeal for a "voice" that may have been enacted within but overshadowed by the violent and "monstrous" acts that were committed during the Los Angeles riots of 1992 could never succeed. This ultimately results, initially at least, in a conservative reading of the film's ending. However, Rebecca is duly eulogized when Harling observes, "She was brave, sir," and Strayn replies, "Braver than you know." And as something of a coda, a voiceover by Harling informs the viewer that Strayn subsequently "escaped from Bowling Green prison and rejoined the Confederate army. . . . Though still an ardent believer in the Southern cause, he made many enemies there by his outspoken stance against slavery." Thus Rebecca is acknowledged to have left a mark on the world and to have had some small impact on race relations more generally.

In terms of African Americans finding a "voice," the 2000s appear to be significant years. Colin Powell (2001–05) and Condoleezza Rice (2005–09) both held the position of America's top diplomat when they served as the Secretary of State and in 2009 Barack Obama became the forty-fourth president of the United States. However, race relations would still continue to be tested. For example, Hillary Potter observes how in 2005 the "devastating effects of Hurricane Katrina revealed to the nation and the world that the United States continues to suffer from considerable racial and class iniquities" when the US government's delayed response to the needs of storm-ravaged New Orleans and its mostly disadvantaged African American population prompted much criticism and outrage (2007: ix).

In the middle of the 2000s, a further American-made Civil War–related horror film was produced, Alex Turner's *Dead Birds* (2004), in which historical depictions of race relations appeared to pass comment on present day America. Set in Alabama in 1863, *Dead Birds* does not reference the Reconciliation Cause tradition—there are no Yankees present for the film's Southern characters to be reconciled with and they are quite happy to kill other Southerners—which might be reflective of the various political divides that were being fostered in America during the 2000s. Equally, there is no reference to the Lost Cause tradition. There is, however, an interesting analogue of an idealized modern American society present here. William (Henry Thomas) leads a band of Southerners who have turned against the Confederacy. Among their number are two of the Western's traditional "Others"—a strong woman, Annabelle (Nicki Aycox), and a free African American, Todd (Isaiah Washington)—who essentially operate on equal terms with the white men (Sam [Patrick Fugit], Clyde [Michael Shannon] and Joseph [Mark Boone Junior]) who make up the rest of the band. However, their anti-Confederacy activities are not altruistic in nature. The gang plans and executes a violent bank robbery, which sees them stealing Confederate gold and killing Confederate soldiers and Southern citizens in the process. Just like the rest of the band, Annabelle and Todd both kill innocent white men during the robbery and—in terms of the "rules" that govern the representation of both strong women and assertive African Americans and the rules that pass judgment on amoral actions in American Westerns (see Broughton 2016b)— their callous and greed-motivated activities suggest that they will be punished later in the film's narrative. Indeed, when William accidentally kills a child as the gang makes its escape, the gang's punishment seems inevitable.

The microcosm of modern American society that the anti-Confederate gang represents also features a further element of significance: racism. When the gang hides out in a remote gothic farmhouse, Clyde secretly begins sowing treacherous thoughts in Joseph's mind and he instills a sense of white privilege in Joseph when he declares, "If William thinks we're taking the same share [of the gold] as that nigger, he's got another thing coming." Later on in the film, racial tensions flare when Clyde and Todd clash. Clyde tries to infantilize Todd and remind him of his slave days by calling him "boy" while Todd assertively stands his ground and calls Clyde a "speculator [slave trader]." These episodes are preceded by one in which the gang encounters two men collecting the dead bodies of deserters. One of them mutters garbled words based on a quote from the Bible—"I have seen servants upon horses, and princes upon the earth"—when he sees Todd ride by on horseback. These episodes represent an initial foregrounding of the Emancipation Cause tradition but it is the film's supernatural aspects and their backstory that really emphasize this tradition. As such the film's supernatural elements can be argued to signal the return of the repressed in the form of the horrors of Southern slavery and racism.

The gang encounters a strange creature that they take to be a shaved wild boar when they first arrive at the farm and most of them subsequently have encounters with the spirits of a white woman and her two children who are able to change into horrific demonic entities. Sam is subsequently visited by the children's Father (Muse Watson), who mutters the cryptic words, "I tried to bring my wife back but they tricked me. They changed my children into demons." However, it is the African American Todd who has the most telling encounters with the supernatural here. When the gang explores the farm and find themselves in the slaves' quarters, it is Todd who is able to determine that a strange book that they discover there contains "Spells. For raising the dead." And it is Todd who subsequently sees a trail of wet boot prints that gradually turns into a trail of large paw prints. Later on, when he tries to determine the source of strange whispers, Todd explores a cellar and finds the instruments of torture associated with the punishment of slaves before discovering an African American woman tied and staked to the floor. He assumes that she is a runaway slave who has been severely whipped with rawhide, a punishment that he indicates he has experienced himself. However, before he is able to free her, the invisible hands of the Father ritually disembowel the terrified woman.

This scene and the imagery that it contains can be read as a metaphor that speaks of racial hierarchies and African American suffering. It is later revealed that the Father ritually tortured and sacrificed several of his slaves in his attempts to bring his wife back from the dead. Here we are ultimately being shown an instance where several black lives have been judged to matter less than the single white life of the woman that the Father wishes to resurrect. This is further stressed when we discover the Father's own fate. When his children become demons, he attempts to destroy them and hides their bodies in a secret location. When a posse of local folk challenges and punishes him for his nefarious actions, they only show concern for the whereabouts of the white children: "Where did you put the bodies? Where are your children?" No mention is made of the black slaves who have also suffered and lost their lives. Interestingly, while all of the white gang members remain physically present but changed in some capacity by their encounters with the demons, Todd is obliterated and scattered into atoms. The instant and total erasure of this African American from the physical world would seem to be another symbolic representation of a racial hierarchy at work.

Dead Birds's narrative is very much concerned with showing how the past impacts on the present. The spirit of the Father occupies the present and channels visions of the past to those who visit the farmhouse. The portal that he opened in the past is still functioning in the present, and new demons possess anyone who visits the farmhouse. Todd is reminded of his past life as an abused slave when he sees the torture and death of the female slave in the cellar. William realizes after-the-fact that Jeffy Hollister (Harris Mann), a jealous and vengeful fellow patient whom he once shared a ward with in a military hospital, had purposefully directed him to the farmhouse with malicious intent. Furthermore, the pain and suffering that is seen to occur at the farmhouse is cyclical and unending: at the film's denouement, William has been transformed into one of the strange creatures (a demon incarnate) that the gang encountered at the film's start and the Confederates who shoot him are last seen heading toward the farmhouse to presumably suffer a similar fate themselves. Thus if the film is taken to be a comment on race relations in America, an allegorical reading might suggest that, despite the establishment of meaningful integration and interracial friendships being possible among right-thinking individuals, the horrors of slavery, the mistreatment of African Americans, and the iniquities of the racial hierarchies associated with America's past will inevitably continue to have some impact on America's present.

Conclusion

This chapter has critically investigated how the Reconciliation Cause, the Lost Cause, and the Emancipation Cause traditions were employed in a range of US Civil War–related films that feature supernatural elements while also considering how those supernatural elements might represent the "return" of the repressed (that being a painful or disturbing memory or action). By determining which of the interpretive traditions were foregrounded in each film and considering what painful or disturbing public memories or actions might be represented by the films' supernatural elements, I have argued that the films reviewed—three American productions and one Italian production—provide unorthodox representations of the US Civil War that in turn provide interesting insights into national unity, race relations, and the state of their respective nations more generally at the time of their production.

Bibliography

Bell, Derrick. *Faces at the Bottom of the Well: The Permanence of Racism.* New York: Basic Books, 1992.

Broughton, Lee. *The Euro-Western: Reframing Gender, Race and the "Other" in Film.* London: I.B. Tauris, 2016b.

Broughton, Lee. "Fighting the North in the Spaghetti West: Peter Lee Lawrence, Italian Westerns and Italian History." In *Mapping Cinematic Norths: International Interpretations in Film and Television*, edited by Jonathan Rayner and Julia Dobson, 155–76. Bern: Peter Lang, 2016a.

Cook, Robert J. *Troubled Commemoration: The American Civil War Centennial, 1961–1965.* Baton Rouge: Louisiana State University Press, 2007.

Davis, John A. *Conflict and Control: Law and Order in Nineteenth-Century Italy.* Basingstoke: MacMillan Education Ltd, 1988.

Freud, Sigmund. *The Standard Edition of the Complete Psychological Works of Sigmund Freud Vol. XIV (1914–1916)*, edited by James Strachey. London: Vintage, 2001 [1957].

Gallagher, Gary W. *Causes Won, Lost, and Forgotten: How Hollywood and Popular Art Shape What We Know About the Civil War.* Chapel Hill: The University of North Carolina Press, 2008.

Gentile, Emilio. *La Grande Italia: The Myth of the Nation in the 20th Century*, translated by Suzanne Dingee and Jennifer Pudney. Madison: The University of Wisconsin Press, 2009.

Greenberg, Matt. "Audio Commentary." *Grey Knight*, Vanguard Cinema DVD, 2004.

Hacker, Andrew. *Two Nations: Black and White, Separate, Hostile, Unequal.* New York: Scribner edition, 2003 [1992].

Heath-Kelly, Charlotte. *Politics of Violence.* London: Routledge, 2013.

Hickenlooper, George. "Audio Commentary." *Grey Knight*, Vanguard Cinema DVD, 2004.

Itagaki, Lynn Mie. *Civil Racism: The 1992 Los Angeles Rebellion and the Crisis of Racial Burnout*. Minneapolis: The University of Minnesota Press, 2016.

Jacobs, Ronald N. *Race, Media and the Crisis of Civil Society: From Watts to Rodney King*. Cambridge: Cambridge University Press, 2000.

Lamb, Richard. *War in Italy 1943–1945: A Brutal Story*. London: John Murray Ltd, 1993.

Miller, Cynthia J., and A. Bowdoin Van Riper. "The Fantastic Frontier: Sixguns and Spectacle in the Hybrid Western." In *Critical Perspectives on the Western: From A Fistful of Dollars to Django Unchained*, edited by Lee Broughton, 27–40. Lanham: Rowman & Littlefield, 2016.

Morgan, Philip. *The Fall of Mussolini: Italy, the Italians and the Second World War*. Oxford: Oxford University Press, 2007.

Pavone, Claudio. *A Civil War: A History of the Italian Resistance*, edited by Stanislao G. Pugliese, translated by Peter Levy and David Broder. London: Verso, 2013.

Potter, Hillary, "Introduction." In *Racing the Storm: Racial Implications and Lessons Learned from Hurricane Katrina*, edited by Hillary Potter, ix–xiii. Lanham: Lexington Books, 2007.

Wills, Brian Steel. *Gone with the Glory: The Civil War in Cinema*. Plymouth: Rowman & Littlefield, 2007.

10

Stranger and Friend:
Non-American Westerns and the Immigrant in the Twenty-First Century

Jenny Barrett

Introduction: The American Dream

James Truslow Adams's most famous words are often quoted as the first published record of the American Dream, wherein he refers to "that American dream of a better, richer and happier life for all our citizens of every rank, which is the greatest contribution we have made to the thought and welfare of the world" (1931: 214). Historian Jim Cullen argues that there are "many American *Dreams*" peculiar to particular eras in American history, suggesting that it is a most ambiguous concept (2003: 7). Embedded within understandings of this Dream is equality, the ambition written large in the Declaration of Independence that "all men are created equal," as long as they are "civilised and white" (Cullen 2003: 51). The Dream also points toward faith in personal transformation, the belief that "anyone can get ahead" (Cullen 2003: 60). Everyone is eligible, according to the Dream, including those who seek its promise from across its borders. The American Dream reaches across the globe in a continuing "saga," as Cullen puts it, in the "Dream of the Immigrant," "a subtext of the Dream of Upward Mobility [which] has long been marked by ambivalence and despair" (2003: 188). In American mainstream cinema, the American Western in particular, the representation of first-generation immigrants regularly circumvents this "ambivalence and despair" in favor of good, stereotyped homesteaders, who defend the promise of equality and upward mobility.

There are unique Westerns in the genre's history, however, that take a cynical turn on the Dream, particularly one that exposes exploitation of the land, resources, and peoples of America. *McCabe and Mrs. Miller* (Robert Altman,

1971), for instance, shows a man failing in his enterprise in competition with corporate power. Sergio Corbucci's *The Great Silence* (*Il grande silenzio*, 1968) casts its bounty hunter, Loco (Klaus Kinski), as a sadist and exposes his trade as an immoral business endorsed by a corrupt Justice of the Peace-cum-opportunistic financier, Henry Pollicut (Luigi Pistilli). Both examples, one American and one Italian, work to dislocate the Western from its traditional celebration of the underdog and his implicit morality, an ideology that confirmed, as Robin Wood (1977) argued, that America is the land where problems are solved. What the films of this chapter will suggest is that recent non-American, often also transnational, Westerns appear to resist a reaffirmation of the American Dream specifically through the person of the immigrant who is lured to the continent by a promise that is rudely unfulfilled or remodeled as fantasy. The films that make up this study are *The Salvation* (Kristian Levring, 2014), *Jauja* (Lisandro Alonso, 2014), and *Slow West* (John Maclean, 2015).

Stranger and Friend

Contemporary European cinema, according to Guido Rings (2016), exhibits a rising interest in the experience of the migrant, in the context of the increasing pace of migration and despite the rise of right-wing anti-immigration politics in recent years. Rings sees this renewed focus in some European films as "potential reflections of popular attitudes, ideas and preoccupations" (2016: 28), showing a "need for a re-definition of the Self in the context of enhanced globalization, international mass migration and expansion of the European Union" (2016: 158). With US rhetoric on migration becoming almost daily headline news since the inauguration of President Donald Trump in 2017, it is a suitable moment to consider one of the cinematic genres that brings together the immigrant and the United States: the Western. To Rings, migrant cinema's strategy is the "individualizing and humanizing" of the migrant in order to disrupt the binaries of monoculturalism and multiculturalism. Taking Rings's conceptions of migrant cinema and the disruptive migrant, and applying them to non-American Westerns that feature an immigrant as the protagonist, one can expose a sharp critique of the American Dream in the second decade of the twentieth century.

The films of this study can be understood as examples of "migrant cinema" if one were to take the definition from Rings who determines European migrant cinema as "films about 'migration' to/from 'Europe,' regardless of the cultural background of director, scriptwriters, producers, cast, or potential viewers" (2016: 28). He sees this very inclusive definition as allowing films from nonimmigrant and non-European personnel to be included. *The Salvation* is a Danish film, with a Danish director and male star, a cast including French and British actors, and shot in South Africa. *Slow West*, the most financially successful of the three films, was funded in the UK and New Zealand, stars a young Australian actor as a Scottish character alongside the Irishman Michael Fassbender, and was shot in New Zealand. *Jauja* was filmed in Argentina by an Argentine director, with a Danish-American star and funding from no less than six countries including Denmark, Argentina, France, and the United States. The films chosen here are migrant cinema by virtue of their central characters who, in each case, have traveled to North or South America from Denmark, Scotland, or Ireland. So, the narratives, personnel, and production contexts mean that these films about the immigrant experience in America are examples of both the transnational Western and migrant cinema.

The central characters each, in some way, bring a disruption to the communities they enter by their very identity as outsiders, people from another nation, and this disruption is manifested in the binaries of mono- and multiculturalism that Rings discusses. "Monoculturalism," Rings writes, is "essentialist, homogeneous and separatist in its link to the notion of a people" (2016: 19), and within this notion the binary oppositions of pure/impure, Self/Other, and superior/inferior exist. This view of cultural difference is one that we might recognize from many classical Westerns in their treatment of Native Americans, Asian Americans, and more. The notion of "multiculturalism" recognizes that several peoples may exist respectfully in proximity, but they live in relative isolation and continue to pursue their cultural mores, what Rings describes as "an agenda of enhanced peaceful coexistence, mutual respect and limited interaction" (2016: 158). Later Westerns, such as *Little Big Man* (Arthur Penn, 1971), attempt to encourage this sort of respectful coexistence with Native Americans, as do many Westerns from the mid-1980s onward. "Transculturalism," however, focuses on what Rings calls the "interconnectedness of our increasingly global environment and on interactions and exchanges that contribute to the development of a pool of global cultures potentially facilitating cultural choices" (2016: 20). This is the more "hybrid" notion of cultures where a form of "fusion" may take place. We might be tempted to conclude that this is how we see European immigrants represented in the classical Western, where the immigrant has perhaps married an American citizen, toils on a homestead, and is raising a family, rather like the Jorgensens in John Ford's *The Searchers* (1956). In fact, Neil Campbell writes that, even from the time of Owen Wister's *The Virginian* in 1902, it was a "diasporic West" (2008: 5), and he encourages us to regard the West as "always, already transnational" (2008: 4).

If we observe Peggy Levitt and Nina Glick Shiller's (2004) conceptualizations of "transnational" and "transcultural," we can see that Rings and Campbell are contributing to the gray area often found in scholarship that is situated between the two terms. They are referring to the identity of the person who has traveled from another nation, and who identities him/herself according to a specific culture, one that may or may not be exclusive to or representative of that nation. Levitt and Shiller write, in reference to the transnational: "Ways of being refers to the actual social relations and practices that individuals engage in rather than to the identities associated with their actions" (2004: 1010). In contrast, they describe the transcultural as "ways of belonging" which, they write, "refers to the practices that signal or enact an identity which demonstrates a conscious connection to a particular group" (2004: 1010). In the Western genre, the two aspects of identity—ways of being and ways of belonging—combine to construct the immigrant as the Stranger from Sweden, Scotland, Ireland, and so forth, whose culture is predominantly signified through accent, name, and perhaps religion, but also, for the character, a conscious identification of them now being "American."

Regardless of the merging of these two concepts in literature about migration and about the Western, it should be noted that what appears to be a transcultural or transnational identity of the immigrant family in the Western is swiftly replaced as they are assimilated, making the shift from what we could call "Stranger" to "Friend," as the immigrant becomes American. As Campbell (2008) confirms, Wister's novel demonstrates exactly this normalizing of difference. Looking at the classical Western, signs of the difference between the two conditions of Stranger and Friend are, principally, effusive faith in the value of America as the land of opportunity (Friend) and, more obviously, an accent (Stranger). Lars Jorgensen (John Qualen), the family patriarch of the transnational family in *The Searchers*, still has his accent while his wife (Olive Carey) and children, Brad (Harry Carey Jr.) and Laurie (Vera Miles), have a generic North American accent. While Mr. Jorgensen frets at their proximity to the frontier ("Oh, Ethan, this country"), he remains there waiting for a better time to come, having faith in his wife's advice: "Someday, this country's gonna be a fine good place to be."

So, the films that will be explored here can be understood as non-American and transnational by virtue of their production contexts, and the Western itself is, from Campbell, "always, already transnational" (2008: 4). Using Rings's understanding, however, we could also describe many Western film narratives as partially transcultural in their depiction of the process of immigrant assimilation. The immigrant in the Western often exists at the boundary between Stranger and Friend, between Self and Other, which is characteristic of monocultural and multicultural perceptions. As the immigrant becomes assimilated, through acquisition of language, loss of accent, and/or by starting a family, his or her different cultural status begins to diminish to the point where only their name signifies their difference. In the case of the Western, this difference is one means of acknowledging transculturalism and ethnic diversity in the narrative of nineteenth-century America, but only insofar as the Stranger/Friend hails from an accepted origin, that is, not African, Chinese, or Asian. As a result, the second generation of the accepted immigrant's family is entirely Self and not Other. But those from an origin that is not accepted will always remain Othered in terms of narrative, casting, and stereotyping, making the US assimilation project less the "development of a pool of global cultures" envisioned by Rings (2016: 20) than a pool of Anglo-Saxon and European cultures.

Roots and Routes

The theme of routes and roots is inspired by the work of Neil Campbell (2008) and his thesis of the "rhizomatic West" which conceptualizes the Western genre in literature and cinema more as a grasslike rhizome, with a global heritage and presence, than a tree with roots only in the United States. One of Campbell's illustrations of transnationalism is Sergio Leone's *Once Upon a Time in the West* (*C'era una volta il West*, 1968), which, he argues, exemplifies Leone's perception of America as "the property of the world" (2008: 141) with its multiple shooting locations and range of ethnicities and cultures represented among the characters, cast, and crew. Within the film Campbell finds a central "concern with migration and mobility" among several of the characters. This theme is one that I believe is central to the three migrant Westerns that I am discussing here: the dialectic between movement and stasis, between the route West and putting down roots in the West, between "routes and roots" (2008: 143). The journey to a home and the putting down of roots is an extension or an outworking of the appeal that

America has to the fictional immigrant: the appeal of the American Dream. The contrast between movement and stasis that this suggests is further complicated in the films of this study. If we recall Rings's claim that migrant cinema humanizes the migrant in order to disrupt ideologies of cultural belonging, it is possible to highlight ways in which these three films disrupt two promises of the American Dream indicated earlier: equality and upward mobility. In each film, as the analysis will demonstrate, the immigrant must either remain in motion (en route), adding a new conceptual layer to Campbell's description of a "diasporic West," or if he stops he must either die or his tale will be enunciated as a fantasy (Once upon a time . . .). Where "upward mobility" is found in the films, it will be either by unethical means such as violence or intimidation, or it will be the manifestation of a fairy tale (Once upon a time . . . again).

The Immigrant Redeemer

Faith in the cluster of ideologies that we call the American Dream is what helps to construct the third and final core structure that this chapter will explore in the films, a trope that is identified by Jonathan J. Cavallero in his study of Frank Capra's films, that of the "immigrant redeemer" (2004). In three urban dramas directed during the 1920s, coinciding with the time of the Immigration Act or Johnson Act of 1924, "Capra looked to the immigrant characters to redeem an American Dream corrupted by greed and materialism," starting a career-long theme in Capra's work of "immigrant redeemers" (2004: 46). Capra, an Italian immigrant director who went on to claim that his heritage had no impact on his filmmaking, was issuing a challenge to audiences in their perception of the immigrant by showing in his 1920s films that "only an innocent and idealistic immigrant, not an American numbed by deceit and greed, could save [the town] and restore traditional American values" (2004: 35). The immigrant's innocence and idealism are not only rewarded with a positive resolution in each of these films, but they are also justified in an affirmation, or redemption, of the American Dream.

As touched upon earlier, the immigrant can be found in the classical Hollywood Western, not as a central character so much as a reassuring presence in the background. The traditional construction of the European immigrant in the classical Hollywood Western is that of the non-threatening, assimilated/ assimilating American. They are dedicated to the ideals of the American Dream, fully aware that their success will be down to hard work and determination, and are consistently grateful for their lot in life. The Fordian immigrant reminds us regularly of an ideology of the United States as the land of opportunity and democracy. Mr. Jorgensen in *The Searchers* may be old and incompetent in the face of danger, and he may be the comic relief with his exclamations of "by golly!," but he is determined for his transcultural family's roots to run deep for the sake of future generations. The Ericsons in *The Man Who Shot Liberty Valance* (John Ford, 1962) are the first at Ranse Stoddart's (James Stewart) makeshift school, proclaiming their faith in a nation ruled by the people. Such overt proclamations do not come from the subjectified Westerner whose ethnicity is effectively "invisible," meaning that part of the function of the immigrant in the classical Western is to draw attention to the American Dream, to act as a redemptive influence in the films' constructions of America.

Jim Kitses discusses the immigrants as the "groundlings" and the "meek" in *Liberty Valance*, made up of "a multicultural mix of reluctant cowboys, proud Swedish immigrants, the eager Mexican-American offspring of Andy Devine's prodigious Link Appleyard, the black Pompey (Woody Strode) and Hallie (Vera Miles) herself" (2004: 31). Kitses believes that Ford's own status as a second-generation Irish immigrant impacted on his treatment of these minor characters, humble people, often disenfranchised or stereotyped, writing that the director "had grown up with the sense of cultural dislocation many ethnicities experienced in a polyglot nation" (2004: 32). But Kitses also recognizes that Ford endorsed Irish stereotypes as much as he challenged them (2004: 32). Ford is certainly very careful to avoid sanctioning the male immigrant with the qualities of the ideal, traditionally masculine Westerner. Peter Ericson in *Liberty Valance*, for example, works in a kitchen, clearly encoded as a feminine space in the film, and although Ranse works as a kitchen hand, his status as hero is the very core of the film's challenge to Western heroics.

For the Fordian immigrant, Kitses writes, "the cornerstone of their world . . . was their powerful sense of family, the nourishing roots of the clan, the importance of home, the pain of exclusion" (2004: 32). Kitses considers the significance of the immigrant in the Western genre, particularly for those who identified as "new" Americans in Ford's audience, who would recognize the "cultural dislocation and the search for roots" in the films. He writes: "Both explicitly and implicitly, Ford's was an ethnic frontier" (2004:.42). He makes an interesting claim which, perhaps, might make us wonder why this topic has not been more fully discussed: "by definition Westerners are travelers, immigrants, pioneers" (2004: 93). Thus part of an essential American identity, as formulated in the classical Western, is travel, the journey. Kitses sees this journeying as paradoxical: "a leaving of home to find a new home, breaking up a family, embracing loss and dislocation, in hope of a better world" (2004: 94). Typically, that better world is confirmed in the classical Western, far less so in the revisionist Western, and is certainly interrogated in the three films of this study.

The three structures outlined earlier, of the immigrant's status as Stranger or Friend, of the fluctuation between following routes and putting down roots, and of the immigrant redeemer, can each be fruitfully explored in *The Salvation*, *Slow West*, and *Jauja*. In doing so, it can be proposed that the films offer a rejection of the American Dream through their tales of the disruptive immigrant in a diasporic West.

The Salvation

The Salvation is part vengeance narrative, part town-tamer, about a Danish immigrant and ex-soldier, Jon (Mads Mikkelson), whose wife and child join him in the American West after seven years of separation while he has been establishing roots there with his brother Peter (Mikael Persbrandt). Jon's family never make it alive to his homestead, the boy murdered and the wife raped then killed by "strangers" on their stagecoach. Jon kills the two men early in the film: vengeance complete. When it is revealed that one of the dead men is the brother of local thug Delarue (Jeffrey Dean Morgan), Jon decides to sell up and move further west. Jon is identified by another immigrant couple in the local town of Black Creek who had seen him on the stagecoach, a concession that not all who have traveled to America are Capra's innocent redeemers. There is no sense of brotherhood between immigrants here, only fear of Delarue who kills random townspeople until his brother's murderer is found. Delarue and the town's Mayor/Undertaker (Jonathan Pryce) are both in the pay of "the Company" which is gradually acquiring land and properties across the area. To more fully establish Delarue's psychopathology, he takes possession of his brother's widow, who he calls "Princess," a scarred, tattooed, and mute ex-captive of Indians played by the enigmatic Eva Green. He rapes her, but talks of it as a beautiful experience and promises that he will parade her in New Orleans. Jon and his brother are arrested and brutalized, but as "men who know war" they have skills that enable them to escape. The term "the man who knows war" is my reformulation of Richard

Slotkin's "the man who knows Indians" in his thesis on frontier mythology (1992: 16). I have adapted his term to describe the war veteran who is found in numerous post–Civil War Westerns, whose fate is influenced by his experience of warfare (Barrett 2009: 74). After Peter is caught and killed, dragged by horses, the final section of the film shows Jon returning to the town and individually eradicating the Mayor, the gang and, finally, Delarue. This last act is with the aid of Princess who shoots Delarue in the back. When the sheriff-priest presents himself to Jon, thanking him for saving the town, Jon expels him at gunpoint. Jon and Princess then ride away from the town.

Depending upon one's view, *The Salvation* is either a collection of clichés or a smart homage with overt references to a number of well-known Westerns of the classical and postclassical canons (*High Noon* [Fred Zinnemann, 1952], *A Fistful of Dollars* [Sergio Leone, 1964], *High Plains Drifter* [Clint Eastwood, 1973], and *Unforgiven* [Clint Eastwood, 1992], just to mention a few). It was not received particularly well at the Cannes Film Festival by reviewer Peter Debruge, who felt that the film depended upon "the new-Western playbook" clichés, and correctly predicted a poor show at the box office (2014). The director, Dogme 95's Kristian Levring, breaks with that movement's technically austere tradition and delivers a highly stylized movie with big name stars. The narrative concerns a Danish immigrant experience, but one that several reviewers accused of as lacking originality. As well as Debruge's critique, Geoffrey MacNab described it as "second-hand" in *The Independent* (2015), and Tim Robey called it "wobbly" and "ugly" in *The Telegraph* (2015). However, the film has more to it than pastiche, particularly in its treatment of the immigrant, that is important to explore.

First, the Stranger/Friend motif is core to the characters and the narrative. Jon and Peter have been in the region of Black Creek for some years and so are regarded as local men (or "Friends"), but their accents still set them apart, so they exist on the border between Stranger and Friend. Jon's wife and son, however, arrive without the ability to speak the language and with complete cultural naivety; they are thus encoded clearly as Strangers. Access to language, similarly, is denied to the Princess, whose tongue was cut out during her captivity. In terms of the immigrant, specifically, the lack of language is something that disempowers. The acquisition of language allows entry into "civilized" society, but until then the non-English speaker in this environment remains an outsider as much as a character with no speech at all. The central character of Corbucci's *The Great Silence*, for example, is set apart by his inability to speak, and he is regularly referred to by others as "Stranger." Without a gun, the character with no voice or language is, essentially, powerless. In fact, in *The Salvation*, all other immigrants in the film are either relatively powerless, as in the couple who reveals Jon's identity, or overly accomplished in violence, such as Eric Cantona's henchman who respects Jon for fighting the Germans, but tortures him anyway. Either way, they are encoded as different from the other American frontier families. Importantly, when Peter asks his brother who killed Jon's wife and child, his brother simply replies "Strangers." The film is building a contrast between innocent, good immigrants, who offer no threat, and corrupt, amoral Americans who are vicious and deadly. The killers are "normal" white Americans, but it is their behavior that sets them apart as dangerous Strangers, thus the more typical structure of Stranger and Friend is disrupted by the film's early events. The contrast seems designed to encourage the viewer to see the immigrants as true Americans and the killers as Un-American.

In some ways *The Salvation* is an inversion of Leone's *Once Upon a Time in the West*: here it is oil, not water, which is the resource that a capitalist and his gunfighter wish to exploit. In Leone's film the immigrant, Jill McBain (Claudia Cardinale), with what for American and British audiences at least was a European accent, ultimately wins out against the "company" and, we assume, goes on to enjoy the fruits of her Irish husband's vision for a lucrative oasis in the wilderness. In *The Salvation*, the immigrants do not, however, recognize or appreciate the value of the town's natural commodity, and the Danish man does not benefit from his victorious battle with the town's corrupt leaders. Unlike the destruction of Morton (Gabriele Ferzetti) and Frank (Henry Fonda) in Leone's film, which allows Jill to take personal possession of her husband's (American) dream, Jon and Princess leave Black Creek to the control of the Company, despite the key antagonists having been killed or drummed out of town. Jon's dream of putting down roots for his family is destroyed by the Company, and he continues his route further west, perhaps never settling, destined to remain a nomad in the diasporic West.

Jon's role as immigrant redeemer is one that is signaled by the film, but is presented with some irony. The town and its inhabitants are signified as guilty even before the Company and its exploits are revealed: the first scene on the main thoroughfare features several buildings painted red, an allusion to the communally guilty town of Lago in *High Plains Drifter*, which was painted red and renamed "Hell." Their guilt, like that of Lago's inhabitants, revolves around the persecution and abuse of landowners and locals for material gain, here through the ownership of oil fields rather than a lucrative mine works. Despite

Delarue's demise, however, Black Creek is not redeemed. In *High Plains Drifter* there is a clear sense of the town's punishment at the hands of the Stranger (Clint Eastwood), permitting, it is implied, a new beginning. No such promise is made in *The Salvation*. The repeated forward-tracking shots, possibly an ironic metaphor for progress or an indication that Jon's journey is not complete, are finally inverted in an extended reverse tracking shot which reveals the town's destiny: a vast oil field. It is a damning verdict on American late capitalism; the corporation will always win out over the common man. On reflection, the only salvation that occurs is for Princess, who leaves the town a free woman but who is, like Jon, now estranged from the town.

Slow West

Slow West, the second film of this study, follows the journey of Scottish teenager Jay (Kodi Smit-McPhee) as he seeks his sweetheart Rose (Caren Pistorius), using the so-called "Immigrant's Handbook," *Ho! For the West!*, as his guide. The film opens with the words "Once upon a time . . ." which not only signals the Western's nature as myth but also draws attention to Jay's naivety in traversing the Wild West in such an underprepared manner and his ignorance of Rose's and her father's guilt as killers on the run. British director John Maclean chooses to use repeated leftward tracking shots here to echo Jay's westward migration through Colorado and this pointed use of a mobile camera brings to mind the one employed in *The Salvation*. Along the journey, Jay's path is crossed by an Irishman, Silas (Michael Fassbender), who becomes his paid protector and eventually a father-like mentor, despite eventually revealing that he is a bounty hunter seeking Rose and her father. Although Jay insists that there is "more to life than just surviving," he learns a harsh lesson in frontier life when a starving immigrant couple, shouting desperately in Swedish, are killed while attempting to raid a grocer's store. When the action cuts to the outside of the store, their two now-orphaned children are revealed. These immigrants function as a means to remind us that life on the frontier often was a matter of survival.

The film's core conflict is between Silas and a multicultural band led by the bounty hunter Payne (Ben Mendelsohn). His traveling community seems to be on a journey motivated by survival that is characterized by lawlessness. Made up of Mexicans, ex-soldiers, and eventually the two orphaned Swedish children, the band is like a nomadic version of the transcultural mix of characters found at Ranse Stoddard's school in *The Man Who Shot Liberty Valance*. Jay's naivety and faith eventually softens Silas, to the extent that he protects Rose against the villainous Payne and his gang. In the film's climax, Rose accidentally kills Jay, not recognizing him. Finally, with Payne's gang destroyed and Rose saved, Silas settles with her in a dreamlike, magical resolution. The words "Once upon a time . . ." found at the start of the film thus foreshadow this precise moment.

Rather like *The Great Silence*, again, there is a problematic relationship between bounty-hunting and the common man. In Corbucci's film Loco's sadistic actions against a band of multiethnic outlaws, who have been barely surviving, expose the heartless, insatiable nature of bounty-hunting as a business. In *Slow West*, Payne is also a bounty hunter and in fact his thick, dark bearskin coat resembles the costume worn by Klaus Kinski's Loco. *Slow West* problematizes *The Great Silence*'s more clear-cut division between moral and immoral characters by showing Payne's own mobile band as a community of ethnically diverse survivors, a group that takes in starving children no less. Where Loco's passion for bounty-hunting was in service of his greed and sadism, Payne and his fellow travelers need the reward of bounty-hunting in order to simply survive. For Silas's American Dream to be fulfilled through settling with Rose, however, Payne and his adult gang members must all die.

As with *The Salvation*, *Slow West* uses the three structures that I have highlighted in its treatment of the immigrant's story. Jay's and Silas's accents set them apart as immigrants from Scotland and Ireland respectively, although they speak the language of the white Americans. Silas is an experienced frontiersman who knows the wild spaces well, whereas Jay's knowledge of the West goes only so far as his Immigrant Handbook, a publication that in itself is more akin to a propaganda text for the settler of some means as opposed to being a genuinely useful survival tool, and so Jay is clearly encoded as Stranger. When Rose fails to recognize him then fatally shoots him, his status as Stranger is made fully tangible. The structure of routes and roots in *Slow West* is at the film's core. Jay's route West is inspired by love and enthusiasm, and sees him journey from boyhood to manhood as he learns something of the "real frontier." Nevertheless, he never loses his single-minded love for Rose and belief in his destiny with her. His goal, to settle, is destroyed—as it is for Jon in *The Salvation*—this time in his own death at the hands of the woman he loves. It is the metaphysical journey of Silas that is the message that is perhaps more telling in *Slow West*. This hardened bounty hunter, described by Jay as a "lonely, lonely man," is deeply affected by the childlike Jay, to such an extent that his metaphysical journey west returns him to an immigrant innocence. He saves/redeems Rose, but in fact he has already been redeemed himself by the immigrant Jay. Silas thus finds his way back to faith in the American Dream, albeit less the promise of equality. Silas's version of the Dream is more the dream of unhindered upward mobility that is signaled by the end of his journeying and a new settled life in a sun-filled homestead.

Jauja

Jauja is not set in the American West and is, like much of Alonso's work, an example of the filmmaking style often referred to as slow cinema. It also refuses to conform to the demands of classical realist filmmaking in its nonlinear and open-ended narrative. Alonso frames the image with a border, akin to early cinema, in a 1.33:1 ratio, summoning an impression of nineteenth-century photography. Despite these characteristics, it has very strong associations with the American Western throughout. Captain Dinesan (Viggo Mortensen) is part of the so-called "Conquest of the Desert," the Danish military campaign in South America that sought to eliminate the Mapuche population (the indigenous people of the area) during the 1870s. Dinesan is a Danish engineer working in Patagonia, living in a tent with his daughter, Ingeborg (Viilbjørk Malling Agger), alongside a small band of workers and Danish military. A renegade by the name of Colonel Zuluaga, who is never seen on screen, has joined forces with the local "gauchos," or bandits, and is in hiding dressed as a woman. Ingeborg begins a relationship with one of the soldiers and they disappear together at night, taking a compass from Dinesan's belongings. Dinesan spends the remainder of the film searching for his daughter, whose lover is found dying of his wounds from an attack by Zuluaga. He eventually crosses a harsh, rocky wilderness to find an elderly woman in a cave (Ghita Nørby). The woman lives alone with her dog, and she is in possession of the missing compass. The dialogue implies that she may be a manifestation of Ingeborg, but Dinesan leaves the old woman and continues on his quest across the nightmarish, desolate landscape. The actress who plays young Ingeborg is seen in a final scene set in contemporary Denmark where she discusses the health of her dog with a man, finds a small toy soldier that had been in the old woman's cave, and throws it away.

The South American countryside locations seen in *Jauja* were filmed in Argentina but they are photographed and referred to in ways that are familiar to the Western, with mention made of a frontier and the wilderness. However,

Jauja's narrative content makes it clear that the landscape depicted is not North America, and this adds a more self-conscious layer of difference to the film. That said, viewers of American and non-American Westerns alike have become somewhat familiar with the general aesthetics of Western-style action that unfolds in "inauthentic" locations since the majority of the genre's films are now filmed outside of the United States. Significantly, signs and symbols of the Western are found in *Jauja* despite its narrative location. Indigenous people are described as savages; one of the military characters describes them as "coconut heads." Mortensen on-screen often draws John Wayne to mind when he is sat astride a horse, with his costume and saber reminiscent of those Wayne wore in John Ford's Westerns such as *She Wore a Yellow Ribbon* (1949). Several reviewers have made note of *Jauja*'s similarities to Ford's *The Searchers* in particular, specifically the search for Ingeborg which echoes Debbie's (Natalie Wood) captivity narrative in that film. But as well as this, shots in *Jauja* appear to be deliberately modeled on moments from the two Ford films. Mortensen's knelt pose, slumped in despair, which was used on some of the film's publicity material, evokes both Wayne's bowed head as Captain Brittles at the side of his dying fellow soldier in *She Wore a Yellow Ribbon* and Wayne's silhouette when Ethan Edwards discovers his dead sister-in-law, Martha, in *The Searchers*. It is an image that returns us to Cullen's verdict on the American Dream of the immigrant, characterized by ambivalence and despair (2003: 188).

In spite of its displaced setting, applying the three immigrant frameworks to *Jauja* does find a film that metaphorically confronts the American Dream through the immigrant. Dinesan is consistently presented narratively, visually and even verbally as a Stranger. An interview for *Sight and Sound* has Mortensen referring to Dinesan's difference through his accent, a Danish man speaking Spanish, which sets him apart (Diestro-Dópido 2015: 22). As well as this, in his search that never ends, he is never settled, he is always moving, consistently en route, following his daughter's route, never putting down roots. After his daughter's disappearance he is never at peace, never comforted, or welcomed except when he finds the elderly cave-dweller. His failure to find his daughter and his ongoing journey resist the resolutions of the films discussed earlier, since the savage Zuluaga is never located and punished, unlike *The Searchers*'s Scar (Henry Brandon). Lastly, Dinesan strives to free or "redeem" his daughter, but his role as immigrant redeemer is characterized by failure in a wild, savage space that overwhelms him. Although the tone is very different from the final scene of *Slow West*, with its overly positive fairy tale resolution, *Jauja* shares a non-realist conclusion, resisting closure in an implication of cyclical, pointless yearning for a better life. There is even an implication that Dinesan's story is part of the dream of a young girl living in contemporary Denmark, potentially allowing a reading of post-imperial guilt.

What is particularly interesting is the film's formulation of the dream of a better future, in some ways akin to the American Dream. The Spanish word "*jauja*" refers to a mystical concept of Paradise which is an illusion. It can be used to refer to concepts as varied as heaven, luxury, and holiday. Those seeking it, according to myth, are lost and confounded. It is unclear from the film whether the Danish immigrants are attempting to turn Patagonia into their "promised land" or whether the search for Ingeborg is Dinesan's quest for Paradise. What can be argued, however, is that the overt references to the American Western in this film allow us to perceive the failed quest to find *jauja* as a measure of the inadequacy of the American Dream. As with the other films of this study, the Dream is exposed as an empty promise, an illusion.

Conclusion

Jon in *The Salvation*, Jay in *Slow West*, and Dinesan in *Jauja* are protagonists who remain more Stranger than Friend because they either die or are forced to keep moving on. For each, their journey does not end with the putting down of roots. For each, their dream of settling, endorsed by faith in the American Dream, is not fulfilled. And although they are immigrant redeemers, functioning to remind other characters that there are good values to defend, none of them benefit from their act of redemption. Instead of offering a Fordian tale of assimilation and celebration of traditional American values, the immigrant's settlement is violently rejected in *The Salvation*, which issues a verdict on America's rapacious exploitation of the world's resources. Despite the apparent bittersweet resolution of *Slow West*, with Silas settling with Rose, the film is overtly encoded as a myth. With the opening words "Once upon a time," the lilting waltz repeatedly playing in the background and the hazy, dreamlike closure, the immigrant's happy ending becomes a fairy tale. *Jauja* recasts the Western with Danish and Argentine characters, and by inference paints the American Dream as a dream of despair for the immigrant.

Other Western formulations of the immigrant and the American Dream have emerged in the same time period as these other films. *Brimstone* (2016), for example, from Dutch director Martin Koolhoven, is a transnational Western about immigrant Joanna (Dakota Fanning). Her Dutch father (Guy Pearce) is the minister of a Puritan settlement in America where he preaches the message of America as John Winthrop's "city upon a hill," the creed of the English Separatists of the seventeenth century, the first American Dream of an ideal nation. The minister is revealed to be a misogynist, sadist, and pedophile, a false immigrant redeemer. As a child, Joanna resists assimilation by continuing to speak Dutch and eventually flees the "roots" put down by her father, is sold into prostitution, escapes and poses as her mute friend Liz, marries, and is finally hunted down by her father again. The film's core focus, it should be acknowledged, is on women as objects or possessions to be controlled, beaten, and caged, quite literally. But it clarifies two matters: First, the equality spoken of in the Declaration of Independence, seen by many as the spirit of the American Dream, was not considered by all to be for women. Second, the Settlers' American Dream of the United States as the "city upon a hill," the model nation to the world, is revealed to be vacuous with the American West depicted as a place of exploitation, greed, and perversion. Despite settling peacefully and prospering after killing her father (Joanna establishes a sawmill and makes plans for her family's future) her fate is not to enjoy the roots that she has put down. Her past finally catches up with her, and she is arrested as "Liz" for the murder of her brothel owner. She chooses to free herself by drowning, leaving, emphatically, a daughter not a son to grow up the beneficiary of her enterprise, possibly a more optimistic closure than one might have expected from such a dark film.

It is important to consider why a focus on the immigrant has emerged in recent transnational Westerns. Given that the films explored (with the exception of *Brimstone*) are pre-Trump era releases, it is clear that a cynical rejection of the American Dream through the person of the immigrant was already part of the zeitgeist and had found its way into public and media discourses prior to Donald Trump's dream of a "great, great wall" (see Rupert Neale 2015). The controversial relationship between the United States and immigration is as old as its history, but what seems to have emerged is a more self-conscious discourse, resisting the subject position of the white American male and instead centralizing the immigrant's subjectivity. This discourse is not restricted to the non-American or transnational Western and can increasingly be found in newscasting, TV dramas, and documentary-filmmaking about the immigrant experience that report on the "tough" approach of some world leaders as they respond to unprecedented numbers of refugees and migrants crossing their borders. The relocation of the immigrant Westerner to a narrative center, as subjective protagonist, allows the Western tale to hold the American Dream of the immigrant to account for its "ambivalence and despair" (Cullen 2003: 188)—a verdict that seems apt in the light of current prospects for so many.

Bibliography

Adams, James Truslow. *The Epic of America*. Boston: Little, Brown and Co., 1931.

Barrett, Jenny. *Shooting the Civil War: Cinema, History and American National Identity*. London: I.B. Tauris, 2009.

Campbell, Neil. *The Rhizomatic West: Representing the American West in a Transnational, Global Media Age*. Lincoln & London: University of Nebraska Press, 2008.

Cavallero, Jonathan J. "Frank Capra's 1920s Immigrant Trilogy: Immigration, Assimilation, and the American Dream." *Melus* 29, no. 2 (2004): 27–53.

Cullen, Jim. *The American Dream: A Short History of an Idea that Shaped a Nation*. Oxford: Oxford University Press, 2003.

Debruge, Peter. "Cannes Film Review: *The Salvation*." *Variety*, May 16 (2014). Available online at: http://variety.com/2014/film/festivals/cannes-film-review-the-salvation-1201182872/ (accessed May 23, 2016).

Diestro-Dópido. "Living the Dream." *Sight and Sound*, 25, no. 5, May (2015): 22.

Hall, Edward H. *Ho! For the West!! The Traveller and Emigrants' Hand-book to Canada and the North-West of the American Union*. 3rd ed. London: Algar & Street, 1858.

Holmlund, Chris. *Impossible Bodies: Femininity and Masculinity at the Movies*. New York & London: Routledge, 2002.

Kitses, Jim. *Horizons West: Directing the Western from John Ford to Clint Eastwood*. London: British Film Institute, 2004.

Kollin, Susan (ed.). *Postwestern Cultures: Literature, Theory, Space*. Lincoln: University of Nebraska Press, 2007.

Levitt, Peggy and Nina Glick Schiller. "Conceptualizing Simultaneity: A Transnational Social Field Perspective on Society." *International Migration Review*, 38, no. 3 (2004): 1002–39.

MacNab, Geoffrey. "*The Salvation* Film Review: Danish-made Western Shot in South Africa is Full of Blood." *Independent*, April 17 (2015). Available online at: http://www.independent.co.uk/arts-entertainment/films/reviews/the-salvation-film-review-danish-made-western-shot-in-south-africa-is-full-of-blood-10183003.html (accessed August 3, 2018).

Neale, Rupert. "Donald Trump Announces US Presidential Run with Eccentric Speech." *Guardian*, June 16 (2015). Available online at: https://www.theguardian.com/us-news/2015/jun/16/donald-trump-announces-run-president (accessed January 8, 2019).

Rings, Guido. *The Other in Contemporary Migrant Cinema: Imagining a New Europe?* London: Routledge, 2016.

Robey, Tim. "*The Salvation* Review: A Waste." *Telegraph*, April 16 (2015). Available online at: http://www.telegraph.co.uk/film/the-salvation/review/ (accessed May 23, 2016).

Slotkin, Richard. *Gunfighter Nation: The Myth of the Frontier in Twentieth-Century America*. New York: Maxwell Macmillan, 1992.

Wister, Owen. *The Virginian*. London and New York: Macmillan, 1902.

Wood, Robin. "Ideology, Genre, Auteur." *Film Comment* 13, no. 1 (1977): 46–51.

11

The Intrusion of Climate in *The Revenant*

Jack Weatherston

Introduction

Defending the use of spectacular violence in his 2015 Western *The Revenant*, director Alejandro González Iñárritu argued that the blood and viscera that marked the film were essential for achieving his stated goal of authenticity: "I've heard people say the movie is violent. . . . But there is no gratuitous violence. These guys were eating animals, wearing animals; they were threatened by accidents, diseases, tribes, wars. This is the real world. This isn't pasteurized" (Segal 2015). The attempt to render the early West in all of its un-sanitized "realness" resulted in a production process defined by an almost masochistic commitment to replicating the grime, discomfort, and gore of the frontiersman existence. The result of this committed engagement with the environment of the West is a film that reveals many of the challenges posed to the Western genre by the creeping intrusion of climate change.

In this chapter, I will show how *The Revenant* gestures toward a productively immersed kind of Western environmental authenticity while also exhibiting the discontinuities and gaps in representation engendered by the changing Western space. The nature and possibility of authenticity is complex in the context of both the Western as a genre and the West as a living environment. The Western genre has been defined by the discourse of authenticity versus inauthenticity, history versus myth. Western writers and filmmakers are often engaged in an attempt to render the reality of the Western space, and yet the West is of course constructed through the interplay of mythology and cultural discourse. Art set in the Western space cannot claim a privileged access to the real. Similarly, ecocritical thought is skeptical of the notion of authentic wilderness that *The Revenant* leans heavily upon. Our conceptions of a landscape or ecology without humanity ignore the persistent trace of human activity and subjectivity. And yet, despite the inherent limitations of representing the frontier, moments of interaction with the authentic do emerge in *The Revenant*. The grueling battle with nature that characterized the film's production process is one example of this tangible encounter with the living frontier. This exuberant interaction with the ecological and social realities of the Western space is also evident in the full-throated environmental advocacy of both Iñárritu and the film's star Leonardo DiCaprio. These impulses are most evident in *A World Unseen: The Revenant* (Eliot Rausch, 2016), the documentary that accompanied the film.

However, on closer examination the complications of representing the primordial West inevitably become apparent. For example, the process of transforming a historical record into a Hollywood script results in a phony resolution that somewhat erases the complexities of the narrative's protagonist, Hugh Glass. Visual style and sound design also have to navigate the complexities of authenticity, attempting to salvage something of the real from a mediated wilderness. Furthermore, the unreal, or hyperreal, is evident in the computer-generated animals that populate and punctuate *The Revenant*. These ghostly impressions of animals are revelatory of the denuded reality of the Western ecosystem. Finally, I will show how the changing climate poses the ultimate challenge to what we might consider the authentic Western. Climate change intruded on the production itself, forcing changes in location and process. Ultimately, the difficulty of making *The Revenant* in a West experiencing the wrenching dislocations of climate change points to a precarious and contingent future for both the landscape and the genre.

The Possibility of Authenticity in the Western Genre and Landscape

The early ideologues of Westward expansion identified the West as both the motivating force of American progress and the location of a truly authentic American character. This is evident in Theodore Roosevelt's autobiography in which he extols the virtues of his former cowboy existence: "I do not believe there ever was any life more attractive to a vigorous young fellow than life on a cattle ranch in those days. It was a fine, healthy life, too; it taught a man self-reliance, hardihood, and the value of instant decision. . . . I enjoyed the life to the full" (2017: 73). Roosevelt grafted the masculinity of the rancher and the Rough Riders onto the frontier thesis of Frederick Jackson Turner (1921).

The phlegmatic sons of the soil that populated Turner's West were joined in Roosevelt's rendering by the heroic patriarchs who wrested the land from the natives for white civilization. Free from the strictures of urban living and the sclerotic institutions of the old East, the character of the Western subject was forged through a rough-and-tumble interaction with the wilderness. The authentic Westerner lived off the land, eschewed the pretensions of the East, was practical, proactive, and an inviolable individual. This figure of stoic authenticity became attractive to a culture that, toward the end of the nineteenth century, was beginning to value the real above the imitative. Miles Orvell identified this transition as being a response to the technological changes that allowed for mass scale reproductions and resulted in a culture of "rounded generalities" (2014: xxvii).

In this reading the movement toward authenticity gave rise to the innovations of modernism. The literature of the West also displays this impulse. Narratives of the West were primarily concerned with historical authenticity and the realness of the forbidding Western landscape. Indeed, Nathaniel Lewis argues that, in the context of the West, authenticity is defined as being "above all, original and real" (2003: 5). Originality was necessary to counteract the reproductive logic of the emerging consumer market while the desire for realness was connected to the rise of the individual. Taking his cues from the thought of ethicist Charles Taylor, Lewis contends that "while modern culture seems to encourage us to explore individually our own higher latitudes, so this thinking goes, it also encourages us to evaluate the hidden depths of public figures" (2003: 4). Western characters came to represent a desirable, sovereign individuality free from the contradictions and compromises of modernity. Lee Clark Mitchell identifies this persistent demand that Western authors concern themselves primarily with authenticity in the cataloging of real locations within fictional narratives when he observes that "cowboy westerns . . . share with other popular genres (spy thrillers, detective novels) a deep investment in assumed authenticity, requiring footnotes be strung around like barbed wire to verify unlikely locales, outrageous garb, and improbable activities all within the realm of the actual, the authentic" (2007: 96). James Fenimore Cooper and later authors such a Wallace Stegner, Ivan Doig, and William Kitteridge are writers who could be accused of fetishizing authenticity at the expense of literary experimentation or literariness itself. Inevitably, the demand that the Western be authentic can potentially limit the ability of Western narratives to respond to their context in novel and provocative ways.

The specter of authenticity also looms over the Western film genre. Westerns, from silent films through to the classical period, presented a history of frontier expansion that bolstered the narrative of manifest destiny and elided the reality of racial conflict and genocide. In his analysis of the early Western Scott Simmon identifies the silent film *The Invaders* (Thomas H. Ince and Francis Ford, 1912) as a point of inflection at which a rough and ready truthfulness was in evidence despite the pressures of the burgeoning settler myth. In Simmon reading the film's narrative of treaty breaking surveyors and their violent interactions with indigenous people is possessed of a primitive form of authenticity that is a result of its proto-Western nature. The film tells multiple stories without centering on the trials of a particular Western hero archetype. Instead the collective nature of the production resulted in a film that represents history as driven by processes and collective action. As Simmon observes, "No single individual is essential to the process of history, just as no one is essential to the process of filmmaking" (2003: 73).

Ultimately, Hollywood would reject this form of redistributive narrative history in favor of established stars and the doctrine of heroic individualism. Simmon hints at the reasons for this in his discussion of the films of Al Jennings and Nell Shipman, two independent Western filmmakers in the mold of Ince and Ford:

> If Jennings and Shipman are the regional dead-ends in independent silent Westerns, it's also because the "real" was never an industry goal. "The Western picture seems a constant temptation to 'realism' of a most undesirable variety," warned *Moving Picture World* in 1911; the filmmakers "give us too close a view of 'hold-ups,' hangings, lynchings, massacres." (Simmon 2003: 68)

To accurately depict the racial violence of the historical frontier would be to reveal the uncomfortable truth of manifest destiny, that the great gains of the frontier were wrested by force from the indigenous inhabitants of the West. Better to lean on a quickly hardening mythology and the sturdy individuals that would come to embody it. The passing of the historical West and the instantiation of the ideologically constructed frontier have created a genre that is well aware of its status as myth while maintaining an almost neurotic attachment to the possibility of authenticity. Moreover, the focus on myth and ideology present in revisionist Westerns is the precise mechanism through which the Western gains access to a vital, contemporary sense of the real. Neil Campbell makes this explicit point in his work on the post-Western when he notes that "the Western genre, rather than collapse, actually found a 'project of positive creation' through which to interrogate the very ideological frameworks that had conjured it into being in the first place" (2013: 3).

One such ideological framework that contemporary Westerns are increasingly compelled to address is the notion of the West as a wilderness. The landscape and ecology of the American West is itself a repository of authenticity, a pristine but wild environment against which the sovereign individuals of the genre can be defined. The frontier's wildness, its untrammeled openness, distinguishes it from both the pastoral, cultivated landscapes of the old world and the industrial development of the Eastern states. Naming the frontier as wilderness was also a feature of colonial ideology. The West was a blank space upon which the operations of manifest destiny could be pursued. Such a framing of course effaces preexisting native cultures, reducing them to just another part of the romantic wilderness, a feature to be overcome in the manner of a river or a mountain range. As the frontier was settled and pacified, and whatever mystery its landscape contained was made known, wilderness came to embody lost notions of masculine identity and authentic American character. Roosevelt oversaw a huge expansion of the national park administration and created the United States Forest Service in 1905. The committed imperialist clearly recognized the value in protecting the dwindling wild spaces of the continent.

The ideologically freighted manner in which wilderness has been deployed historically is reflected in the contemporary critical debates around the term. For some in the environmental movement, unspoiled nature has stood as a bulwark against the failures and compromises of contemporary industrial society. In reaction to modernity some environmentalists and ecocritics have constructed a monolithic wilderness invested with metaphysical significance. William Cronon identifies the overarching motivation of these wilderness advocates when he notes that

> wilderness is the natural, unfallen antithesis of an unnatural civilization that has lost its soul. It is a place of freedom in which we can recover our true selves we have lost to the corrupting influences of our artificial lives. Most of all, it is the ultimate landscape of authenticity. (1996: 80)

The attractive idea of escaping into wilderness in order to experience an authenticity not present elsewhere is complicated by the reality of the persistent human presence. Existence in the wild requires the apparatuses and support of contemporary society and economic relations. Tents, kayaks, parasails are all products of the "non-authentic" world outside. And furthermore, the presence of human subjects in remaining wild spaces ensures the kind of demystification that wilderness enthusiasts are attempting to avoid. And yet, these spaces possess an immense value on their own terms, as areas of ecological diversity and geological history, as well as zones of aesthetic wonder. Undoubtedly they should be protected and stewarded through the climate upheavals of the coming decades.

Greg Garrard argues that the problematic status of wilderness, the tension between utilitarian exploitation and pseudo-religious mystification, can be overcome through pragmatic engagement with wilderness spaces when he observes that

> the choice between monolithic, ecocidal modernism and reverential awe is a false dichotomy that ecocriticism can circumvent with a pragmatic and political orientation. The fundamental problem of responsibility is not what we humans are, nor how we can "be" better, more natural, primal or authentic, but what we *do*. (2012: 59)

Wilderness, as a place of authenticity, is a construct that obscures the real value of the living West. As the climate changes, Edenic conceptions of the Western environment risk erasing human agency and stifling action. What might be called for is a committed engagement with wilderness that records whatever scraps of the authentic that might still persist.

Making *The Revenant*: Difficulty and Authenticity

The story of the production of *The Revenant* would certainly seem to indicate a committed engagement with the Western environment. The film is a loose retelling of the story of nineteenth-century fur trapper Hugh Glass. Set in 1823 in the unorganized territories that would become Montana and South Dakota, the narrative follows Glass (Leonardo DiCaprio) as he acts as a guide for a group of fellow trappers, led by Captain Andrew Henry (Domhnall Gleeson), who are on an expedition into hostile country. While preparing their spoils for transport the group is attacked by an Arikara war party and forced to flee. While scouting ahead to facilitate their escape Glass is attacked and critically injured by a grizzly bear protecting its cubs. Promised a reward for staying behind to look after the seemingly mortally wounded Glass, John Fitzgerald (Tom Hardy) is left with an inexperienced party member Jim Poulter and Glass's mixed race son, Hawk (Forest Goodluck). Eager to leave and claim his reward Fitzgerald attempts to smother Glass but ends up killing Hawk, who had tried to protect his father. Fitzgerald lies to Poulter and convinces him to leave Glass for dead. However, Glass miraculously recovers and proceeds to drag himself across the frozen landscape back toward Fort Kiowa and salvation. Surviving many trials and tribulations along the way, Glass makes it back to the fort where he is informed that Fitzgerald murdered Hawk. Glass sets out into the frozen wilderness with Captain Henry in order to track and kill Fitzgerald, who has since fled.

The Revenant achieved a mostly laudatory critical response, with particular praise being given to its brutal and visceral evocations of the antediluvian frontier and the human and animal suffering that existence there entailed. In *The Guardian* Peter Bradshaw (2015) wrote that the film "expose[s] you to the elements. You are out in a piercingly painful cold, under an endless, pitiless sky. This is not an immersion that feels like a sensual surrender; it's closer to having your skin peeled." Iñárritu was awarded the Oscar for best director, while DiCaprio received the best actor commendation. Praise was heaped on the film in part due to its professed authenticity that stemmed from a desire to faithfully represent the harsh material reality of its subject matter. To do this required an almost absurd level of commitment. Iñárritu shot in natural light in extremely challenging weather conditions, pushing both the budget and the release schedule to breaking point. DiCaprio's suffering became the stuff of Hollywood legends, with the actor hauling one hundred pound bearskins up mountainsides and consuming a raw bison liver (DiCaprio is a vegetarian). Quoted in *The Hollywood Reporter* unknown crewmembers described the shoot as "a living hell" (Masters 2015).

Iñárritu's commitment to shooting outdoors and away from green screens and digital effects caused the production to overrun on time and budget. His response to the complaints was blunt: "If we ended up in greenscreen with coffee and everybody having a good time, everybody will be happy, but most likely the film would be a piece of shit" (Masters 2015). This kind of muscular, uncompromising, filmmaking is reminiscent of other auteur driven productions such as *Apocalypse Now* (Francis Coppola, 1979) and *Fitzcarraldo* (Werner Herzog, 1982), both films in which the difficulty of their creation ultimately contributed to their positive critical regard. However, these films differ from *The Revenant* partly because the difficulties in their making have been associated with their filming locations in the global south, the Philippines in the case of

Apocalypse Now and Peru and Brazil for *Fitzcarraldo*. By contrast it was issues emanating from the familiar environment of the American West that dogged Iñárritu's film.

Iñárritu has explicitly stated the rationale behind the masochistic difficulty of the filming process. He argues that such extreme techniques were essential for accessing an authentic representation of wilderness and were also an essential part of the film's environmental advocacy. These sentiments are most clearly stated in the documentary that accompanied the film entitled *A World Unseen: The Revenant*. *A World Unseen* structures the making of story of *The Revenant* around a journey made by the actor Forest Goodluck (who plays Glass's son, Hawk) and his family to the Fort Berthold reservation in North Dakota in order to "explore their history and the lasting realities of their ancestral home" (*A World Unseen* 2016). Goodluck's family and forebears have born witness to the environmental changes wrought by white settlers and extractive industry, and Goodluck reveals the hurt caused by a dam that flooded historic tribal lands. The experiences of Native Americans animate the environmentalism of the production; Goodluck's reconnection with the lost landscapes of his past is presented as an expression of authenticity. The documentary deploys the trope of the ecological Indian to support and cement the critique developed in *The Revenant* itself.

Alongside Goodluck's narrative the documentary presents foreboding imagery of the contemporary West, in particular the gas flaring from plants processing fossil fuels of the Bakken shale region. Historic environmental exploitation is thus linked to both the present and the future. DiCaprio argues that the fur trappers were the antecedents of the contemporary carbon rush economy, equally heedless of the long-term consequences of their acquisitiveness. The looming uncertainties of climate change were clearly present in the construction of *The Revenant*'s ecological conscience. This pragmatic concern for the future of the Western space coupled with straightforward calls for action that incorporate the perspectives of Native Americans is a valuable example of what a progressive Western might aim to achieve amid a changing climate. However, Iñárritu also claims that going out into the West, as it now exists, is a form self-actualizing therapy when he observes that "you have to be a little, kind of, crazy to embark on a film like this. The physicality of it, the setting, the nature as a transformative experience [*sic*]. That was exactly what I wanted, personally, to go through. In my personal life" (*A World Unseen* 2016). Here Iñárritu reflects the simplified, transactional relationship with the living world present in reductive forms of environmentalism. This is an impulse that threatens to override productive engagement with the changing West in favor of the mystifying rhetoric of self-help and authenticity.

There are other crucial areas in *The Revenant* where authenticity as a modus operandi becomes less apparent. For example, there are a number of discrepancies between the narrative of the film and the historical record of Glass's journey. Of course it would be wrong to overly criticize the film for the necessary changes enforced by the adaptation process, and in any case Glass's own account of his escape was written down years later and may have been embroidered. However, the adaptation does contain some problematic embellishments. *The Revenant* gives Glass as son, Hawk, who works alongside him as a scout and trapper. Glass is also given a tragic backstory in which American soldiers murdered Hawk's mother, a nameless Pawnee Indian woman. By adding this sentimental backstory and character motivation Glass is softened and made more sympathetic. As opposed to a driven loner on the outskirts of society he is a family man, and, ultimately, a victim. It also allows for a, perhaps too easy, conflation of Glass's personal tragedy and suffering with the destruction of Native peoples and their culture. Here, *The Revenant* falls into the same trap as Western's like *Dances with Wolves* (Kevin Costner, 1990), in which a white male character acts as a savior or proxy for noble but ultimately doomed Native Americans.

The film also deviates from the historical record in its conclusion. The real Hugh Glass did not get his revenge: in the end he let the two men who betrayed him go. Iñárritu cannot help but reach for narrative closure, which again seems at odds with the stated goal of authenticity. The moral compromises and failures of life on the historical frontier are elided in favor of a more compelling revenge fantasy. What then are we to make of the director's reasoning for the self-imposed difficulty and discomfort of his filmmaking process? Iñárritu claims that "we are less and less used to be exposed to the real elements and try to solve it with the reality [*sic*]. . . . It's a transforming experience" (*A World Unseen* 2016). The search for forms of authentic experience in the West—through committed, material immersion—is certainly a project that has value and yet such efforts are inevitably complicated by anthropocentric discourses. However, it is possible to discern productive moments of immersion and revelation in *The Revenant*. And beyond that, the pressures of environmental disruption and climate change have the capacity to intrude into the narrative, disrupting the very identity of the "authentic" West.

Moments of Immersion

Leonardo DiCaprio makes the claim that the grueling methodology of the filmmaking process resulted in a particularly involving final product, a film with the capacity to immerse the audience in a faithful representation of the frontier: "What Alejandro accomplishes is . . . his ability to put you there . . . this almost virtual reality where you really feel like you're out in the elements with these characters" (*A World Unseen* 2016). And it is indeed evident that the film does employ a range of techniques to expand the frame and envelop the viewer's senses. The opening shot of a river running beneath trees is accompanied by a lush, aural landscape where the sound of water envelopes the visuals in the absence of any musical score. This is the first of a series of scenes in which Glass is entirely submerged in water (the later submergences occur when Glass is escaping from the Arikara and during his final showdown with Fitzgerald). These literal immersions, and the cloaking soundtrack of moving water that accompany them, have the effect of anchoring the film in a visceral sense of physicality. The sound of icy running water produces an empathic reaction in viewers, an innate understanding of that moment's discomfort. Additionally, letting natural sounds takeover from non-diegetic musical inputs creates a sense of a dynamic, living environment oblivious to human trials and suffering.

The film's rerecording mixer Jon Taylor confirmed that natural sound was privileged in the mixing process, observing that "the film is about nature so music never just takes over, it always has spaces so that the nature can come through and co-exist" (Woodhall 2016). Here *The Revenant* has something in common with other contemporary Westerns that choose to employ a minimalist or modernist sound design. The production's primary concern with issues of environment meant that the sounds of frontier nature were a foundational part of its sound design. This is again indicative of a good faith attempt to wrest something of substance from the uncooperative and always mediated wilderness. The impossibility of achieving an entirely "natural" soundscape does not devalue this partial but rugged commitment to the real.

Immersion is also a property of scale in *The Revenant*. The visual style of the film is defined by the contrast between wide shots of the sublime landscape and highly detailed close-ups. A shot of mountains illuminated by shafts of winter sun is set against the persistent, tight close-up of Glass's scabbed, and filthy face, surrounded by a halo of ragged furs. The camera also picks out smaller natural details, such as shriveled plant life in the snow or the movement of ants. In much the same way Glass is often shown as tiny figure trudging through an overwhelming space. This is a conscious attempt to minimize the human and to demonstrate a natural world that is utterly oblivious to the morality tale that happens to be occurring within it. However, the painterly quality of these landscape compositions, their beauty and symmetry, also has the effect of implying the human trace. Indeed the concept of immersion itself can have negative valence.

The James Cameron science fiction epic *Avatar* (2009), which prompted a renaissance in three-dimensional films, is perhaps the premier contemporary example of self-consciously immersive cinema. However, the postcolonial critic Gautam Basu Thakur has persuasively shown that *Avatar*'s narrative deploys colonial ideology in a way that would not be unfamiliar to the Western by noting that although "its plot appears to do just the opposite—that is, galvanize opinion against violence perpetrated against indigenous populations of the globe—the film is rife with recognizable and clandestine acts of violent othering of the Other" (2016: 89). The "white savior" plot of *Avatar* reflects that of revisionist Westerns, such as *Dancing with Wolves*. It is also possible to read the immersion aspects of *The Revenant* in a similar manner. Glass is an explorer in an exoticized world of racial difference, one in which he inhabits the privileged position of interlocutor and peacemaker between the colonizers and the colonized. There is no doubt that the project of immersion is a worthwhile one and can work affectively to more fully represent the Western space. However, the indulgence of immersion as an ideologically neutral act of exploration ignores the colonial power dynamics inherent to the act.

The visual language of *The Revenant* is most effective when it clearly articulates a message of environmental plunder and gestures to the changing climate. Two instances of this in particular bear much of the weight of the film's critique. First, in a fever dream Glass is presented with a pyramid of skulls taken from the great buffalo herds that were in the process of being wiped out by Glass's contemporaries. The shot echoes photos taken from the mid-nineteenth century featuring men standing on meters-tall piles of buffalo carcasses (the Detroit Public Library holds a particularly stark example from 1892). As a symbol of the excesses of settler plundering the images could not be any starker. Glass is himself awestruck by the extent of the pillaging that the pyramid represents. A link is also made with the contemporary West as the last pockets of biodiversity are squeezed by deregulation and environmental stresses exacerbated by climate change. The skulls stand for the continuity of violence and ecocidal mania in the history of the frontier. The ominously totemistic quality of the pyramid works alongside another sign in the film, namely the persistent imagery of melting ice and dripping water. Despite the obvious signs of coldness that are presented on-screen, the landscape of *The Revenant* is revealed to be experiencing persistent change. The sound of this dissolution produces a palpable anxiety, emerging at moments of crisis in the narrative, most significantly when Glass sets out to hunt down Fitzgerald. The snowy West of *The Revenant* is dissolving into new forms that may yet prove to be even more hostile than those endured by Glass.

CGI Animals Haunting the Frontier

Iñárritu's attempt to exhibit the reality of the frontier and the wilderness is continually confounded by the ideological underpinnings of the Western genre and the persistence of the human presence in the landscape. Nevertheless moments of insight do emerge in *The Revenant* when environmental crisis is expressed with clarity. This play, between the desire for authenticity and denial of the West as it is currently constituted, is most apparent in the way in which the film depicts animals through the use of computer-generated imagery (CGI). The scene in which the mother bear attacks Glass while defending her cubs is shockingly violent and realistic, and only made possible through the use of computer graphics. In practical terms, the fur and saliva of the creature are effectively recreated, while a stunt man mimicked its movements. The heightened viciousness of this encounter functioned as exploitative publicity for the film. Such was the frisson surrounding the scene that the distributors were compelled to deny rumors regarding its content:

> Arguably, the most unnerving, gaze-averting scene is the bear attack, which could do for the woods what "Jaws" did for the ocean. The horrors of this sequence are so rattling that Fox, in response to a preposterous report by The Drudge Report, released a statement that said, essentially, No, Mr. DiCaprio was not raped by a bear in the course of the film. (Segal 2015)

The fight with the grizzly was traumatizing enough to be read as an act of violation, an extreme form of sexual assault. And yet the creature itself did not exist. The scene was again praised for its authenticity, as a brutal evocation of what such an attack would be like. Yet again the "reality" discourse around *The*

Revenant constructs a notion of the authentic built on something that cannot possibly be real.

There are many more such encounters with CGI creatures, including a herd of bison being attacked by wolves. The wolves in this instance arrive after Glass's pyramid of skulls dream. The animals' balletic hunting is contrasted with the industrial slaughter committed by the colonists. Later, in his hunger, Glass takes a stick and mimes shooting a gun at a herd of moose crossing a river. The stick-as-gun imagery is perhaps a small acknowledgment of the film's equally contrived representations of animals. Of course Glass is a hunter, and wild animals were common and dangerous in the West of the 1820s, and it would have been highly impractical to film these sequences without the use of CGI. However, there are occasions in which the appearance of CGI animals seems gratuitous. A raven is framed looking down on Glass as he lies by the river but as it moves its wings it becomes clear that it is computer generated. A dislocation is immediately created between the naturally lit, pristine authenticity of the wilderness landscape and the awkwardly animated raven approximation, squatting in the center of the screen.

In *The Revenant* an attempt has been made to populate an empty landscape with long-dead fauna. Interestingly, William Brown, in his analysis of the function of CGI in film, argues that digital technologies have allowed the development of a "Nonanthropocentric Character" in contemporary cinema (2013: 52). Following Deleuze and Guattari's conception of becoming, Brown shows how the morphing capabilities of CGI destabilize the settled notion that it is the human that is the subject of film:

> The fact that digital cinema is a cinema in which fixed identity is replaced by the constantly shifting and fluid identities of non- or posthuman characters allows us easily to grasp the ways in which digital cinema is also potentially an antihumanist cinema. (2013: 77)

The Revenant, however, seems to employ CGI in order to reinstate a relational hierarchy that was actually extinguished by human action. The visual effects in the film represent an effort to recreate a Western space that is prelapsarian. The sense of awe that spectators experience when the human characters interact with the CGI animals in *The Revenant* is clearly linked to the film's striking on-screen resurrection of an exuberantly vital biosphere that has now been lost forever.

The digital animals that shamble through *The Revenant* seem to be indicative of a cinematic natural world that makes claims to authenticity and yet is ultimately constructed. The world of the film seems to conform to Jean Baudrillard's notion of simulation and hyperreality. In the post-modern world, Baudrillard argues, the proliferation of communication technologies and the subsequent ubiquity of images, signs, and codes has created a simulated world that has supplanted the real one: "The territory no longer precedes the map, nor does it survive it" (1994: 1). In modernity images were designed to represent a thing that was presumed to exist in the real world. However, in our condition of postmodernity the image has no referent outside of other images. These simulacra reflect one another in an endless and inescapable hall of mirrors. In this hermetic worldview we live in a state of hyperreality, in which the play of signs and images is both more real and more inherently attractive than any claims toward truth, the real or the natural.

Indeed the skepticism toward stable truth and the real that Baudrillard's thought represents challenges the very existence of a natural world beyond the simulated. Ultimately, Baudrillard identifies contemporary environmentalism as a symptom of the end of nature when he observes that "the great signified, the great referent Nature, is dead, replaced by environment" (1981: 201). This is of course problematic for any analysis that is concerned with real threats to this environment. The risk of climate change and environmental destruction would seem to intensify the enfolding of the natural into the simulated since landscapes and ecosystems become further removed and abstracted from us as they are changed. The CGI beasts of *The Revenant* may be indicative of an attempt to mask the absence of those animals and create the ultimate simulation that is the Western landscape. Baudrillard depicts the silence of animals as a form of dissent against the logic of reason that leads to their exploitation by humans (1994: 137–38). Animals, as beings without language, are able to fully inhabit their own territory, free from the anxieties that afflict rootless humanity. The bear, the moose, the bison, and the raven in Iñárritu's rendering are perhaps indicators of the impossibility of authentic nonhuman representation.

Acknowledging the echoes of simulation and the hyperreal in *The Revenant* risks an enervating sense of despair, as climate change only exacerbates the disconnection between the play of signs and the diminishing world outside. The failure of authenticity that the film represents could point to the essential futility of narratives that seek to represent the challenges facing the natural world. The Western genre faces the absence of the Western landscape. However, we can accept that claims to truth that rely on an essentialized "nature" should be subject to skepticism while also accepting a non-anthropocentric world possessed of inherent value, and that we can hope to preserve it. As Greg Garrard notes, when "oriented toward practical problems of responsibility, we need not accept the dichotomy between backpacking in the Adirondacks and a cyborg existence on a simulated Earth" (2012: 130). For all of its confusion around the desire for and possibility of authenticity, *The Revenant* maintains a practically oriented position with regards to the environment of the West.

The Value of Making Westerns in the Anthropocene

Despite the naive claims it makes to authenticity *The Revenant* may provide an example of a Western that acknowledges the constructed nature of the West as wilderness, while nevertheless passionately advocating for an ethical engagement with a real and contingent nature. Both Iñárritu and DiCaprio have spoken about the film as containing environmental themes and a concern for the rapid denuding of a once pristine wilderness. DiCaprio has fronted two documentaries—*The 11th Hour* (Leila Conners Petersen and Nadia Conners, 2007) and *Before the Flood* (Fisher Stevens, 2015)—specifically about climate change and the necessity of ameliorating its worst effects. While it is easy to dismiss such efforts as the affectations of Hollywood liberals it is clear that *The Revenant* was undertaken with a commitment to representing a living world that is under immense pressure.

The behind-the-scenes documentary *A World Unseen* makes an explicit connection between the acquisitive impulses of the fur trappers and the contemporary rush to exploit shale oil and tar sands in the West. However, the most significant thing that the documentary and reporting around the film revealed was the way in which the production experienced the effects of climate change firsthand. For the look and narrative of the film Iñárritu required wilderness locations that were snowbound. The vast majority of filming for *The Revenant* was scheduled to take place in Canada around the city of Calgary. However, there was an unprecedented lack of snow in the region. DiCaprio detailed how locals he talked to had never experienced anything like it: "When we were shooting in Calgary the natives from there, they were telling us they had never experienced that weather they were going through. Never in their lives" (*A World Unseen* 2016). The production was forced to undertake a "global search for snow" (Miller 2015), ultimately landing on the southern tip of Argentina.

Similar problems beset Quentin Tarantino's Western *The Hateful Eight* (2015), with a lack of snow at high altitude in Colorado hampering the shooting schedule. It seems clear that the kinds of landscapes in which the Western was developed and defined visually are now becoming increasingly inhospitable to Western narratives and filmmakers. One response could be a retreat inside and onto the green screen. Animated Westerns like *Rango* (Gore Verbinski, 2011) show that this might even produce thoughtful and creative films. But the Western is a genre that necessitates venturing out into the West and experiencing, firsthand, the incongruities and changes rapidly proliferating in the anthropocene. Climate change poses a myriad of representational challenges while disrupting notions of authenticity. But, in spite of this, it is still possible for an environmentally responsible Western to be made in the wilderness and—in doing so—pass comment on the changing climate. The Western has always been about the interplay of signs, symbols, and tropes (the black hat, the gun, the horse) but it has also always acknowledged the truth of lives lived in a particular landscape.

Conclusion

The task faced by Western filmmakers is a daunting one. How can genre films continue to be set and produced in a region that is becoming increasingly hostile to the process of filmmaking? It is easy to imagine future scenarios in which production is forced away from a particular location due to excessive heat or the effects of flooding. The ecology of what we consider the Western space is also threatened. As populations of larger vertebrates have dwindled so have those of the smaller creatures. Monarch butterflies, who roost in enormous numbers across California, have had their migration routes disrupted by changing weather patterns (Holson 2019). Other changes in vegetation are occurring. For example, Robinson Meyer's (2017) study suggests that climate change may play a role in the movement of tree populations westward, a strange echoing of historical settler movements and the frontier. The flora and fauna that have provided the backdrop for Western narratives for over one hundred years are rapidly disappearing or changing and Westerns that seek to depict an authentic version of the frontier past will be compelled to address the absence of anything resembling the historical West in which to tell their stories. As I have shown, *The Revenant* demonstrates two possible responses to climate change in the Western.

First, the film is deeply animated by the desire for authenticity and attempts to create an immersive Western through visual and sound design with some success. However, this obsession with a "real" West ignores the extent to which the frontier and the idea of wilderness have been constructed and deployed for ideological ends. With the rapid changes that the West is experiencing, authenticity may prove to be a dead end for the Western film. However, *The Revenant* also shows the value of a full-blooded engagement with the landscapes of the West. By heading out into the changing spaces of the genre, the makers of *The Revenant* were able to experience firsthand the discontinuities and dislocations of climate change. This may well indicate the value of the Western, as chronicle of loss and change, in the anthropocene.

Bibliography

A World Unseen: The Revenant. [Film] Dir. E. Rausch, USA: Twentieth Century Fox, 2016.

Baudrillard, Jean. *For a Critique of the Political Economy of the Sign*, translated by Charles Levin. St. Louis: Telos Press, 1981.

Baudrillard, Jean. *Simulacra and Simulation*, translated by S. F. Glaser. Ann Arbor: University of Michigan Press, 1994.

Bradshaw, Peter. "The Revenant Review—Gut-churningly Brutal, Beautiful Storytelling." *The Guardian*, December 4 (2015). Available online at: https://www.theguardian.com/film/2015/dec/04/the-revenant-review-gut-churningly-brutal-beautiful-storytelling (accessed August 5, 2017).

Brown, William. *Supercinema: Film-Philosophy for the Digital Age*. Oxford: Berghahn, 2013.

Campbell, Neil. *Post-Westerns: Cinema, Region, West*. London: University of Nebraska Press, 2013.

C.D. 1892 Glueworks, Office Foot of 1st st., Works at Rougeville, Michigan 1892. Detroit Public Library, Detroit. Available online at: https://digitalcollections.detroitpublic library.org//islandora/object/islandora:151477 (accessed February 2, 2019).

Cronon, William. "The Trouble with Wilderness; or, Getting Back to the Wrong Nature." In *Uncommon Ground: Rethinking the Human Place in Nature*, edited by William Cronon, 69–90. London: Norton, 1996.

Garrard, Greg. *Ecocriticism*. Oxford: Routledge, 2012.

Holson, Laura M. "With 86% Drop, California's Monarch Butterfly Population Hits Record Low." *The New York Times*, January 9 (2019). Available online at: https://www.nytimes.com/2019/01/09/science/monarch-butterfly-california.html (accessed February 2, 2019).

Lewis, Nathaniel. *Unsettling the Literary West: Authenticity and Authorship.* London: University of Nebraska Press, 2003.

Masters, Kim. "How Leonardo DiCaprio's 'The Revenant' Shoot Became 'A Living Hell."' *The Hollywood Reporter*, July 22 (2015). Available online at: https://www.hollywood reporter.com/news/how-leonardo-dicaprios-revenant-shoot-810290 (accessed August 7, 2017).

Meyer, Robinson. "American Trees Are Moving West, and No One Knows Why: Climate Change Explains only 20 Percent of the Movement." *The Atlantic*, May 17 (2017). Available online at: https://www.theatlantic.com/science/archive/2017/05/ go-west-my-sap/526899/ (accessed September 10, 2017).

Miller, Julie. "Leonardo DiCaprio Slept in Animal Carcasses and Ate Bison Body Parts for The Revenant: Beat that, Johnny Depp." *Vanity Fair*, October 20 (2015). Available online at: https://www.vanityfair.com/hollywood/2015/10/leonardo-dicaprio-the-revenant (accessed September 12, 2017).

Mitchell, Lee Clark. "What's Authentic about Western Literature? And, More to the Point, What's Literary." In *Postwestern Cultures: Literature, Theory, Space*, edited by Susan Kollin, 95–112. London: University of Nebraska Press, 2007.

Orvell, Miles. *The Real Thing: Imitation and Authenticity in American Culture, 1880–1940*. Chapel Hill: UNC Press, [1989] 2014.

Roosevelt, Theodore, and Henry Cabot Lodge. *The Complete Works of Theodore Roosevelt*, edited by Joseph Bucklin Bishop. USA: e-artnow, 2017.

Segal, David. "About That Bear: Alejandro G. Iñárritu Discusses Making the Revenant." *The New York Times*, December 22 (2015). Available online at: https://www.nytimes. com/2015/12/27/movies/about-that-bear-alejandro-g-inarritu-discusses-making-the-revenant.html (accessed August 5, 2017).

Simmon, Scott. *The Invention of the Western Film: A Cultural History of the Genre's First Half-Century*. Cambridge: Cambridge University Press, 2003.

Thakur, Gautam Basu. *Postcolonial Theory and Avatar*. New York: Bloomsbury Academic, 2016.

Turner, Frederick Jackson. *The Frontier in American History*. New York: Henry Holt and Company, 1921.

Woodhall, Woody. "Creating the sounds for The Revenant." *ProVideo Coalition*, January 2 (2016). Available online at: https://www.providecoalition.com/ creating-the-sounds-for-the-revenant/ (accessed September 12, 2017).

12

"Hand in Hand We'll Get There":
—the Racial Politics of *The Hateful Eight*

Thomas Moodie

Introduction

The Hateful Eight (2015) is the third of Quentin Tarantino's films in which a narrative of fantasy revenge unfolds against a historical backdrop of hostile race relations, in this case the immediate aftermath of the American Civil War. As with his previous films *Inglourious Basterds* (2009) and *Django Unchained* (2012), *The Hateful Eight* features an array of allusions to other cinematic and literary texts, an aesthetic eclecticism, frequent tonal shifts between humor and horror, and moments of extreme violence, all of which have long been recognized as part of the director's signature style. These diverse, often conflicting elements present a critical challenge to the viewer with regard to the films' politics. The central question when watching these films is whether they have serious things to say about their subject matter, or whether they merely exploit their historical settings in the service of superficial entertainment.

Critical responses to these films include accusations of historical insensitivity, the glorification of violence, and an emphasis on style as a substitute for sustained critical thought. Jonathan Rosenbaum, for example, argues that the historical revisionism of *Inglourious Basterds*, in which the Second World War ends prematurely with the assassination of the Nazi High Command in a cinema, is tantamount to Holocaust denial (2009), while director Spike Lee made a case for boycotting the theatrical release of *Django Unchained* on the grounds that the film reduces historical atrocities to a stylized genre piece (Carroll 2018). Similarly, Mark Kermode argues in his review of *The Hateful Eight* that Tarantino is primarily concerned with witty dialogue and references to other films, which as a consequence relegates the political thought in the film to secondary importance (2016).

This chapter responds to some of the hostility toward Tarantino's work with an exploration of *The Hateful Eight*'s cinematic and historical allusions. Through this, I contend that the film operates as a broad allegory of US race relations which satirizes the divisions of its Reconstruction Era setting and resonates with its contemporary moment. Its many references to other Western texts form part of this subversive project, with their coexistence rendering visible the political diversity of depictions and constructions of national history on the screen. After an overview of the promotion of community in American post–Civil War Westerns, I provide a close reading of the film's extensive dialogues on racial politics. What emerges from this analysis is a satirical strategy in which inequalities are articulated only for the potential for reconciliation to be frustrated by the characters' sustained prejudice. The failure of community is presented through a violent allegory of societal collapse as the result of this entrenched ideological division, which in the film's final moments is transcended by an ironic alliance predicated on misogyny and sadism rather than restorative communal values. The film thus subverts the unifying impulse common in the genre by presenting a cynical vision of the United States.

Reconstruction in the West

The defeat of the Confederate States of America at the end of the Civil War presented the challenge of how to unify the defeated Southern states with the North, quell old grievances, and restore the South's economy in the absence of the slave system, as well as the not insignificant task of absorbing five million former slaves into the fabric of democratic society. In the decade after the war, Abraham Lincoln and successive presidents undertook a project of national unification that sought to promote a new patriotism in order to reunite former enemies and ensure the survival of the nation. Several editorials from the time reflect this effort in their optimistic prophesies of a United States in which the divisions of the conflict would soon be erased. Writing in the April 14, 1865, edition of the New York *Tribune*, editor Horace Greeley declared "the path of Peace opens pleasantly before us" ([1865] 2003: 5). Similarly, on April 20, 1865, Samuel Bowles for the *Republican* argued "the restoration of the Union is a simple and straight forward process, and it will be speedy and permanent" ([1865] 2003: 11). In spite of efforts toward peace, ideological resistance to the restored union continued, and prophesies of a unified nation proved premature. As historian

W. E. B. Du Bois writes, paramilitary organizations roamed the Southern states with the objective of terrorizing recently emancipated African Americans in opposition to their enfranchisement, as well as to revenge themselves on the perceived injustices carried out on white citizens ([1935] 1995: 676–77). Among these, the Ku Klux Klan emerged as one of the most notorious white supremacist groups with its aim of disenfranchisement through intimidation, violence, and murder. In addition to these vigilante groups, many Southern states elected former Confederate officers to positions of power (Dickerson 2003: 16), and President Johnson's gamble to pardon thousands of rebels enabled what Donna L. Dickerson calls "the old planter class" (2003: 193) to reassume political control over the South. Although the war had ended and slavery was abolished, the union remained fragile and racial division endured.

The Reconstruction Era is commonly viewed as the period between 1865 and 1877, ending with the Compromise of 1877 which saw the withdrawal of Federal troops from Southern states. However, the project of Reconstruction has arguably never finished. From its inception, cinema has played a significant role in this project as a vehicle for shaping cultural attitudes and understanding. It is a basic observation that Westerns reflect the sensibilities of their age, with the genre being one in which contemporary values and tensions play out against the backdrop of national history and the semi-mythic space of the frontier. This makes the genre particularly well-suited to this national enterprise, with several scholars noting its role in the promotion of social unity. The basic formula of many films set in the aftermath of the Civil War is the reconciliation of former opponents as they cooperate against an external threat. Past ideological divisions must be set aside in order to ensure the characters' survival, and as a consequence a new, revitalized American community emerges. As Jenny Barrett argues, the position of these films is that "the North/South line of conflict cannot be seen to endure because in the new united nation there can be no North or South" (2009: 88). By contrast, Lee Broughton has noted the ways in which Italian-made Westerns set in the post–Civil War era routinely reject stories of reconciliation. Broughton argues that Italy's long-standing and still unresolved history of North-South antagonisms is thus reflected in the films' narratives of ongoing North-South conflict (2016a) rather than evaded as in the US tradition.

In their promotion of reconciliation through the diversion of the conflict onto a new threat antithetical to the community, Hollywood Westerns implicitly (and often explicitly) establish which groups are acceptable and which are intolerable to the nation. In *Stagecoach* (John Ford, 1939) and *The Searchers* (Ford, 1956) it is the Apache and Comanche who present an existential danger; in *Major Dundee* (Sam Peckinpah, 1965) and *The Undefeated* (Andrew V. McLaglen, 1969) it is the Mexicans and the French army against whom united former opponents must contend. If these films promote community, it is principally a community of their white characters and those they represent, with Native Americans and other minorities demonized or absent. A xenophobic logic thus underpins these films, with a "white *centrality*" (Coyne 1998: 4, emphasis in original) common across the genre if not an explicit white supremacy. Moreover, African American characters have always been a rarity in the post–Civil War Western.

Indeed, Lee Broughton's work on the representation of African Americans in Hollywood Westerns found just a handful of post–Civil War Westerns that featured a major black presence (2016b). And, as Jenny Barrett notes (2009: 90–91), the addition of the Civil War to the genre has rarely challenged the tendency for the causes of the conflict to be obscured, with very few films commenting on the racist ideologies that underpinned the war and its legacy. In those that do depict characters unable to move beyond the war, such as *The Searchers*, those who hold onto the divisions of the past are ultimately rejected from society; Ethan Edwards (John Wayne), with his Confederate uniform and saber three years after the war ended, cannot rejoin the homestead at the film's conclusion. In sidestepping the legacy of slavery to focus on other supposed threats to white society, these films contribute to the marginalization, misrepresentation, and erasure of minority groups in their constructions of a predominantly white national history. Thus Gary W. Gallagher's definition of the "Reconciliation Cause Tradition"—which "represented an attempt by white people North and South to extol the *American* [Gallagher's emphasis] virtues both sides manifested during the war, to exalt the restored nation that emerged from the conflict, and to mute the role of African Americans" (2008: 2)—can be seen to play out in most Hollywood Westerns that feature references to the Civil War.

A reworking of the episode "Fair Game" (Irvin Kershner, 1960) from the Nick Adams vehicle *The Rebel* (1959–61), *The Hateful Eight*'s premise is deceptively simple. In both, a bounty hunter transporting a woman in chains takes shelter in a coach station, only to stumble into a conspiracy to free the woman that transforms the station into a site of paranoia, collective distrust, and poisoned beverages. Where "Fair Game" is a relatively straightforward mystery— essentially a reworking of an Agatha Christie plot into a half-hour television slot—*The Hateful Eight* adds complexity to the premise by exploring the shifting power dynamics of the unlikely community assembled in Minnie's haberdashery in order to comment on the racial inequalities of its Reconstruction Era setting. As such, it soon becomes clear that mapping Gallagher's blueprint for stories that depict reconciliation in the post–Civil War West onto the narrative of Tarantino's film would be an increasingly difficult proposition.

After the opening credits sequence, *The Hateful Eight* immediately alludes to John Ford's classic Western *Stagecoach* in its introduction of Major Warren (Samuel L. Jackson). Not only is his introduction similar to the first appearance of John Wayne's Ringo, the stagecoaches appear to be from the same company, with the Overland Stage Line in Ford's film and the Butterfield Overland Stage Line in Tarantino's. This is more than a straightforward homage. In *Stagecoach*, a diverse community is compelled to interact with each other in their journey across the frontier, with each character representing a different element of white society in the United States. The stagecoach dislocates the characters from their own environments and requires a renegotiation of preexisting hierarchies as they face challenges and threats to their survival. Their journey is given the allegorical weight of an odyssey through which the nation learns to recognize and accept its diversity to form a new, unified community. As Michael Coyne notes, this is not an entirely optimistic vision; as well as presenting Dallas (Claire Trevor) and Ringo as "paradigm citizens in a harsh society," he argues that the film implies "there is no room for the timid, the unhealthily ancient, the corrupt, or the malignant" (1997: 22) as the characters who embody these qualities are either wounded or arrested, or they perish. Moreover, the community necessarily disbands once they reach their destination. What the film offers is not an affirmation of a community achieved but the potential for it, an allegorical vision of the pursuit of a unified society with an awareness of the challenges which continue to prevent it. In referencing this community-based Western in its opening scenes, *The Hateful Eight* creates the expectation that it too will function as an allegory of the nation. However, the "collectivist heroic drama" (Kitses 2004: 49) of Ford's film is substituted with a far more pessimistic allegory in which communal values are unable to be entertained, let alone sustained.

Any expectations created by these allusions to *Stagecoach* are complicated by further references to several anti-mythologizing films which function as cynical allegories of US society. In its narrative of societal collapse in the wake of collective paranoia and opportunism, it shares similarities with Sergio Corbucci's Western *The Great Silence* (*Il grande silenzo*, also known as *The Big Silence*, 1968). Major Warren's introduction shares similarities to a scene in which Tigrero

(Klaus Kinski) asks for assistance transporting the bodies of his bounties in the snow, and the entire conversation between Major Warren and John Ruth (Kurt Russell) about the practicalities of transporting bounties mirrors that between Tigrero and Sheriff Burnett (Frank Wolff). In its cynical vision of capitalist society, individual heroism is an insufficient response to a world corrupted by greed and opportunism. Here the film's already wounded and incapacitated protagonist, Silence (Jean-Louis Trintignant), is unceremoniously gunned down by Tigrero in a subversion of the traditional showdown in which the better man always triumphs against the odds. The second European Western with which *The Hateful Eight* shares similarities is Joaquín Luis Romero Marchent's hybrid horror-Western *Cut-Throats Nine* (*Condenados a vivir*, 1972), an obscure exploitation film in which the failed transportation of chained prisoners leads to a spectacle of graphic, nihilistic violence, with a final act set in a cabin not unlike Minnie's haberdashery. As a heavy-handed anti-capitalist allegory (the prisoners are literally chained together by gold), *Cut-Throats Nine* is devoid of communal values and heroic impulses, its characters instead motivated by self-preservation, greed, and sadism. Like *Cut-Throats Nine*, *The Hateful Eight* often crosses into the horror genre. Indeed, *The Hateful Eight* includes several allusions to John Carpenter's *The Thing* (1982). In Carpenter's film, the characters face a literal Other, an extraterrestrial monster capable of using humans as hosts that causes collective paranoia and a breakdown in its isolated Antarctica-based community. Ennio Morricone reuses some of his unused score for the earlier film, and this, combined with the casting of main star Kurt Russell as bounty hunter John Ruth, invites comparisons between these snow-filled studies of paranoia and existential threat.

Where *Stagecoach* depicts the formation of a community, these later films examine the disintegration of society through prejudice, market forces, and paranoia. In evoking both *Stagecoach* and *The Great Silence* in its opening sequences, the film sets up an intertextual tension between competing visions of the United States, with Major Warren a composite of Ringo and Tigrero. The coexistence of these allusions challenges their radically divergent depictions of nationhood in the United States and renders them vulnerable to interrogation, their politics made visible by their amalgamation. Through its allusions to various films in the Western genre and beyond, the film reveals itself not only as part of an allegorical tradition within the genre, with its stagecoach and haberdashery microcosms of society, but also as a critique of the diverse cultural constructions of US society that have preceded it.

Restaging the Civil War

In marked contrast to the majority of post–Civil War Westerns which bypass the racial politics of the conflict to focus on new threats to the nation, *The Hateful Eight* focuses on the war's legacy as its characters negotiate on racial terms, discuss the war and its ideologies, and remain, for the most part, devoted to its divisions. In his review of the film, critic Mark Kermode suspects that the extensive conversations about race in the film, although they often resonate with contemporary politics, are ultimately "just talking because no one reigned this stuff in" (2016). By contrast, I contend that the lengthy dialogue sequences, whether the result of the screenwriter's indulgence or not, have a significant function within the film's satirical project. The characters repeat themselves ad nauseam as they obsess over minor details and exchanges to an absurd degree, negotiating who is admitted onto the stagecoach, who is chained, and who is armed. Their repetitive negotiations are often humorous and serve to make clear their paranoia, as does their reliance on bounty bills, letters, and business cards to establish authority and legitimacy. Although their discussions frequently touch on race and hint at the possibility of mutual respect, these moments of potential unity are frustrated by their inability to develop in any meaningful way, an absurdist political stasis that is only ruptured by extreme violence.

The introduction of Major Warren establishes the film's exploration of power dynamics in a white supremacist society. Warren is an African American former Union cavalry officer, and when asked to identify himself he offers his full military title. He also refers to himself as "a servant of the court," a euphemism for his current work as a bounty hunter. His introduction ties him to the US military and justice systems, yet the reality of historical racial inequality cuts through; in response to John Ruth's suggestion that Warren should be shown respect, his prisoner Daisy (Jennifer Jason Leigh) responds with a blunt "howdy nigger." John Ruth's response, an earnest attempt at political correctness, equally falls short: "Don't you know darkies don't like being called niggers anymore? They find it offensive."

Warren is admitted onto the stagecoach through an agreement with Ruth that they will protect the other's bounties, but also because he carries a letter purportedly written by Abraham Lincoln (while the film is not set in a specific year, a reference to John Wilkes Booth implies the film is set after the president's assassination). Through the letter's reception, the film depicts the enduring inequalities of the Reconstruction Era. Although its contents are not revealed until the end of the film, Ruth's excitement to read it, as well as his hesitation and embarrassment to ask, signifies its importance not only as a presidential artifact but also as a letter of passage. Its white authority engenders respect, with Warren's blackness made palatable to Ruth as a result. This alliance is predicated on prior white acceptance, the higher authority of the president, and the revelation of the letter's inauthenticity disrupts their relationship. Oswaldo Mobray (Tim Roth) and Chris Mannix (Walton Goggins), respectively a white Englishman and the son of a Southern paramilitary leader, express disbelief at the notion that a black man shared correspondence with the president. Mobray's high-pitched exclamation "the nigger? In the stable? Has a letter? From Abraham Lincoln?" emphasizes the unlikelihood of the situation, as does Mannix's incredulous word-for-word repetition. Mannix's interrogation of Warren at the dinner table is equally repetitive to the point of absurdity:

> You got a letter from Abraham Lincoln? The Abraham Lincoln? Abraham Lincoln, the President of the United States? Of America? Wrote you a letter, personally? Personally as in "Dear Major Warren? Dear Marquis," Abraham Lincoln, the President?

Although such moments are played for laughs, they articulate the sociopolitical realities of the era; slavery may have been abolished, but Lincoln was certainly never pen pals with an African American officer. The revelation of the letter's artificiality provides an opportunity for Ruth to experience empathy, as Warren defends the deception as a survival mechanism. His argument "the only time black folks are safe is when white folks is disarmed, and this letter had the desired effort" exposes Ruth to his own complicity in racist dynamics and the disparities that have informed their interactions. Warren is hyperaware of his position as a black man, and expresses the challenges he faces trying to negotiate his way through a racist society. However, the potential for empathy and reconciliation is frustrated as Ruth's prejudice not only endures but is entrenched, with his retreat into the racist stereotype of black men as deceitful in his response: "I guess it's true what they say about you people; can't trust a fucking word comes out of your mouths." This is the last time the men talk to each other.

The film continues its exploration of racial inequality in its allusions to historical Civil War atrocities and their legacy. In an attempt to deflate the tension between the pro-Confederates and the pro-Unionists, Mobray proposes to divide the haberdashery, with one side the Northern Side, the other the South, and the dinner table neutral territory. This recreation of the North-

South division signals a return to the conflict of the past, as the geography of the room is made an explicitly allegorical site. When Major Warren crosses the line to enter "Georgia" with a bowl of stew for General Smithers (Bruce Dern), a former Confederate officer, it appears initially to be a peace offering rather than an incursion. Major Warren and General Smithers are ideological opposites, a division emphasized by the unsubtle symbolism of the black and white chessboard placed between them. Once again, the possibility of racial tolerance appears possible as the two men discuss life after the war. Smithers offers up details of his life as he nostalgically dotes on his late wife, his peach orchards, and his ponies. This softer side is a stark contrast to his earlier use of an intermediary to communicate with Warren and his stubborn refusal to recognize "niggers in cavalry officer uniforms." Throughout this scene, Bob (Demián Bichir) plays the Christmas carol "Silent Night" on the piano, one of many Christian motifs in the film with attendant connotations of reconciliation and redemption. However, just as Bob is unskilled at the piano and grows frustrated as he plays the wrong notes, any suggestion of reconciliation is undermined as Warren takes revenge on the general for his war crimes.

In a standard Western conceit, Warren places his gun next to Smithers and goads him into reaching for it by telling the story of his rape and murder of Smithers' son. Warren's revenge is the atrocity hidden in the film's title, a pun on the sexual assault he describes at length: the hateful fellatio, or the *hate fellate*. Here Tarantino reworks the desert march from Sergio Leone's *The Good, the Bad, and the Ugly* (*Il buono, il brutto, il cattivo*, 1966) with Smithers' son forced to crawl naked through the snow for miles before he is raped, refused a blanket, and murdered. In both films, the sadism of the act is dwelled upon, yet in Leone's film there is never any doubt that Blondie (Clint Eastwood) will eventually escape from Tuco (Eli Wallach), however unlikely it appears. Where the earlier film allows for a degree of excitement in anticipation of Blondie's escape, Warren's revenge is solely horrific. Smithers' eyes are overlaid on the first shot of the march, and the combined images give the scene a subjective quality in which the audience shares the old man's perspective. Warren's line "starting to see pictures, ain't ya?" is delivered directly into the camera, as though he has broken the fourth wall to terrorize the audience. This is more than a straightforward homage but a complex scene of horror that merges the assault on Smithers' son with the assault on Smithers and the assault on the audience.

It is worth noting that there is no way to know whether Warren is telling the truth here, especially since what we see is less a flashback than Smithers' imagining of events. Warren's strength lies in his keen understanding of the racist pathologies of the people he encounters, and his ability to manipulate their racism against them gives him an unusual degree of agency. He succeeds in tricking Ruth into accepting his friendship with Lincoln, and here he avenges the execution of black soldiers by exploiting Smithers' racist beliefs. With its use of the stereotype that depicts black men as a sexual threat to white society, a greater fantasy of black revenge could not be imagined by this white supremacist character. Later, Warren deduces that Bob killed Minnie (Dana Gourrier) because of her refusal to admit Mexicans to her establishment, yet in the film's flashback sequence she shows no signs of animosity toward him, suggesting that this particular anecdote may be a fiction too, thus raising further doubts about Warren's other claims.

Curiously, Tarantino locates Warren's animosity toward Smithers in the 1862 Battle of Baton Rouge, a real historical event which did not feature black soldiers. Although the Militia Act of 1862 was enacted on July 17 that year, which allowed for the participation of African Americans in the military, it was not until September 27 that General Benjamin F. Butler commanded the first black regiment to fight for the Union. In spite of this anachronism, Smithers' fictional war crime echoes several high-profile atrocities carried out against black soldiers during the conflict. As Gregory J. W. Urwin writes, Confederate forces treated captive black soldiers with less respect than their white counterparts "not so much for any crimes they may have committed but for who they were and the social revolution that they represented" (2004: 7). For example, the Fort Pillow massacre in April 12, 1864, saw the murder of the majority of a Union garrison in spite of their surrender, with the Confederate army's refusal to acknowledge them as prisoners. Led by Major General Nathan Bedford Forrest, Confederate forces were reported to have "set fire to tents containing Federal wounded, and committed other terrible atrocities" (Castel 2004: 89). The reports include accounts of black soldiers "buried alive" (Castel 2004: 98), a controversial claim given some credence by a Confederate soldier's account of the battle and its aftermath. Similarly, accounts of the conditions in the Confederate-operated prisoner-of-war camp in Andersonville describe black prisoners subjected to especially cruel treatment even within the already neglectful and dehumanizing conditions of the camp (Coles 2004: 78). While the specifics of Smithers' war crime are anachronistic fiction, it is rooted in this long legacy of white supremacist military violence against minorities across the nation's history.

This is far from the enjoyable fantasy revenge of *Django Unchained*. In the earlier film, there is a marked shift in its approach to violence as it moves from depictions of slavery to a conventional Western shoot-out. As Anne-Marie Paquet-Deyris perceptively notes, the unrealistic spurts of blood in the final act "point toward the complete de-realization of the type of violence that was depicted earlier in the film" (2016: 163). Django (Jamie Foxx) asks Cora (Dana Gourrier) to say goodbye to her owner, and seconds later Miss Lara (Laura Cayouette) is shot and flies out of frame at an impossible speed and direction. Soon after, Django is unharmed by the explosion of the Candie mansion and Broomhilda's (Kerry Washington) horse barely flinches. The ending stresses its own fictiveness by employing the clichéd Hollywood narrative of the hero defeating the villains and rescuing his love interest. This exaggerated fantasy fulfillment allows the audience to enjoy the spectacle because the finale's violence is separated from the historically rooted violence that preceded it. In contrast, in *The Hateful Eight* the sadism and sexual transgression of Warren's act temper any ironic enjoyment of his revenge. As with the relationship between Ruth and Warren, this interaction teases reconciliation between its prejudiced characters only to be frustrated when they remain defiant. After the general's death Bob closes the piano lid, a sign that once again the potential for reconciliation and redemption has eluded the travelers.

Ironic Post-Racial Harmony

After these dialogues on race are frustrated, the film presents a violent allegory of intolerance as the fragile community descends into extreme violence and cruelty. The failure to reconcile differences and to cooperate is depicted as an existential threat to society, with a great deal of its violence absurdist in its excess. Ruth and the stagecoach driver O. B. (James Parks) vomit gratuitous amounts of blood after being poisoned; jelly beans scatter as one of Minnie's helpers is shot at point-blank range; Daisy and Ruth engage in slapstick violence while chained to one another; a parody of Doris Day's *Calamity Jane* (David Butler, 1953) character is swiftly dispatched; Daisy hacks off Ruth's arm in an attempt to escape; Mannix faints; Bob's head explodes.

The film dwells on this violence, with the shoot-out between Warren, Mannix, and Mobray presented in slow motion so that each bullet wound is registered. This has a similar effect to the temporal manipulation found in Sam Peckinpah's work, undoubtedly an influence here. As Jim Kitses writes with regard to Peckinpah, "The audience is compelled to experience the thrill and the brutality, the sustained excess ideally keying spectatorship's uncomfortable insight into its own complicity," part of a strategy "to elicit a critical awareness" (2004: 203). The absurdist quality of these scenes emphasizes their unreality, encouraging the viewer to look beyond the narrative to their allegorical qualities. These are, for the whole, incomplete characters, far less developed than those in *The Wild Bunch* (Peckinpah, 1969) or *Django Unchained*. Warren is given some complexity in his ability to manipulate racial prejudice to survive and exact revenge, but otherwise the film is populated with stock characters onto whom extreme violence and suffering are inflicted. This is a point emphasized in some of the advertising for the film. In the posters, trailers, and playbills used to promote the film, the characters are described as archetypal figures: the sheriff, the hangman, the prisoner, the bounty hunter, the Mexican, the little man, the confederate, and the cow puncher. Because each character's authenticity is in doubt, there is a critical distance between the viewer and the action. Straightforwardly, Tim Roth's exaggerated portrayal of a bandit posing as an impossibly posh Englishman with a twirly mustache gives the viewer little reason to care about Oswaldo Mobray as he writhes on the floor after being shot. This is arguably the closest Tarantino's work has come to realizing the charges of gratuitous violence leveled against it, yet excess is precisely its purpose within its allegory of a nation doomed by its divisions.

This absurdist violence culminates in a scene of ironic post-racial harmony. As discussed earlier, Hollywood Westerns have often been used to cultivate an idealized, sanitized image of the nation which moves beyond its divisions toward a unified community with renewed purpose. To this end, *The Hateful Eight* offers teases that point toward the prospect of racial harmony right from the early, unsubtle shots that show black and white horses pulling O. B.'s stagecoach as a team. However, when the teases involve the film's characters, they end with reconciliation being rejected. In contrast to such earlier episodes, Mannix and Warren eventually combine forces in order to survive the common threat of Daisy's gang, setting aside their prejudices for the purpose of survival and, when survival becomes an impossibility, in order to inflict pain on Daisy. Warren prevents Mannix from providing her with a swift death by arguing that she should be hanged in tribute to John Ruth. As they hang her, they frame the death as an act of justice and respect, with Mannix proudly declaring it his first and last act as the Sheriff of Red Rock. However, this is far from the dispassionate justice discussed earlier in the film. The justification rings hollow; there have been no strong bonds of friendship that explain the sudden desire to honor Ruth, and it is never entirely clear if Mannix's official position of authority is genuine. This transition away from racial hostility toward cooperation is predicated on their hatred for Daisy, an inescapably misogynistic shift disguised as justice. Daisy throughout the film has been the recipient of beatings, insults, and abuse, and the pair's act is preceded by gendered insults as they repeatedly refer to her as a "bitch." Her death is neither redemptive nor regenerative, and looks closer to something out of a horror film. Drenched in at least three people's blood, Daisy's wide-eyed face makes for a striking image that brings to mind Carrie's (Sissy Spacek) face at the height of her ultimate humiliation in Brian de Palma's *Carrie* (1976).

In this sadistic moment, Christian iconography returns and is once again undermined. Daisy's hanged body is framed with two snow shoes behind her, giving her the appearance of an angel with wings. This recalls an earlier scene in which Mannix mocks the relationship between Ruth and Warren and asks if they will "make snow angels together." Here, her death is a response to the post-racial unison that Mannix previously disparaged, a final alliance achieved through misogyny and sadism. This is a far cry from the angel in John Gast's iconic 1872 painting "American Progress" with its attendant symbolism of hope and promise. Instead Tarantino offers a surreal and sacrilegious image of an exterminated angel in the wake of societal collapse.

The film's pessimistic indictment of a nation beset with insurmountable divisions and cruelty is epitomized by its final moment of ironic tragicomedy. A lone bugle plays a patriotic military tune while Mannix recites the Lincoln letter, an artificial but nonetheless authentic expression for the desire of racial acceptance, equality, and friendship:

> Dear Marquis, I hope this letter finds you and in good health and stead. I'm doing fine, although I wish there were more hours in a day. There is just so much to do. Times are changing slowly, but surely it is men like you who will make a difference. Your military success is a credit not only to you but your race as well. I'm very proud every time I hear news of you. We still have a long way to go, but hand in hand I know we'll get there. I just want to let you know you're in my thoughts. Hopefully, our paths will cross in the future. Until then, I remain your friend. Old Mary Todd's calling, so I guess it must be time for bed. Respectfully, Abraham Lincoln.

On the line "We still have a long way to go, but hand in hand we'll get there," the camera slowly pulls back to reveal John Ruth's severed arm still attached to Daisy's.

Conclusion: A More Perfect Union

In his analysis of *Stagecoach*, Michael Coyne argues that the film works as "a parable of 1939 America" through its parallels to the aftermath of the Depression and the growing political crisis in Europe, with its characters representing a cross section of contemporary society. Like *Stagecoach*, *The Hateful Eight* can be viewed as a parable of 2015 America, albeit a far bleaker vision than Ford's. Along with *Django Unchained* it emerged as part of a renewed cultural interest in the historical inequalities of the United States, which also saw films such as *Lincoln* (Steven Spielberg, 2012) and *12 Years a Slave* (Steve McQueen, 2013) explore slavery and the Civil War with critical success. Although it is difficult to ascribe direct influence, these films resonate with the aftermath of Barack Obama's landmark 2008 presidential victory, which saw prophesies of a post-racial society in which "race no longer mattered in American politics" (Tesler and Sears 2010: 159). If *Django Unchained*'s ironic fantasy of racial empowerment reflected the optimism of its era, *The Hateful Eight* reflects the disillusionment of that dream. Hundreds of racist incidents were recorded around the time of Obama's first election (Marable 2009: 9–10), while the Ku Klux Klan expanded from 72 chapters to 190 between 2014 and 2015 (Potok 2017: 38). Meanwhile, Obama's legitimacy as president was called into question by the Birther Movement, with future far-right president Donald Trump a significant exponent of this theory. *The Hateful Eight* itself garnered controversy after Tarantino gave a speech at a rally in New York against police brutality toward minority groups; perceiving his comments to be anti-police, the president of the Patrolmen's Benevolent Association of the City of New York called for a boycott of the film in response, while the Fraternal Order of Police claimed to have "something in the works" for its theatrical release (Nigel M. Smith 2015).

As the previous examples show, *The Hateful Eight* forms part of a critical moment in which the United States saw an intensification of an ideological battle over the future of the nation. This chapter has explored some of the film's historical and cinematic allusions in order to make the case that it operates as a satirical allegory of race relations in its Reconstruction Era setting which resonates with its contemporary moment. While it must be remembered that it is entirely possible to watch this film without taking into account its allegorical impulses or identifying every allusion, a critical approach which takes intertextuality as a serious interpretive challenge rather than a superficial gimmick reveals a subversive political project with a stark warning to a nation divided on matters of history, nationhood, and race.

Bibliography

Barrett, Jenny. *Shooting the Civil War: Cinema, History and American National Identity*. London: I.B. Tauris, 2009.

Bowles, Samuel. "Restoration of the Union." *The Republican*, April 20 (1865). Reproduced in *The Reconstruction Era: Primary Documents of Events from 1865 to 1877*, edited by Donna L. Dickerson, 10–11. Westport: Greenwood Press, 2003.

Broughton, Lee. *The Euro-Western: Reframing Gender, Race and the "Other" in Film*. London: I.B. Tauris, 2016b.

Broughton, Lee. "Fighting the North in the Spaghetti West: Peter Lee Lawrence, Italian Westerns and Italian History." In *Mapping Cinematic Norths: International Interpretations in Film and Television*, edited by Jonathan Rayner and Julia Dobson, 155–76. Bern: Peter Lang, 2016a.

Carroll, Rory. "'I Think People are Really Disgusted'—Quentin Tarantino Faces Hollywood Backlash." *The Guardian* [online], February 7 (2018). Available online at: https://www.theguardian.com/film/2018/feb/07/quentin-tarantino-hollywood-baclkash-uma-thurman-roman-polanski (accessed September 5, 2018).

Castel, Albert. "The Fort Pillow Massacre: An Examination of the Evidence." In *Black Flag over Dixie*, edited by Gregory J. W. Urwin, 89–103. Carbondale: Illinois University Press, 2004.

Coles, David J. "'Shooting Niggers Sir': Confederate Mistreatment of Union Black Soldiers at the Battle of Olustee." In *Black Flag over Dixie*, edited by Gregory J. W. Urwin, 65–88. Carbondale: Illinois University Press, 2004.

Coyne, Michael. *The Crowded Prairie: American National Identity in the Hollywood Western*. London: I.B. Tauris, 1998.

Dickerson, Donna L. *The Reconstruction Era: Primary Documents of Events from 1865 to 1877*. Westport: Greenwood Press, 2003.

Du Bois, W. E. B. *Black Reconstruction in America*. 1935. Reprint: New York: Touchstone, 1995.

Gallagher, Gary W. *Causes Won, Lost, and Forgotten: How Hollywood and Popular Art Shape What We Know About the Civil War*. Chapel Hill: University of North Carolina Press, 2008.

Greeley, Horace. "The Dawn of Peace." *New York Tribune*, April 14 (1865). Reproduced in *The Reconstruction Era: Primary Documents of Events from 1865 to 1877*, edited by Donna L. Dickerson, 5. Westport: Greenwood Press, 2003.

Kermode, Mark. "BBC Radio 5 Live—Kermode and Mayo's Film Review, with Eddie Redmayne, Mark Kermode Reviews The Hateful Eight." BBC, January 8 (2016). Available online at: http://bbc.in/2bKTQ14 (accessed June 28, 2018).

Kitses, Jim. *Horizons West*. London: British Film Institute, 2004.

Marable, Manning. "Introduction: Racializing Obama: The Enigma of Postblack Politics and Leadership." In *Barack Obama and African-American Empowerment: The Rise of Black America's New Leadership*, edited by Manning Marable, and Kristin Clarke, 1–12. New York: Palgrave Macmillan, 2009.

Paquet-Deyris, Anne-Marie. "Glorious Basterds in Tarantino's *Django Unchained*." In *Critical Perspectives on the Western: From a Fistful of Dollars to Django Unchained*, edited by Lee Broughton, 153–66. London: Rowman & Littlefield, 2016.

Potok, Mark. "The Year in Hate and Extremism." *Intelligence Report*, 160 (2017): 36–42.

Rosenbaum, Jonathan. "Recommended Reading: Daniel Mendelsohn on the New Tarantino." *Blog*, August 17 (2009). Available online at: http://www.jonathanrosenbaum.net/2009/08/recommended-reading-daniel-mendelsohn-on-the-new-tarantino/ (accessed August 12, 2018).

Smith, Nigel M. "Quentin Tarantino wants to 'Go Further' with his Anti-police Violence Protests." *The Guardian* [online], December 7 (2015). Available online at: https://www.theguardian.com/film/2015/dec/07/quentin-tarantino-anti-police-violence-protests-hateful-eight (accessed August 23, 2018).

Tesler, Michael, and David O. Sears. *Obama's Race: The 2008 Election and the Dream of a Post-Racial America*. Chicago: University of Chicago Press, 2010.

Urwin, Gregory J. W. "'A Very Long Shadow': Warfare, Race, and the Civil War in America." In *Black Flag over Dixie*, edited by Gregory J. W. Urwin, 213–46. Carbondale: Illinois University Press, 2004.

Filmography

The 11th Hour (2007), [Film] Dir. Leila Conners Petersen and Nadia Conners, USA: Warner Independent Pictures.

12 Years a Slave (2013), [Film] Dir. Steve McQueen, USA: Plan B Entertainment / River Road Entertainment / Film 4.

2001: A Space Odyssey (1968), [Film] Dir. Stanley Kubrick, UK / USA: MGM / Stanley Kubrick Productions.

A Clockwork Orange (1971), [Film] Dir. Stanley Kubrick, UK / USA: Warner Brothers / Hawk Films.

A Fistful of Dollars / Per un pugno di dollari (1964), [Film] Dir. Sergio Leone, Italy / Spain / West Germany: Jolly Film / Constantin Film / Ocean Films.

A Man Called Horse (1970), [Film] Dir. Elliot Silverstein, Mexico / USA: Cinema Center Films.

A World Unseen: The Revenant (2016), [Film] Dir. Eliot Rausch, USA: RauschFilms.

Adiós, Sabata / The Bounty Hunters / Indio Black, sai che ti dico...sein un gran figlio di... (1970), [Film] Dir. Gianfranco Parolini (as Frank Kramer), Italy: Produzioni Europee Associate (PEA).

The Apartment (1960), [Film] Dir. Billy Wilder, USA: United Artists.

Apocalypse Now (1979), [Film] Dir. Francis Coppola, USA: United Artists.

Avatar (2009), [Film] Dir. James Cameron, USA: 20th Century Fox.

Barbarosa (1982), [Film] Dir. Fred Schepisi, USA: ITC Entertainment / Associated Film Distribution / Universal Pictures.

Before the Flood (2016), [Film] Dir. Fisher Stevens, USA: National Geographic Documentary Films.

Blazing Saddles (1974), [Film] Dir. Mel Brooks, USA: Crossbow Productions / Warner Bros.

Blood Brothers / Blutsbrüder (1975), [Film] Dir. Werner W. Wallroth, East Germany: Deutsche Film-Aktiengesellschaft (DEFA).

Bonanza (1959–73), [Television Series, NBC] USA: National Broadcasting Company.

Bone Tomahawk (2015), [Film] Dir. S. Craig Zahler, USA / UK: Caliber Media Company / Platinum Platypus / Realmbuilders Productions / The Jokers Films / Twilight Riders.

Boot Hill / La collina degli stivali (1969), [Film] Dir. Giuseppe Colizzi: Finanziaria San Marco S.p.A. / Crono Cinematografica S.p.A / B.R.C.

Brimstone (2016), [Film] Dir. Martin Koolhoven, Netherlands / France / Germany / Sweden / UK: N279 Entertainment / X-Filme / Backup Media / Filmwave / Prime Time / Jokers Films.

Broken Arrow (1950), [Film] Dir. Delmer Daves, USA: Twentieth Century Fox.
Bronco (1958–62), [Television Series, ABC] USA: Warner Bros. Television.
The Buccaneer (1958), [Film] Dir. Anthony Quinn, USA: Paramount Pictures.
Buchanan Rides Alone (1958), [Film] Dir. Budd Boetticher, USA: Columbia Pictures.
Buffalo Bill and the Indians, Or Sitting Bull's History Lesson (1976) [Film] Dir. Robert Altman, USA: United Artists.
Butch Cassidy and the Sundance Kid (1969), [Film] Dir. George Roy Hill, USA: Twentieth Century Fox / Campanile Productions / Newman-Foreman Company.
Calamity Jane (1953), [Film] Dir. David Butler, USA: Warner Bros.
Carrie (1976), [Film] Dir. Brian de Palma, USA: Red Bank Films.
Casablanca (1942), [Film] Dir. Michael Curtiz, USA: Warner Bros.
Cast a Giant Shadow (1966), [Film] Dir. Melville Shavelson, USA: United Artists.
Closely Watched Trains / Ostře sledované vlaky (1966), [Film] Dir. Jirí Menzel, Czechoslovakia: Filmové Studio Barrandov.
Curse of the Undead (1959), [Film] Dir. Edward Dein, USA: Universal International Pictures.
Cut-Throats Nine / Condenados a vivir (1972), [Film] Dir. Joaquín Luis Romero Marchent, Spain: Films Triunfo S.A.
Dances with Wolves (1990), [Film] Dir. Kevin Costner, USA: Trig Productions / Orion Pictures.
Days of Violence / I giorni della violenza (1967), [Film] Dir. Alfonso Brescia (as Al Bradley), Italy: Concord Film.
Dead Birds (2004), [Film] Dir. Alex Turner, USA: Silver Nitrate Pictures / Dead Birds Films.
Death of a Salesman (1951), [Film] Laszlo Benedek, USA: Columbia Pictures.
The Deer Hunter (1978), [Film] Dir. Michael Cimino, USA: EMI / Universal Pictures.
Django (1966), [Film], Dir. Sergio Corbucci, Italy / Spain: B. R. C. Produzione Film / Tecisa.
Django Kill … If You Live, Shoot! / Se sei vivo spara (1967), [Film] Dir. Giulio Questi, Italy / Spain: GIA Società Cinematografica / Hispamer Films / Rewind Film.
Django the Bastard (1969), [Film] Dir. Sergio Garrone, Italy: Società Europea Produzioni Associate Cinematografiche (SEPAC) / Tigielle 33.
Django Unchained (2012), [Film] Dir. Quentin Tarantino, USA: The Weinstein Company / Columbia Pictures Corporation.
Doc (1971), [Film] Dir. Frank Perry, USA: United Artists.
Dodge City (1939), [Film] Dir. Michael Curtiz, USA: Warner Brothers.
Easy Rider (1969), [Film] Dir. Dennis Hopper, USA: Pando Company Inc. / Raybert Productions.
El Topo (1970), [Film] Dir. Alejandro Jodorowsky, Mexico: Producciones Panicas.
Fando y Lis (1968), [Film] Dir. Alejandro Jodorowsky, Mexico: Producciones Panicas.

Fear Eats the Soul / Angst essen Seele auf (1973), [Film] Dir. Rainer Werner Fassbinder, West Germany: City Film / Tango Film.

Fitzcarraldo (1982), [Film] Dir. Werner Herzog, West Germany: Filmverlag der Autoren.

For a Few Dollars More / Per qualche dollaro in piu (1965), [Film] Dir. Sergio Leone, Italy / Spain / West Germany: Produzioni Europee Associate (PEA) / Arturo Gonzalez Producciones Cinematograficas / Constantin Film.

Fox and His Friends / Faustrecht der Freiheit (1975), [Film] Dir. Rainer Werner Fassbinder, West Germany: Filmverlag der Autoren / Tango Film.

The Good, the Bad and the Ugly / Il buono, il brutto, il cattivo (1966), [Film] Dir. Sergio Leone, Italy / Spain / West Germany: Produzioni Europee Associate (PEA) / Arturo Gonzalez Producciones Cinematograficas / Constantin Film.

The Great Silence / Il grande silenzio / The Big Silence (1968), [Film] Dir. Sergio Corbucci, Italy / France: Adelphia Compagnia Cinematografica / Les Films Corona.

Grey Knight / The Killing Box (1993), [Film] Dir. George Hickenlooper, USA: Motion Picture Corporation of America.

Guns for Hire: The Making of The Magnificent Seven (2000), [Television Programme, Channel 4] Dir. Louis Heaton, UK / USA: Channel 4 Television Corporation / October Films.

The Hateful Eight (2015), [Film] Dir. Quentin Tarantino, USA: Double Feature Films / Visiona Romantica / FilmColony.

Heaven's Gate (1980), [Film] Dir. Michael Cimino, USA: Partisan Productions / United Artists.

High Noon (1952), [Film] Dir. Fred Zinnemann, USA: Stanley Kramer Productions.

High Plains Drifter (1973), [Film] Dir. Clint Eastwood, USA: Malpaso Company.

The Hired Hand (1971), [Film] Dir. Peter Fonda, USA: Universal Studios.

The Holy Mountain (1973), [Film] Dir. Alejandro Jodorowsky, Mexico / USA: ABKCO Films / Producciones Zohar.

Hombre (1967), [Film] Dir. Martin Ritt, USA: Hombre Productions.

In a Year with 13 Moons / In einem Jahr mit 13 Monden (1978), [Film] Dir. Rainer Werner Fassbinder, West Germany: Filmverlag der Autoren / Pro-ject Filmproduktion / Tango Film.

Inglourious Basterds (2009), [Film] Dir. Quentin Tarantino, USA: Universal Pictures / The Weinstein Company / A Band Apart.

The Invaders (1912), [Film] Dir. T. H. Ince and Francis Ford, USA: Mutual Film.

Jauja (2014), [Film] Dir. Lisandro Alonso, Denmark / Argentina / France / Mexico / Netherlands / USA: 4L / Arte / Bananeira Filmes / Canal Brasil.

Katzelmacher (1969), [Film] Dir. Rainer Werner Fassbinder, West Germany: Antiteater-X-Film.

Last Train from Gun Hill (1959), [Film] Dir. John Sturges, USA: Paramount Pictures.

The Lawman (1958–62), [Television Series, ABC] USA: Warner Bros. Television.
Lemonade Joe or the Horse Opera / Limonádový Joe aneb Koňská opera (1964), [Film] Dir. Oldřich Lipský, Czechoslovakia: Filmové Studio Barrandov.
The Leopard / Il gattopardo (1963), [Film] Dir. Luchino Visconti, Italy / France: Titanus / S.N. Pathe Cinema / Societe Generale de Cinematographie (S.G.C.).
Lincoln (2012), [Film] Dir. Steven Spielberg, USA: DreamWorks / Twentieth Century Fox / Participant Media.
Little Big Man (1970), [Film] Dir. Arthur Penn, USA: Cinema Center Films / National General Pictures.
Long Riders, The (1980), [Film] Dir. Walter Hill, USA: Huka Productions / United Artists.
McCabe and Mrs. Miller (1971), [Film] Dir. Robert Altman, USA: Warner Bros.
The Magnificent Ambersons (1942), [Film] Dir. Orson Welles, USA: RKO Pictures.
Magnificent Obsession (1954), [Film] Dir. Douglas Sirk, USA: Universal Pictures.
The Magnificent Seven (1960), [Film] Dir. John Sturges, USA: United Artists.
Major Dundee (1965), [Film] Dir. Sam Peckinpah, USA: Jerry Bresler Productions.
The Man Who Shot Liberty Valance (1962), [Film] Dir. John Ford, USA: Paramount Pictures.
Maverick (1957–62), [Television Series, ABC] USA: Warner Bros. Television.
My Darling Clementine (1946), [Film] Dir. John Ford, USA: Twentieth Century Fox.
Ned Kelly (2003), [Film] Dir. Gregor Jordan, Australia / UK / USA / France: Universal Pictures.
Never So Few (1959), [Film] Dir. John Sturges, USA: Metro-Goldwyn-Mayer.
Night of the Living Dead (1968), [Film] Dir. George Romero, USA: Image Ten / Laurel Group / Market Square Productions / Off Colour Films.
Once Upon a Time in the West / C'era una volt il West (1968), [Film] Dir. Sergio Leone, Italy / USA: Rafran Cinematografica / Finanzia San Marco / Paramount Pictures.
One, Two, Three (1961), [Film] Dir. Billy Wilder, USA: United Artists.
Pale Rider (1985), [Film] Dir. Clint Eastwood, USA: The Malpaso Company / Warner Brothers.
The Professionals (1966), [Film] Dir. Richard Brooks, USA: Columbia Pictures Corporation.
The Proposition (2005), [Film] Dir. John Hillcoat, Australia / UK: Surefire Films / Autonomous / Jackie O Productions.
The Quick and the Dead (1995), [Film] Dir. Sam Raimi, USA: Japan Satellite Broadcasting / InterProd Company Production / TriStar Pictures.
Raise Your Hands, Dead Man, You're Under Arrest / Su le mani, cadavere! Sei in arresto (1971), [Film] Dir. Leon Klimovsky, Italy / Spain: Dauro Films / Sara Film.
Rango (2011), [film] Dir. Gore Verbinski, USA: Paramount Pictures / Nickelodeon Pictures / Blind Wink / GK Films / Industrial Light & Magic.

The Rebel (1959–1961), [Television Series, ABC] episode "Fair Game" (1960), Dir. Irvin Kershner, USA: Mark Goodson-Bill Todman Productions / Celestial Productions / Fen-Ker-Ada Productions.

Red River (1984), [Film] Dir. Howard Hawks, USA: Monterey Productions / United Artists.

The Revenant (2015), [Film] Dir. A. G. Iñárritu, USA: Twentieth Century Fox.

The Road (2009), [Film] Dir. John Hillcoat, USA: Dimension Films / 2929 Productions / Nick Wechsler Productions / Chockstone Pictures.

Rocco and his Brothers / Rocco e i suoi fratelli (1960), [Film] Dir. Luchino Visconti, Italy / France: Titanus / Les Films Marceau.

The Salvation (2014), [Film] Dir. Kristian Levring, Denmark / UK / South Africa: Zentropa Entertainments 33 / Forward Films / Spier Films / Danish Film Institute / Nordisk Film & TV Fond / Film i Väst.

The Searchers (1956), [Film] Dir. John Ford, USA: C.V. Whitney Pictures.

Seven Samurai / Shichinin no samurai (1954), [Film] Dir. Akira Kurosawa, Japan: Toho.

Shane (1953), [Film] Dir. George Stevens, USA: Paramount Pictures.

She Wore a Yellow Ribbon (1949), [Film] Dir. John Ford, USA: Argosy Pictures.

Silverado (1985), [Film] Dir. Lawrence Kasdan, USA: Delphi III Productions / Columbia Pictures.

Sing, Cowboy, Sing (1937), [Film] Dir. Robert N. Bradbury, USA: Boots and Saddles Pictures.

Sing, Cowboy, Sing (1981), [Film] Dir. Dean Reed, German Democratic Republic: Deutsche Film-Aktiengesellschaft (DEFA).

Slow West (2015), [Film] Dir. John Maclean, UK / New Zealand: DMC Film / Film4 Productions / New Zealand Film Commission / See-Saw Films.

Some Like it Hot (1959), [Film] Dir. Billy Wilder, USA: United Artists.

The Sons of Great Bear / Die Söhne der großen Bärin (1966), [Film] Dir. Josef Mach, East Germany: Deutsche Film-Aktiengesellschaft (DEFA).

The Soul of Nigger Charley (1973), [Film] Dir. Larry G. Spangler, USA: Paramount Pictures.

Stagecoach (1939), [Film] Dir. John Ford, USA: Walter Wanger Productions / United Artists.

The Story of the Kelly Gang (1906), [Film] Dir. Charles Tait, Australia: Johnson and Gibson / J. and N. Tait.

Sugarfoot / Tenderfoot (1957–61), [Television Series, ABC] USA: Warner Bros. Television.

Sweet Sweetback's Baadasssss Song (1971), [Film] Dir. Melvin Van Peebles, USA: Yeah.

The Texas Chainsaw Massacre 2 (1986), [Film] Dir. Tobe Hooper, USA: Cannon Films / Golan-Globus Productions.

The Thing (1982), [Film] Dir. John Carpenter, USA: Universal Pictures / Turman-Foster Company.

The Third Generation / Die dritte Generation (1979), [Film] Dir. Rainer Werner Fassbinder, West Germany: Filmverlag der Autoren / Pro-ject Filmproduktion / Tango Film.

Thunderbolt and Lightfoot (1974), [Film] Dir. Michael Cimino, USA: The Malpaso Company / United Artists.

Tom Horn (1980), [Film] Dir. William Wiard, USA: First Artists / Solar Productions / Warner Brothers.

Tombstone (1993), [Film] Dir. George P. Cosmatos, USA: Hollywood Pictures / Cinergi Pictures / Buena Vista Pictures.

The True Story of Jesse James (1957), [Film] Dir. Nicholas Ray, USA: Twentieth Century Fox.

Two Thousand Maniacs! (1964), [Film] Dir. Herschel Gordon Lewis, USA: The Jacqueline Kay, Inc. / Friedman-Lewis Productions.

The Undefeated (1969), [Film] Dir. Andrew V. McLaglen, USA: Twentieth Century Fox.

U.S. Marshal (1958–60), [Television Series, NTA] USA: Desilu Productions.

Unforgiven (1992), [Film] Dir. Clint Eastwood, USA: Malpaso Productions / Warner Brothers.

Vera Cruz (1954), [Film] Dir. Robert Aldrich, USA: United Artists.

Viva La Muerte (1971), [Film] Dir. Fernando Arrabal, France / Tunisia: Isabell Films / SATPEC.

Viva Zapata! (1952), [Film] Dir. Elia Kazan, USA: Twentieth Century Fox.

The Walking Dead (2010- present), [Television Series, AMC] USA: Circle of Confusion / Valhalla Motion Picures / Darkwoods Productions / AMC Studios / Idiot Box.

West Side Story (1961), [Film] Dir. Jerome Robbins and Robert Wise, USA: United Artists.

Westworld (2016-present), [Television Series, HBO] USA: Bad Robot / Jerry Weintraub Productions / Kilter Films / Warner Bros. Television.

Whity (1971), [Film] Dir. Rainer Werner Fassbinder, West Germany: Antiteater-X-Film / Atlantis Film.

Wichita Town (1959–60), [Television Series, NBC] USA: Four Star Productions / Mirisch/McCrea Productions.

The Wild Bunch (1969), [Film] Dir. Sam Peckinpah, USA: Warner Bros. / Seven Arts.

Winchester Does Not Forgive / Buckaroo: il winchester che non perdona (1967), [Film] Dir. Adelchi Bianchi, Italy: Magister Film.

Wyatt Earp (1994), [Film] Dir. Lawrence Kasdan, USA: Kasdan Pictures / Tig Productions / Warner Brothers.

Yojimbo / Yojinbo (1961), [Film] Dir. Akira Kurosawa, Japan: Kurosawa Production Co. / Toho Company.

Young Guns (1988), [Film] Dir. Christopher Cain, USA: Morgan Creek Productions / 20th Century Fox.

About the Editor and the Contributors

Lee Broughton is a freelance writer, critic, film programmer, and lecturer in film and cultural studies. He is the author of *The Euro-Western: Reframing Gender, Race and the "Other" in Film* (2016) and the editor of *Critical Perspectives on the Western: From* A Fistful of Dollars *to* Django Unchained (2016). Lee edits the *Current Thinking on the Western* blog online and is the convener of the International Scholars of the Western Network. His research interests include the Western, horror films, exploitation films, the gothic tradition, and cult movies more generally. A former Leverhulme Trust Early Career Fellow, Lee is currently writing a monograph that critically interrogates the representations of North and South that are found in Italian Westerns and explores how and why they might differ to those that are typically found in American Westerns.

* * *

Jenny Barrett is Reader in Film and Popular Culture at Edge Hill University. Her research interests include the American Civil War on-screen, genre theory, the Western and transatlantic slavery. She has published on ethnicity, American national identity, and both American and non-American Westerns. Her most recent book is *Shooting the Civil War: Cinema, History and American National Identity* (2009).

Hamish Ford is senior lecturer in Film, Media, and Cultural Studies at the University of Newcastle, Australia. The author of *Post-War Modernist Cinema and Philosophy: Confronting Negativity and Time* (2012), his research focuses on modernist postwar European cinema, film and philosophy, and contemporary world cinema, across numerous articles and book chapters. He also provided an audio commentary for Fassbinder's 1975 film, *Fox and His Friends* (Madman 2008, Arrow 2016). His current projects include coediting a special journal issue on the global responses to Ingmar Bergman's cinema and a sole-authored book on Bergman's 1960s films.

Peter J. Hanley studied medicine and worked in hospitals for several years before switching his attention to the study of heart muscle and immune cells. He is a researcher in the Institute of Molecular Cell Biology at the University of Münster, Germany. In his spare time he carries out research on Sergio Leone's *Dollars* films and the filming locations of Spaghetti Westerns. He is the author of the book *Behind-the-scenes of Sergio Leone's The Good, the Bad and the Ugly* (2016).

Paul Kerr is a senior lecturer in the Media Department at Middlesex University. His research interests include Hollywood, independent production in film and television, documentary, and "quality television." He was a TV producer-director for the BBC and Channel 4 in the UK for almost twenty-five years, and he produced a Channel 4 documentary about the making of *The Magnificent Seven*. He is the editor of *The Hollywood Film Industry* (1986) and his next book is a study of the Mirisch Company to be published by Bloomsbury in 2020.

Craig Ian Mann is an associate lecturer in Film and Television Studies at Sheffield Hallam University. He is broadly interested in the cultural significance of popular genre cinema, including horror, science fiction, action, and the Western. His research has been published in *Science Fiction Film and Television*, *Horror Studies* and the *Journal of Popular Film and Television* as well as several edited collections. He is co-organizer of the Fear 2000 conference series on contemporary horror media.

Matt Melia is a senior lecturer in Film, TV, and English Literature at Kingston University. He wrote his PhD on "Architecture and Cruelty in the Writing of Jean Genet, Samuel Beckett and Antonin Artaud" and his research is now focused on the work of the film directors Ken Russell and Stanley Kubrick. His work has been published in journals such as *Screening the Past* and *Frames Cinema Journal*. He is currently coediting a book on *Jaws* with I. Q. Hunter for Bloomsbury where he is contributing a chapter on the relocation of the Western in Spielberg's film.

Cynthia J. Miller is senior faculty in the Institute of Liberal Arts at Emerson College. She is a visual anthropologist whose areas of expertise are horror, Westerns, genre mash-ups, and cult film. She is the editor or co-editor of over fifteen scholarly volumes which include *Undead in the West: Vampires, Zombies, Mummies, and Ghosts on the Cinematic Frontier* (2012), *Undead in the West*

II: They Just Keep Coming (2013), and *International Westerns: Re-Locating the Frontier* (2013). Her most recent book is *Dark Forces at Work: Essays on Social Dynamics and Cinematic Horrors* (2019).

Thomas Moodie is a freelance writer and script supervisor in the UK film industry. He holds an MA in English from King's College, Cambridge University, and an MA in Film Studies from University College London.

Sonja Simonyi is a Hungarian-born independent scholar. Her research interests focus on the visual cultures of late socialist Eastern Europe. She has published on socialist Westerns, as well as the region's experimental cinemas, in the journals *Film History*, *Third Text* and *Frames Cinema Journal* and in the edited collection *International Westerns: Re-Locating the Frontier* (2013). Her coedited volume on experimental Eastern European film will be published by Amsterdam University Press in 2020.

Jack Weatherston is an independent scholar who has recently completed a PhD at Northumbria University. His research focuses on contemporary American literature and film, ecocriticism, and the Western.

Chelsea Wessels is Assistant Professor and Co-Director of the Film Studies minor at East Tennessee State University. She received her PhD from the University of St Andrews in Scotland, where her work focused on the emergence of the Western as a political and popular genre in global cinema. Her research interests include local cinema history and archives, global film genres, and feminist film. Her publications include writing for the National Film Registry, journal articles in *Transformations* and *Frames Cinema Journal*, and chapters in *Teaching Transnational Cinemas* (2016) and *The Western in the Global South* (2015).

Index